THE PALEOZOIC ERA

DIVERSIFICATION OF

PLANT AND ANIMAL LIFE

THE PALEOZOIC ERA
DIVERSIFICATION OF
PLANT AND ANIMAL LIFE

EDITED BY JOHN P. RAFFERTY, ASSOCIATE EDITOR, LIFE AND EARTH SCIENCES

Britannica®
— Educational Publishing —

IN ASSOCIATION WITH

ROSEN
EDUCATIONAL SERVICES

Published in 2011 by Britannica Educational Publishing
(a trademark of Encyclopædia Britannica, Inc.)
in association with Rosen Educational Services, LLC
29 East 21st Street, New York, NY 10010.

Distributed exclusively by Rosen Educational Services.
For a listing of additional Britannica Educational Publishing titles, call toll free (800) 237-9932.

First Edition

Britannica Educational Publishing
Michael I. Levy: Executive Editor
J.E. Luebering: Senior Manager
Marilyn L. Barton: Senior Coordinator, Production Control
Steven Bosco: Director, Editorial Technologies
Lisa S. Braucher: Senior Producer and Data Editor
Yvette Charboneau: Senior Copy Editor
Kathy Nakamura: Manager, Media Acquisition
John P. Rafferty: Associate Editor, Life and Earth Sciences

Rosen Educational Services
Alexandra Hanson-Harding: Senior Editor
Nelson Sá: Art Director
Cindy Reiman: Photography Director
Matthew Cauli: Designer, Cover Design
Introduction by Catherine Vanderhoof

Library of Congress Cataloging-in-Publication Data

The Paleozoic era : diversification of plant and animal life / edited by John P. Rafferty.
    p. cm.—(The geologic history of Earth)
"In association with Britannica Educational Publishing, Rosen Educational Services."
Includes bibliographical references and index.
ISBN 978-1-61530-111-9 (lib. bdg.)
1. Geology, Stratigraphic—Paleozoic. 2. Paleoecology—Paleozoic. I. Rafferty, John P.
QE654.P2413 2010
561'.112—dc22

2009051123

Manufactured in the United States of America

On the cover: Plants such as ferns (above) and ancient creatures such as the trilobite (below) were common during the Paleozoic era. *SSPL via Getty Images (above); Sinclair Stammers/Photolibrary/Getty Images (below and pages 5, 29, 36, 93, 138, 187, 245, 285, 325, 326, 329, 331)*

On page 18: Fallen pine trees in Emerald Lake, reflecting the Burgess Shale, British Columbia, Canada. *Shutterstock.com*

Contents

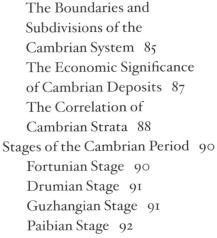

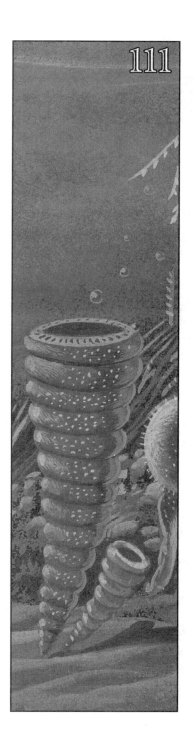

139

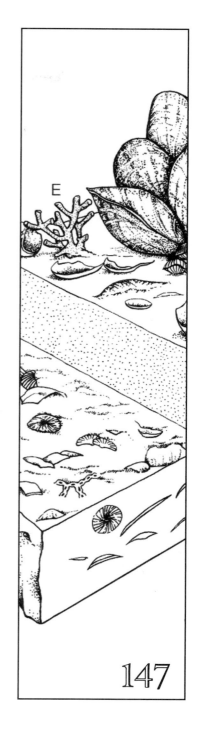

147

189

196

211

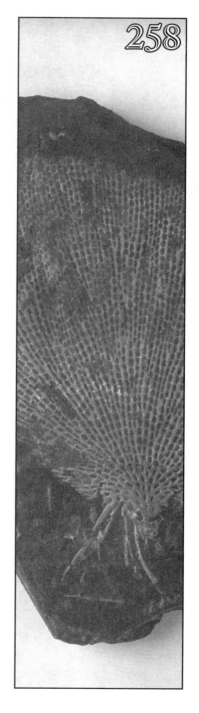

258

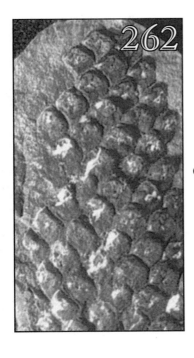

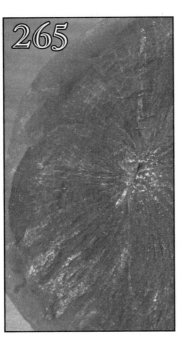

309

312

INTRODUCTION

The Paleozoic Era is probably less familiar and perhaps less dramatic than the age of the dinosaurs that would dominate the Mesozoic Era that followed. However, the Paleozoic Era contained one of the most intense increases in biodiversity in Earth's history, the Cambrian explosion and the subsequent Ordovician radiation. It also contained the largest extinction event the world has ever known, the Permian extinction, which wiped out more than 90 percent of marine species and roughly 70 percent of species on land. It was also a time of great geological changes as landmasses migrated and collided, eventually creating the supercontinent called Pangea. Sea levels rose, drowning whole continents, fell, and rose again. Some of Earth's oldest mountain ranges, such as the Appalachians and the Urals, were formed during the Paleozoic. Life moved from the oceans to dry land and insects took wing for the first time. Many evolutionary advances took place, which set the stage for life as we know it today. Some of these advances include the development of plants with seeds, shelled eggs, and organisms capable of breathing air. So in geologic history the Paleozoic Era was pretty dramatic after all. In the pages that follow, all of these developments, as well as the clues that scientists have used to decipher the history of Earth's changes, will be explored.

Spanning nearly 300 million years of history, from 542 to 251 million years ago, the Paleozoic Era covers more than half of the Phanerozoic Eon, also known as the Age of Life—the geologic time in which humans still live. Scientists divide the Paleozoic into a number of smaller periods, beginning with the Cambrian, approximately 542 million to 488 million years ago, followed by the Ordovician, Silurian, Devonian, Carboniferous, and Permian periods. Most of these names are derived from the locations in which rocks and fossils from that time were first discovered and studied. The exception is the Carboniferous period, so named because it was the period in which great coal beds were formed all around the world. These coal beds still provide a significant portion of the world's energy needs today.

The Cambrian period, the first period of the Paleozoic Era, was a time of great transition in the Earth's environment. Global temperatures, which had been cooler than today, suddenly warmed to average temperatures of 22 C (72 F), much warmer than today's global temperatures of approximately 14 C (57 F). There were no polar ice caps, and the oceans flooded over large portions of the world's continents. These changes led to increased levels of oxygen in the ocean waters. This increase in turn set the stage for the Cambrian explosion – a sudden burst of evolutionary development leading to an amazing diversification of life in the sea. Although some primitive life forms existed prior to this time, they have left little information in the fossil record. In the Cambrian period, however, life forms such as trilobites and other species with hard skeletons left fossils that can be found in present-day rocks throughout the world.

The most famous fossil field for studying the Cambrian period is the Burgess Shale, a formation in western Canada. The rock in this area is thought to have beenformed from a giant mudslide that rolled into the sea and buried a huge area of the ocean floor. Instantly, the mudslide killed all living organisms unlucky enough to live beneath it and preserved their remains as the mud hardened into rock. The fossils in the Burgess Shale are therefore extremely detailed and include soft body parts and animals without an exoskeleton that would normally have decomposed before becoming fossilized. This remarkable find has given scientists a much more complete picture of life in the Cambrian period than would be afforded by more typical fossil formations. More than 60,000 specimens have been identified from fossils in the Burgess Shale. Many of these organisms have no living counterparts today.

The Ordovician period, approximately 488 to 443 million years ago, is when almost every modern phylum of marine invertebrate began to appear, as well as the first fishes. During this period, the first land plants occurred. Scientists contend that the earliest terrestrial animals, early arthropods similar to millipedes, also appeared. Scientists have not found any fossils of these animals, but have found fossilized burrows, which, evidence suggests, could have been created by such creatures.

Besides the diversification of life forms, the Ordovician period was also characterized by significant geological activity. Tectonic shifts caused extensive and created vast ridges deep in the ocean floor. The continental landmasses were all in motion, shifting their positions on the globe. Significant parts of the continents were submerged during a good portion of this period due to rising sea levels and high global temperatures

Sedimentary rock from this period continues to contain a multitude of fossils. These rocks reveal much about life on earth and in the seas, but much of the Ordovician rock layer attests to the volcanic eruptions that characterized this period. Comparison of the makeup of the volcanic rocks from different regions allows scientists to estimate the incredible magnitude of these eruptions. Studying the rock layers from this period also provides evidence of huge hurricanes and typhoons across the oceans. The Ordovician period ended with a mass extinction second only to the Permian extinction some 200 million years later.

By contrast, the Silurian period (443.7-416 million years ago) was relatively quiet. Shallow seas extended over most of the world. Marine life rebounded after the

GEOLOGIC TIME SCALE

Left vertical scale: Paleozoic Era / Mesozoic Era / Cenozoic Era — present; Precambrian time; 1,000¹, 2,000¹, 3,000¹, 4,000¹, 4,600¹

Eonothem/Eon	Erathem/Era	System/Period	Series/Epoch	Stage/Age	mya¹
Phanerozoic	Cenozoic	Quaternary	Holocene		0.0117
			Pleistocene	Tarantian	0.126
				"Ionian"	0.781
				Calabrian	1.806
				Gelasian	2.588
		Neogene	Pliocene	Piacenzian	3.600
				Zanclean	5.332
			Miocene	Messinian	7.246
				Tortonian	11.608
				Serravallian	13.82
				Langhian	15.97
				Burdigalian	20.43
				Aquitanian	23.03
		Paleogene	Oligocene	Chattian	28.4 ± 0.1
				Rupelian	33.9 ± 0.1
			Eocene	Priabonian	37.2 ± 0.1
				Bartonian	40.4 ± 0.2
				Lutetian	48.6 ± 0.2
				Ypresian	55.8 ± 0.2
			Paleocene	Thanetian	58.7 ± 0.2
				Selandian	~61.1
				Danian	65.5 ± 0.3
	Mesozoic	Cretaceous	Upper	Maastrichtian	70.6 ± 0.6
				Campanian	83.5 ± 0.7
				Santonian	85.8 ± 0.7
				Coniacian	~88.6
				Turonian	93.6 ± 0.8
				Cenomanian	99.6 ± 0.9
			Lower	Albian	112.0 ± 1.0
				Aptian	125.0 ± 1.0
				Barremian	130.0 ± 1.5
				Hauterivian	~133.9
				Valanginian	140.2 ± 3.0
				Berriasian	145.5 ± 4.0

Eonothem/Eon	Erathem/Era	System/Period	Series/Epoch	Stage/Age	mya¹
Phanerozoic	Mesozoic	Jurassic	Upper	Tithonian	145.5 ± 4.0
				Kimmeridgian	150.8 ± 4.0
				Oxfordian	~155.6
			Middle	Callovian	161.2 ± 4.0
				Bathonian	164.7 ± 4.0
				Bajocian	167.7 ± 3.5
				Aalenian	171.6 ± 3.0
			Lower	Toarcian	175.6 ± 2.0
				Pliensbachian	183.0 ± 1.5
				Sinemurian	189.6 ± 1.5
				Hettangian	196.5 ± 1.0
		Triassic	Upper	Rhaetian	199.6 ± 0.6
				Norian	203.6 ± 1.5
				Carnian	216.5 ± 2.0
			Middle	Ladinian	~228.7
				Anisian	237.0 ± 2.0
			Lower	Olenekian	~245.9
				Induan	~249.5
	Paleozoic	Permian	Lopingian	Changhsingian	251.0 ± 0.4
				Wuchiapingian	253.8 ± 0.7
			Guadalupian	Capitanian	260.4 ± 0.7
				Wordian	265.8 ± 0.7
				Roadian	268.0 ± 0.7
			Cisuralian	Kungurian	270.6 ± 0.7
				Artinskian	275.6 ± 0.7
				Sakmarian	284.4 ± 0.7
				Asselian	294.6 ± 0.8
		Carboniferous	Pennsylvanian² Upper	Gzhelian	299.0 ± 0.8
				Kasimovian	303.9 ± 0.9
			Pennsylvanian² Middle	Moscovian	306.5 ± 1.0
			Pennsylvanian² Lower	Bashkirian	311.7 ± 1.1
			Mississippian² Upper	Serpukhovian	318.1 ± 1.3
			Mississippian² Middle	Visean	326.4 ± 1.6
			Mississippian² Lower	Tournaisian	345.3 ± 2.1
					359.2 ± 2.5

¹ Millions of years ago.
² Both the Mississippian and Pennsylvanian time units are formally designated as sub-periods within the Carboniferous Period.
³ Several Cambrian unit age boundaries are informal and are awaiting ratified definitions.

Encyclopædia Britannica, Inc. Source: International Commission on Stratigraphy (ICS)

Eonothem/Eon	Erathem/Era	System/Period	Series/Epoch	Stage/Age	mya[1]
Phanerozoic	Paleozoic	Devonian	Upper	Famennian	359.2 ± 2.5
					374.5 ± 2.6
				Frasnian	385.3 ± 2.6
			Middle	Givetian	391.8 ± 2.7
				Eifelian	397.5 ± 2.7
			Lower	Emsian	407.0 ± 2.8
				Pragian	411.2 ± 2.8
				Lochkovian	416.0 ± 2.8
		Silurian	Pridoli		418.7 ± 2.7
			Ludlow	Ludfordian	421.3 ± 2.6
				Gorstian	422.9 ± 2.5
			Wenlock	Homerian	426.2 ± 2.4
				Sheinwoodian	428.2 ± 2.3
			Llandovery	Telychian	436.0 ± 1.9
				Aeronian	439.0 ± 1.8
				Rhuddanian	443.7 ± 1.5
		Ordovician	Upper	Hirnantian	445.6 ± 1.5
				Katian	455.8 ± 1.6
				Sandbian	460.9 ± 1.6
			Middle	Darriwilian	468.1 ± 1.6
				Dapingian	471.8 ± 1.6
			Lower	Floian	478.6 ± 1.7
				Tremadocian	488.3 ± 1.7
		Cambrian[3]	Furongian	Stage 10	~492.0
				Stage 9	~496.0
				Paibian	~499.0
			Series 3	Guzhangian	~503.0
				Drumian	~506.5
				Stage 5	~510.0
			Series 2	Stage 4	~515.0
				Stage 3	~521.0
			Terreneuvian	Stage 2	~528.0
				Fortunian	542.0 ± 1.0

Eonothem/Eon	Erathem/Era	System/Period	mya[1]
Precambrian	Proterozoic	Neoproterozoic	Ediacaran	542
			Cryogenian	~635
				850
			Tonian	1,000
		Mesoproterozoic	Stenian	1,200
			Ectasian	1,400
			Calymmian	1,600
		Paleoproterozoic	Statherian	1,800
			Orosirian	2,050
			Rhyacian	2,300
			Siderian	2,500
	Archean	Neoarchean	2,800
		Mesoarchean	3,200
		Paleoarchean	3,600
		Eoarchean	4,000
		Hadean (informal)	4,600

Published with permission from the International Commission on Stratigraphy (ICS). International chronostratigraphic units, ranks, names, and formal status are approved by the ICS and ratified by the International Union of Geological Sciences (IUGS).
Source: 2009 International Stratigraphic Chart produced by the ICS.

Ordovician extinction, and similar types of life forms thrived worldwide. Coral reefs were common, and fish were widely distributed. Also present in this period were now-extinct giant arthropods known as sea scorpions. These creatures grew up to 2.5 metres (8 feet) in length with large grasping pincers to trap their prey. On land, plants continued to evolve, although most were still quite small—just a few inches in height—and confined to areas near the coastline. These early plants did not yet have leaves or seeds. They consisted of smooth branched stems with spore sacs for reproduction.

Rocks from the Silurian period include a crystallized rock called dolomite. Dolomite is harder than the shale that characterized much of the sedimentary rock from earlier periods. It is rare for dolomite to be formed today. Dolomite can be observed in such natural features as Niagara Falls, formed by erosion washing away the underlying shale below a layer of harder Silurian stone.

The Devonian period, spanning 416 million to 359 million years ago, is sometimes called the "Age of Fishes" but also sees the emergence of the first land-based vertebrates. Fossil evidence also indicates the presence of forests by the end of this period, signifying a rapid surge in the evolution of plant life.

Devonian fish could be found in both saltwater and freshwater environments. Many Devonian fish had external armor or scales. These exoskeletons allowed for excellent fossil preservation of those species. By the end of the period, most of these armored fish had become extinct, however. Of more importance for evolutionary history are early sharklike fishes, lungfishes, and a group of fish known as rhipidistians. Although the Rhipidstia became extinct by the early Permian period, many scientists maintain that their body features suggest that these were most likely the branch from which early amphibians and all later terrestrial vertebrates developed. This issue, however, is not settled.

An even more dramatic evolutionary development was taking place in the plant world, however. By the end of the Devonian period, plants had established themselves throughout the land masses, not only at the margins of the sea, and had evolved from primitive leafless forms to a wide variety of ferns, leafy stemmed plants, and even the first true woody trees, some with trunks up to 1.8 metres (6 feet) in diameter. Fossils of plant forms from this period are frequently found in a layer of rock known as "Old Red Sandstone," characteristic of the Devonian period. The preserved remains are both beautiful in their detail and extremely important for scientists to understand the anatomy and function of these early plants.

The presence of this sandstone rock layer in diverse areas of the globe also helps scientists to understand the movement of the continents during this period, which featured the creation of a single Northern Hemisphere continent named Laurussia, comprising most of North America and Europe. Laurussia was formed by the union of two smaller landmasses—Laurentia and Baltica. South America, Africa, India, Australia, and Antarctica were all part of a single supercontinent in the Southern Hemisphere called Gondwana.

The vast coal deposits across Europe, Asia, Australia, and North America that gave the Carboniferous period its name formed as giant swamps full of vegetation gradually and repeatedly decayed. The movements of the continents during this period (from 359-299 million years ago) eventually joined the two major landmasses of Laurussia and Gondwana, forming the Appalachian mountain range at the point of their collision. A later collision of Siberia with Eastern Europe formed the Urals. The movement of the continents also changed the global climate, causing the formation of glacial ice in Gondwana. These ice sheets emerged and retreated, causing times of continental flooding interspersed with times of drier terrestrial terrain, particularly during the latter half of this period.

With the increase of terrestrial habitats, several important evolutionary advances occurred during the Carboniferous period. Perhaps the most important of these was the development of amniotic eggs (that is, eggs that were encased in shells to prevent drying). The Carboniferous period was the time of peak amphibian development and the emergence of the reptiles (which lay amniotic eggs). One of the earliest reptiles, Hylonomus, was recovered from Lower Pennsylvanian tree stumps in Nova Scotia.

The Carboniferous period also saw the first winged insects. By the Pennsylvanian subperiod (the second half of the Carboniferous period), dragonflies and mayflies were abundant and had reached large sizes. Fossils of more advanced insects capable of folding their wings, particularly cockroaches, have been dated to the Pennsylvanian subperiod. Other Pennsylvanian insects include the ancestral forms of grasshoppers and crickets and the first terrestrial scorpions.

The Permian period (from 299 to 251 million years ago) ended the Paleozoic Era, and ended it in dramatic fashion with the largest extermination event in Earth's history. The cause of this massive disruption was most likely climate change, perhaps caused in part by the continuing unification of continental landmasses. During the Early Permian period this process was largely complete, with the merging of Gondwana and Laurussia.

Worldwide climate warmed throughout the Permian period, and much of the world became drier. There were also significant drops in sea level and the shallow surface waters of Permian seas warmed, which would have destroyed the habitat of many marine species. The warmer and drier climate during the early to middle Permian period also allowed for increasing diversity and development of many types of flora and fauna, however, particularly those suited to the terrestrial environment. Early coniferous plants and the precursors to flowering plants all appeared in the Middle and Late Permian periods. As plants diversified and spread, so did the insect populations that adapted to these new species.

The Permian period also saw the emergence of several important reptile types, including early ancestors of dinosaurs, crocodiles, and birds, as well as precursors to snakes, lizards, turtles, and other reptile species. The fossil record from this period also reveals a group of transitional reptiles called synapsids that had begun to show mammal-like tooth and bone features. Evidence of these animals at relatively high and colder latitudes would suggest that they also had the ability to maintain an elevated body temperature, another feature that separates mammals from reptiles.

By the end of the Permian period, the overwhelming majority of marine and terrestrial species had become extinct. Marine invertebrates were especially hard hit, and several life forms that had been common since the early Paleozoic period disappeared from the fossil record. All life on Earth today is descended from the survivors of the Permian extinction.

Our understanding of the Paleozoic Era comes from about 175 years of work with fossils and the various rock layers that contained. There is still much to learn about the Paleozoic world, and several debates still need to be resolved. This book will reveal what scientists do know about the Paleozoic Era, how they know it, and what still remains to be explained.

CHAPTER I
AN OVERVIEW OF PALEOZOIC TIME

S panning nearly 300 million years, the Paleozoic Era was one of the defining intervals shaping life on Earth. It was characterized by the sudden emergence of multitudes of new life-forms as well as the migration of several of Earth's continents from the Southern Hemisphere to the Northern Hemisphere. By the end of the era, all of Earth's major landmasses were merged into one. The Paleozoic was a time in which many bizarre creatures thrived. Long, tubular *Hallucigenia* floated through ancient seas along with trilobites and armoured fishes, while early amphibians first crawled onto solid ground. These were just a few of the notable members of Paleozoic faunas. However, life on Earth was subjected to three of the most severe extinctions of all time.

The Paleozoic Era was a major interval of geologic time that began 542 million years ago with the Cambrian explosion, an extraordinary diversification of marine animals, and ended 251 million years ago with the end-Permian extinction, the greatest extinction event in Earth history. The major divisions of the Paleozoic Era, from oldest to youngest, are the Cambrian (542 to 488.3 million years ago), Ordovician (488.3 to 443.7 million years ago), Silurian (443.7 to 416 million years ago), Devonian (416 to 359.2 million years ago), Carboniferous (359.2 to 299 million years ago), and Permian (299 to 251 million years ago) periods. The Paleozoic takes its name from the Greek word for ancient life.

PALEOZOIC LIFE

The story of the earliest Paleozoic animals is one of life in the sea. Presumably simple fungi and related forms existed in freshwater environments, but the fossil record provides no evidence of these modes of life. The terrestrial environment of the early Paleozoic was barren of the simplest of life-forms.

The Cambrian explosion was a sharp and sudden increase in the rate of evolution. About 542 million years ago, at the onset of the Cambrian Period, intense diversification resulted in more than 35 new animal phyla. However, new discoveries show that the "explosion" started roughly 575 million years ago, near the end of the Proterozoic Eon, with the Ediacara fauna. The biota rapidly diversified throughout the Cambrian and Ordovician

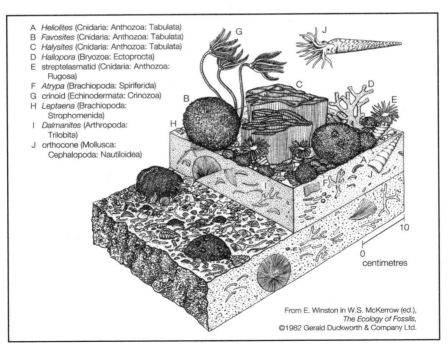

A *Heliolites* (Cnidaria: Anthozoa: Tabulata)
B *Favosites* (Cnidaria: Anthozoa: Tabulata)
C *Halysites* (Cnidaria: Anthozoa: Tabulata)
D *Hallopora* (Bryozoa: Ectoprocta)
E streptelasmatid (Cnidaria: Anthozoa: Rugosa)
F *Atrypa* (Brachiopoda: Spiriferida)
G crinoid (Echinodermata: Crinozoa)
H *Leptaena* (Brachiopoda: Strophomenida)
I *Dalmanites* (Arthropoda: Trilobita)
J orthocone (Mollusca: Cephalopoda: Nautiloidea)

10
0
centimetres

From E. Winston in W.S. McKerrow (ed.),
The Ecology of Fossils,
©1982 Gerald Duckworth & Company Ltd.

An early Silurian coral-stromatoporoid community.

periods as life-forms adapted to virtually all marine environments. In numbers of described marine species, fossils of trilobites dominate Cambrian rocks, whereas brachiopods (lamp shells) predominate in strata from the Ordovician through the Permian Period.

Several different kinds of organisms adapted independently to life on land, primarily during the middle Paleozoic. Leafless vascular plants (psilophytes) and invertebrate animals (centipede-like arthropods) were both established on land at least by Silurian time.

The lone tree with horizontal grooves in the right foreground is a jointed sphenopsid (Calamites). The large trees with scar patterns are lycopsids. Courtesy of the Department Library Services, American Museum of Natural History, neg. #333983

Vertebrate animals made the transition to land via the evolution of amphibians from air-breathing crossopterygian fish during Devonian times. Further conquest of the land became possible during the Carboniferous Period, when plants and animals evolved solutions to overcome their dependence on moist environments for reproduction: waterborne spores were replaced by seeds in plants of seed-fern origin, and shell-less eggs were replaced by amniote eggs with protective shells in animals of reptilian origin. Flight was first achieved also during the Carboniferous Period as insects evolved wings.

The Permian extinction, at the end of the Paleozoic Era, eliminated such major invertebrate groups as the blastoids (an extinct group of echinoderms related to the modern starfish and sea lilies), fusulinids, and trilobites. Other major groups, which included the ammonoids, brachiopods, bryozoans (small colonial animals that produce a skeletal framework of calcium carbonate), corals, and crinoids (cuplike echinoderms with five or more feathery arms), were severely decimated but managed to survive. It has been estimated that as many as 95 percent of the marine invertebrate species perished during the late Permian Period. Extinction rates were much lower among vertebrates, both aquatic and terrestrial, and among plants. Causes of this extinction event remain unclear, but they may be related to the changing climate and exceptionally low sea levels of the time. Although of lesser magnitude, other important Paleozoic mass extinctions occurred at the end of the Ordovician Period and during the late Devonian Period.

PALEOZOIC GEOGRAPHY

On a global scale, the Paleozoic was a time of continental assembly. The majority of Cambrian landmasses were gathered together to form Gondwana, a supercontinent made up of the present-day continents of Africa, South America, Australia, and Antarctica and the Indian subcontinent. It extended from the northern tropics to the southern polar regions. With the exception of three major cratons (landmasses forming the stable interiors of continents) not part of the initial configuration of Gondwana, the remainder of Earth was covered by the global Panthalassic Ocean.

Laurentia, a craton primarily made up of present-day North America and Greenland, was rotated 90° clockwise from its present orientation and sat astride the paleoequator during Cambrian times. Laurentia (a name derived from Quebec's portion of the Canadian Shield) was separated from Gondwana by the Iapetus Ocean. The smaller Baltica craton was positioned within the Iapetus Ocean, lying to the south of Laurentia and just off the northern margin of Gondwana. Baltica was made up of much of Scandinavia and western Europe. To the east of Laurentia, the Siberian craton was positioned just south of the paleoequator between Laurentia and the western coast of Gondwana. Until the late Carboniferous Period, Siberia was rotated 180° from its present orientation.

While a portion of Gondwana was positioned at or near the South Pole, there is no evidence of glaciation during Cambrian time. While little is known about the finer details of the Cambrian climate, geologic evidence shows that the margins of all continents were flooded by shallow seas. It is in the rock formed within these shallow seas that the greatest explosion of life ever recorded occurred. By Ordovician time, part of Gondwana had begun to move over the South Pole. The distribution of extensive glacial deposits, which formed later in the Paleozoic, has been used to track the movement of parts of Gondwana over and around the South Pole.

Siberia, Baltica, and Laurentia also moved to new locations during the course of the Paleozoic. Siberia, essentially the large Asian portion of present-day Russia, was a separate continent during the early and middle Paleozoic, when it moved from equatorial to northern temperate latitudes. Baltica moved across the paleo-equator from southern

Devonian volcanics formed Ancient Wall. Once the floor of a shallow ocean, it now juts up to a peak in Canada's Jasper National Park. Jonathan S. Blair/ National Geographic/Getty Images

cool temperate latitudes into northern warm latitudes during the Paleozoic Era. It collided with and joined Laurentia during the early Devonian Period. The beginnings of such mountainous regions as the Appalachians, Caledonides, and Urals resulted from the Paleozoic collision of the lithospheric plates. By the end of the Paleozoic, continued tectonic plate movements had forced these cratons together to form the supercontinent of Pangea. Large areas of all continents were episodically inundated by shallow seas, with the greatest inundations occurring during the Ordovician and early Carboniferous (Mississippian) periods.

Paleozoic rocks are widely distributed on all continents. Most are of sedimentary origin, and many show evidence of deposition in or near shallow oceans. Among the more useful guide fossils for correlation are trilobites (an extinct group of aquatic arthropods), for Cambrian through Ordovician strata; graptolites (small, colonial, planktonic animals), for rocks dated from Ordovician through Silurian times; conodonts (primitive chordates with tooth-shaped fossil remains), for Ordovician to Permian rocks; ammonoids (widely distributed extinct mollusks resembling the modern pearly nautilus), for Devonian through Cretaceous strata; and fusulinids (single-celled amoeba-like organisms with complex shells), for rocks dating from the Carboniferous through the Permian Period.

CHAPTER 2

THE CAMBRIAN PERIOD

The earliest time division of the Paleozoic Era was the Cambrian Period, an interval extending from about 542 to 488.3 million years ago. The Cambrian Period is divided into four stratigraphic series: Series 1 (542 to 521 million years ago), Series 2 (521 to 510 million years ago), Series 3 (510 to 501 million years ago), and the Furongian Series (499 to 488.3 million years ago).

Rocks formed or deposited during this time are assigned to the Cambrian System, which was named in 1835 by English geologist Adam Sedgwick for successions of slaty rocks in southern Wales and southwestern England. These rocks contain the earliest record of abundant and varied life-forms. The corresponding period and system names are derived from Cambria, the Roman name for Wales. As originally described, the Cambrian System was overlain by the Silurian System, which was named, also in 1835, by Scottish geologist Roderick I. Murchison. Subsequent disagreement between Sedgwick and Murchison over the definition and placement of the Cambrian-Silurian boundary led to a bitter controversy that involved many British geologists. The problem persisted until after the deaths of both Sedgwick and Murchison in the 1870s and the eventual adoption of an intervening system, the Ordovician, which was proposed in 1879 by English geologist Charles Lapworth.

The Cambrian world differed greatly from that of the present, but it was also quite different from the preceding

Proterozoic Eon (2.5 billion to 542 million years ago) in terms of climate, geography, and life. Average global temperatures during much of the Neoproterozoic Era (1 billion to 542 million years ago) were cooler (around 12°C [54°F]) than the average global temperatures (around 14°C [57 °F]) of the present day, whereas the global temperature of Cambrian times averaged 22°C (72°F). Low temperatures during the Neoproterozoic helped to sustain a series of worldwide events known as the Sturtian (748 to 713 million years ago), Marinoan (650 to 600 million years ago), and Gaskiers (595 to 565 million years ago) glaciations. Climate studies suggest that Cambrian temperatures were the norm for most of the Phanerozoic Eon (the last 542 million years), and these were exceeded only by a brief increase during the Permian Period near the end of the Paleozoic Era. Cooler periods, similar to the average global temperature of the present day, occurred during the end of the Ordovician, Late Carboniferous, Early Permian, Late Jurassic, and Early Cretaceous periods, as well as near the end of the Oligocene Epoch.

Just prior to the beginning of the Neoproterozoic Era, Earth experienced a period of continental suturing that organized all of the major landmasses into the huge supercontinent of Rodinia.

Rodinia was fully assembled by one billion years ago and rivaled Pangaea (a supercontinent that formed later during the Phanerozoic Eon) in size. Before the beginning of the Cambrian, Rodinia split in half, resulting in the creation of the Pacific Ocean west of what would become North America. By the middle and later parts of the Cambrian, continued rifting had sent the paleocontinents of Laurentia (made up of present-day North America and Greenland), Baltica (made up of present-day western Europe and Scandinavia), and Siberia on their separate ways. In addition, new collisional events led to the formation of Gondwana, a supercontinent composed of what would become Australia, Antarctica, India, Africa, and South America.

The tectonic events involved in the breakup of Rodinia also modified the ocean basins, forcing their expansion and flooding portions of many continents. The melting of the Varanger glaciers during the Neoproterozoic Era also played a role in the flooding of continents. This episode represented one of the largest and most persistent rises in sea level of the Phanerozoic Eon. Though the extent of continental flooding varied, for most continents sea level reached its maximum by the middle and later parts of the Cambrian time. This flooding, combined with the elevated Cambrian temperatures and changes in Earth's geography, led to increased rates of erosion that altered ocean chemistry. The most notable result was an increase in the oxygen content of seawater, which helped set the stage for the rise and later diversification of life — an event that has come to be known as the "Cambrian explosion."

THE CAMBRIAN ENVIRONMENT

Known from rocks and fossils surrounding three of the period's major landmasses, the Cambrian was a time of volcanism across Gondwana and several other continents, ice-free polar regions, and warmer conditions than today. Scientists contend that global sea levels dropped and rose relatively suddenly during this period that created as well as destroyed many biological communities.

PALEOGEOGRAPHY

The geography of the Cambrian world differed greatly from that of the present day. The geographic reconstruction is based on integrated geologic and biological evidence. Fossils in continental-shelf deposits indicate the presence of at least three major faunal provinces (or biogeographical regions) during much of the Cambrian Period.

The most distinct faunal province surrounded the continent of Laurentia. Paleomagnetic evidence indicates that Laurentia was located over the paleoequator during most or all of Cambrian time. This geographic interpretation is supported by the presence of thick, warm-water carbonate-platform deposits that accumulated in a broad belt encircling the continent. These carbonates are commonly flanked on the inner shelf by lagoonal shale and nearshore sandstone deposits. On the outer shelf, the carbonates commonly grade into laminated mudstone and shale that accumulated in deeper water. At times, two almost mutually exclusive ecosystems are separated by temperature and salinity barriers in the shallow water on the carbonate platforms. Inner restricted-shelf deposits were characterized by sparse low-diversity communities that tended to be highly endemic (confined to a particular region). Outer open-shelf deposits are characterized by high-diversity ecosystems that were widely distributed around the continent. Fossils are usually most abundant and most diverse near the outer margins of the carbonate platform. Because Laurentia remained nearly intact structurally, it is ideal for studying the relationships between Cambrian environments and communities of organisms around a low-latitude Cambrian continent.

Another Cambrian faunal province surrounded the small continent of Baltica, which was located in middle to high southern latitudes. Cambrian shelf deposits of Baltica are relatively thin, rarely exceeding 250 metres (820 feet) in thickness, and are composed primarily of sandstone and shale. Seemingly as a consequence of cool-water environments, carbonate deposits are relatively minor and very thin. The wide distribution of many species from the nearshore to deep-shelf environments of Baltica suggests that no significant restrictions in shelf dispersal occurred, unlike the shallow carbonate platforms of Laurentia.

The largest Cambrian faunal province is located around Gondwana, which extended from the low northern latitudes to the high southern latitudes, just short of the South Pole. The rocks and fossil assemblages of Gondwana show major changes that correspond to its great size and wide range of climates and environments. The Antarctic and Australian sectors of Gondwana rested in low latitudes during the Cambrian and have extensive carbonate deposits, although those of Antarctica are poorly exposed through the present-day polar ice cap. Differences in their fossil assemblages in addition to paleomagnetic evidence suggest that present-day North and South China were on separate tectonic plates. However, extensive carbonate deposits in both regions indicate that both plates were found in low latitudes during the Cambrian. The fossil assemblages of South China have strong similarities with those of both Australia and Kazakhstan, but details of the Cambrian geographic relationships remain unclear.

Several terranes (fault-bounded fragments of the Earth's crust) seem to have been located near or attached to the margin of the northern Africa sector of Gondwana in the high southern latitudes, but many details of their Cambrian geographic relations are unknown. These terranes now make up much of southern Europe and parts of eastern North America. Cambrian deposits in all the terranes are chiefly sandstone and shale and include few or no carbonates. Their faunas closely resemble those of Baltica at generic and higher taxonomic levels, but differences at the species level suggest some geographic separation.

Siberia was a separate continent located in the low latitudes between Laurentia and Gondwana. Fossil similarities between this continent and Gondwana suggest that it was positioned relatively close to the equatorial region of Gondwana. Present-day Kazakhstan seems to be composed of several microcontinental blocks that were in all likelihood separated during the Cambrian. These blocks became amalgamated after the Cambrian, and the subsequent composite continent known as Kazakhstania collided with Siberia during the late Paleozoic Era.

Few Cambrian faunas from continental-slope and deep-ocean environments are known. Limited information from these is important, however, for demonstrating affinities between deep, cool-water ecosystems at all latitudes and shallow, cool-water communities of higher latitudes. There exists a close similarity between the observed distribution patterns of Cambrian and modern marine arthropods. This has been used as persuasive evidence for the existence of thermally stratified Cambrian oceans in lower latitudes with a thermocline separating warm-water from cool-water layers. This inferred thermocline and the wide oceanic separation of biogeographic regions are seen as the likely causes for the high endemism of the biological communities surrounding Laurentia. This interpretation is supported by deposits that date back to the middle of the Cambrian in northern Greenland where, within a few tens of kilometres (miles), normal Laurentian shelf-margin trilobite (distinctive three-lobed marine arthropods) communities grade into deepwater faunas like those in the shallow-shelf deposits of Baltica. Similarly, trilobite species in later Cambrian deepwater faunas found in the western United States also appear in southeastern China, whereas shallow-water communities of the two regions have few genera in common.

As large tectonic plates continued to move during the Phanerozoic Eon, terranes of various sizes were displaced. Endemic Cambrian fossils, in conjunction with other geologic evidence such as physical stratigraphy, have been useful for identifying the geographic origins of some terranes, particularly those that have undergone substantial displacement. Examples of displaced terranes include northern Scotland and west-central Argentina (Precordillera) with Laurentian fossils, eastern Newfoundland with fossils from Baltica, and southern Mexico (Oaxaca) with Gondwanan (South American) fossils.

Another important consequence of continued plate movement has been the formation of large mountain ranges at the sites of plate collision. Pressure and heat generated during collisions since the Cambrian have folded, faulted, and metamorphosed significant volumes of Cambrian rock, especially from the outer margins and slopes of many continental shelves. No crustal rocks found in today's oceans are older than the Mesozoic Era (251 to 65.5 million years ago). Most pre-Mesozoic deposits that accumulated in the deep ocean basins are thought to have been destroyed after they subducted into Earth's interior.

Relatively abrupt changes in sea level may have significantly influenced Cambrian environments and life. A global drop in sea level is suggested by extensive unconformities (interruptions in the deposition of sedimentary rock). The time represented by such unconformities in sectors of Laurentia and Baltica bounding the Iapetus Ocean has been called the Hawke Bay event. An apparent absence of a coeval unconformity in western North America seems to be an anomaly. Thick uninterrupted shelf deposits in this sector of Laurentia, however, may have resulted from abnormal shelf subsidence caused by the cooling of crustal rocks following a late Precambrian plate-rifting event. The timing of unconformities found in widely separated continents cannot be correlated with precision. However, it is perhaps significant that a number of characteristic animal groups from the early portions of the Cambrian were either exterminated or severely restricted in their geographic distribution at about the same time in the world's shallow-shelf environments. Among biostratigraphically important trilobites, the olenellids were exterminated near Laurentia, the holmiids went extinct at the margins of Baltica, and the redlichiids vanished from the shallow-shelf ecosystems near Gondwana. Also, diverse and abundant reef-dwelling archaeocyathans (extinct group of sponges thought to have helped construct the first reefs) disappeared from most low-latitude warm-water continental shelves.

The significant rise in sea level is suggested by rather abrupt and extensive displacements in sedimentary environments and biotas during the middle of the Cambrian (the *Ptychagnostus gibbus* zone). Lowland areas were flooded, as in parts of Baltica. In warm-water shelf sections of the world, coarse-grained, shallow-water, carbonate rocks were abruptly overlain by fine-grained, deeper-water, laminated limestone or shale. Adaptive radiation of the pelagic agnostoid trilobites was greatly accelerated in open-oceanic environments following this event, perhaps in response to newly expanded habitats.

In Laurentia, a significant drop in sea level near the end of the Cambrian is suggested by both the disappearance of some faunas and a single unconformity that defines the boundary between the Dresbachian and Franconian stages, two regional stages in peripheral areas of North America. However, there is no evidence for a comparably large change in sea level at or near the Cambrian-Ordovician boundary. Associated minor unconformities have made it difficult to select a defining Global Standard Section and Point (GSSP) for the boundary, which ideally should be located in an uninterrupted stratigraphic section.

Several regions of Cambrian volcanism have been identified. Australia was especially active. Large areas in the northern and central regions were covered by flood basalts during the early parts of the Cambrian with residual activity extending into the middle of the period. Basalts and mafic intrusives (molten rock derived from basic magmas) in southeastern Australia formed in a volcanic island arc setting during the early and middle parts of the Cambrian. Volcanic suites of similar age are also present in New Zealand and in parts of Antarctica (northern Victoria Land, Ellsworth Mountains, and Pensacola Mountains). Other significant Cambrian volcanic deposits occurring during the early and middle parts of the period are found in southern Siberia and western Mongolia (Altai and Sayan mountains), eastern Kazakhstan and northwestern China (Tian Shan), and northeastern China. Cambrian volcanics are scattered along the easternmost margin of the United States, but most are probably island arc deposits that were accreted to Laurentia after the Cambrian. In the southern United States (Oklahoma), granitic intrusives and basaltic and rhyolitic extrusives are associated with a large tectonic trough that was formed by rifting, or crustal extension, throughout the first half of the period.

Minor volcanic deposits, mainly ash beds and thin flows, are widely known. In general, these have received little study, but some are suitable for the determination of isotopic ages. Zircons from a lower Lower Cambrian (pre-trilobite) volcanic ash bed in New Brunswick, Can., have a uranium-lead age of 531 million years. Volcanic tuffs near inferred Tommotian-Atdabanian boundaries (Russian designations for the pretrilobite and trilobite portions of the Cambrian explosion) in both Morocco and southwestern China have yielded similar dates of 521 million years.

The tectonic history of the Precambrian is not as well known as that of the Paleozoic. In general, however, late Precambrian history seems to have been characterized by continental fragmentation, whereas Paleozoic history was characterized by the continental accretion of terranes. The Cambrian was a period of transition between those tectonic modes, and continents were scattered, apparently by the fragmentation of Rodinia. Major Cambrian and early Ordovician tectonism affected large areas of Gondwana in what are now Australia, Antarctica, and Argentina. Multiphase tectonism in Antarctica is called the Ross Orogeny, and in Australia it is known as the Delamerian Orogeny. At least some of the volcanic activity noted previously, particularly that of volcanic island arcs, is evidence that seafloor spreading and crustal subduction were active geologic processes.

PALEOCLIMATE

Global climate during the Cambrian time was probably warmer and more equable than today. An absence of either land or landlocked seas at the Cambrian poles may have prevented the accumulation of polar ice caps. The general absence of glacial till deposits of the Cambrian age is more notable, because these deposits are common and widespread in upper Precambrian strata. They accumulated again during the Ordovician Period in northern Africa as Gondwana began to move over the South Pole. Otherwise, the presence of persistent and widespread limestone deposits found on the margins of a centralized transcontinental arc in North America, for example, indicates that a subtropical climate existed in latitudes between 30°N and 30°S. In addition, arid to semiarid conditions at latitudes around the Tropics of Cancer and Capricorn (approximately 23°27' N and S latitude, respectively) are suggested by deposits that include sandstone with quartz grains frosted by abrasion through wind transport, ventifacts (wind-polished stones), and evaporites.

More sophisticated research on paleoclimates relies on the detection of changing patterns in the amounts of isotopic oxygen, carbon, and strontium retained in limestone samples to correlate the timing of different geological events. Much remains to be accomplished regarding this promising line of research on Cambrian strata, but certain trends and events are becoming better defined. Strong reductions in isotopic carbon (^{13}C), for example, are correlated from Lower Cambrian strata at localities as distant from one another as the Lena River area of Siberia and the Atlas Mountains of Morocco. Another substantial drop in ^{13}C is believed to mark the transition between the early and middle parts of the Cambrian in the Great Basin of North America. Such decreases may represent a global rise in temperature occurring at the same time as a rise in global sea level. In addition, the delivery of anoxic (oxygen-depleted) ocean waters with reduced amounts of ^{13}C also may have been aided by the rising sea level.

CAMBRIAN LIFE

The long history of life on Earth has been punctuated by relatively abrupt changes. Some have argued that the greatest change of all occurred in marine environments near the Precambrian-Cambrian boundary. Fossils from

Cambrian rocks include the oldest representatives of most animal phyla having mineralized shells or skeletons. A lack of observed connecting links suggests that processes of biomineralization (specifically, the formation of bones, shells, and teeth) evolved independently in several phyla. Whether or not soft-bodied representatives of some of these phyla originated during the Precambrian Era but have no preserved record is a debated question. Nevertheless, the hard parts of Cambrian animals had a much greater potential for preservation than the soft parts, and they mark the beginning of a diverse fossil record.

THE FOSSIL RECORD OF THE PRECAMBRIAN-CAMBRIAN TRANSITION

The preservation of the record of the Precambrian-Cambrian transition was significantly affected by global changes in sea level. During the latest Precambrian time, the sea level was relatively low, resulting in spatially restricted oceans and expanded continents. Throughout much of the Cambrian, rising seas gradually flooded vast land areas. Sediment was eroded from the continents and deposited in adjacent seas. Because of low sea level, the sedimentary and fossil records of the Precambrian-Cambrian transition are generally most complete toward the outer margins of continental shelves. As a corollary, the time gaps, represented by the boundary surface, generally increase in landward directions. This has led to an absence or serious incompleteness of the transitional record in most areas, particularly in those of classical Cambrian studies. As a result, it is thought that this incompleteness, combined with a general deficiency in knowledge—prior to the mid-1900s—of Precambrian communities, contributed significantly to the long-held notion of an abrupt or sudden appearance of Cambrian fossils.

Considering the biological importance of the Precambrian-Cambrian transition, it is somewhat surprising that the primary impetus for its detailed study came from a project designed to establish a suitable international boundary stratotype (a rock layer that serves as a benchmark of geologic time). Before the project was initiated in 1972, reasonably complete stratigraphic sections across the transition were either largely unrecognized or ignored. Since 1972, information about the transition has accumulated at an accelerating rate. Although many details remain to be learned, the general history of this momentous interval is becoming clear.

The Precambrian-Cambrian biotic transition, once thought to be sudden or abrupt, has been found to include a succession of events spread over many millions of years. It commenced with the appearance of the animal kingdom (i.e., multicelled organisms that ingest food), but the date and details of that event remain obscure. At least three informal phases in the transition can be identified by progressively more diverse and complex biological communities.

The earliest phase of the late Precambrian age is characterized by fossils of soft-bodied animals known from many localities around the world. Based on fossils of animal embryos, it is thought that elements of the Ediacaran fauna appeared as early as 590 to 600 million years ago. The fossils are predominantly the imprints of soft-bodied animals. Their extraordinary preservation, usually in sandstone or shale, was probably the result of rapid burial and protection by smothering sediment. Most of the fossils are relatively simple, and many resemble worms, sea pens, and jellyfish. Dwelling traces (fossilized burrows and other excavations) like those of modern sea anemones are also common. Placing Ediacaran fauna in higher (more generalized) taxonomic levels is controversial, however, because critical diagnostic features are not evident. Some paleontologists have assigned Ediacaran body fossils to the extant phyla Annelida, Coelenterata, and Arthropoda, whereas others have regarded them as members of extinct taxonomic groups of high rank. Some adherents of this latter viewpoint have suggested that the Ediacaran fauna was terminated by a major extinction event, but direct evidence of an abrupt replacement of species has not been found in the geologic record.

Other kinds of fossils also provide valuable clues about life during Ediacaran time. Photosynthetic organisms include unicellular blue-green algae (cyanobacteria) and acritarchs (probable algae), both of low diversity. Individuals of some species were probably abundant, however, and may have been an important source of food for Ediacaran animals. Hard parts of animals, primarily known from Africa and China, are mainly dwelling tubes composed of calcium carbonate and other compounds. Most were probably secreted by sessile, filter-feeding, wormlike animals. Although rare and of low diversity, these forms are significant because they signal the advent of biomineralization. The oldest unequivocal trace fossils, mainly crawling trails, are also of Ediacaran age. The trails suggest that locomotion of the trace makers was accomplished by waves of muscular contraction, like that in annelids and sea slugs, and not by legs. All but the latest Ediacaran trace fossils are relatively simple, suggesting limited and primitive behaviour patterns. Their low diversity further suggests that few kinds of mobile animals lived on the Ediacaran seafloor.

The second phase of the Precambrian-Cambrian biotic transition is characterized by a marked increase in the diversity of its shelly fauna and a lack of trilobites. It is near the lowest stratigraphic occurrence of this fauna that the Precambrian-Cambrian boundary stratotype has been placed. The fauna includes that of the Tommotian Stage, as applied in Russia, and it has often been referred to as the Tommotian fauna. It is known from many localities around the world, but time correlations lack precision. A general acceleration in biotic diversity during this second phase is the beginning of the Cambrian explosion.

Fossils of the second phase, which may be locally abundant, represent several new animal groups of Paleozoic aspect. Calcified archaeocyathans (extinct group of sponges thought to have helped construct the first reefs) diversified rapidly and were the first skeletal metazoans (multicellular animals with differentiated tissues) to develop a modular growth habit. They also evolved a complex symbiotic relationship with reef-building blue-green algae. Mollusks, preserved in both shale and limestone, include at least four classes (Monoplacophora, Gastropoda, Hyolitha, and Rostroconchia). Brachiopods (lamp shells) made their appearance but are low in diversity. Several groups are represented by an astonishing array of small mineralized tubes, scales, and spicules. The presence of arthropods, the first animals to develop legs, is indicated by characteristic trace fossils. The skeletal remains of arthropods are not preserved in

Now extinct, the small, conical-shelled hyoliths are usually only found preserved in Cambrian rocks. O. Louis Mazzatenta/National Geographic/ Getty Images

the fauna, however, presumably because they were not mineralized. Other trace fossils show a marked increase in abundance and diversity as well as an expansion of behaviour patterns that reflect improvements in locomotion, greater ability to penetrate sediment, and new foraging strategies.

The third phase of the Precambrian-Cambrian biotic transition commenced with the appearance of mineralized trilobite skeletons. The subsequent adaptive radiation of the trilobites was exceptional, and their remains dominate most later Cambrian deposits. For this reason, the Cambrian Period has sometimes been called the "Age of Trilobites."

The known Cambrian biota was restricted to marine environments. At least 11 extant animal phyla (Annelida, Arthropoda, Brachiopoda, Chordata, Ctenophora, Echinodermata, Hemichordata, Mollusca, Onychophora [velvet worms], Porifera, and Priapulida), including most of those with a fossil record, first appear in Cambrian rocks. Most of these rapidly diversified as they seemingly adapted to numerous unfilled ecological niches. Another five phyla (Nemertea, Phoronida, Platyhelminthes, Pogonophora, and Sipuncula) may also trace their origin back to the Cambrian fossils, though questions still remain about them. The only extant animal phylum with a good fossil record that is not known from Cambrian rocks are the Bryozoa (moss animals), which first appear in rocks of Early Ordovician age. A summary of the principal biotic groups of the Cambrian is given below.

PHOTOSYNTHETIC ORGANISMS

Cambrian photosynthetic organisms, the primary food of animals, are entirely unicellular. These organisms include a variety of prokaryotic (nonnucleated) and eukaryotic (nucleated) bacteria and algae. Their evolution, like that in associated animals, shows a marked acceleration in adaptive radiation and biomineralization near the base of the Cambrian. A new calcareous bottom-dwelling flora dominated by blue-green algae appeared. Some of these organisms formed mounds on the seafloor. Others formed small, concentrically laminated, marble- or biscuit-shaped structures called oncoids, which were locally abundant. Although it was rarely preserved, there existed a non-calcareous benthic flora that also was dominated by blue-green algae. By at least the middle of the Cambrian, some noncalcareous green algae (Chlorophyta) had become common. In North America and Siberia, the axes of one species, *Margaretia dorus*, exceeded 2 centimetres (0.8 inch) in diameter and were probably more than 1 metre (3.3 feet) in height. Such large size is attained by modern green algae only in warm, equatorial oceans. The phytoplankton, consisting of acritarchs and blue-green algae, also diversified near the base of the Cambrian. Acritarchs are widespread in many kinds of marine rocks and seem to have the potential for an improved zonation of Lower Cambrian rocks. They are difficult to study, however, because of their microscopic size.

FAUNA

Cambrian faunas, like those of the present day, are commonly dominated in numbers and kind by members of the phylum Arthropoda. Calcification of skeletons by the beginning of Atdabanian time contributed to an abundant fossil record of the class Trilobita, of which some details have been discussed above. Many hundreds of genera and thousands of species of Cambrian trilobites have been described worldwide. Rates of evolution in Cambrian trilobites were relatively rapid, resulting in short stratigraphic ranges and giving them much value for biostratigraphic correlation. Representatives of the class Ostracoda, characteristically enclosed by a bivalved carapace, also appeared near the base of the Atdabanian. Compared with trilobites, however, ostracods are generally rare and of low diversity throughout the Cambrian, except in some rocks of Australia and China. Extraordinary preservation at rare localities indicates that many other kinds of arthropods were at least locally more abundant and more diverse than the trilobites. These other arthropods had unmineralized skeletons, and some may represent extinct classes.

Sponges (phylum Porifera) are commonly represented in Cambrian faunas. Archaeocyathan sponges, characterized by cup-shaped skeletons with double calcareous walls and numerous pores, are abundant and diverse in some early Cambrian deposits. They have been used for provincial biostratigraphic zonation, especially in Australia and Siberia. Archaeocyathans are common only in regions that were positioned in low latitudes during the Cambrian — Antarctica, Australia, China, Kazakhstan, Siberia, and North America. Their latitudinal distribution is similar to that of modern colonial corals, suggesting adaptations to similar ecological controls in warm shallow seas. Archaeocyathans nearly disappeared about the middle of the Cambrian, but rare species survived until much later in the period, after which the group became extinct. Other common Cambrian sponges had skeletons of siliceous (silica-derived) spicules, which readily disaggregated after death, making their identification at lower taxonomic levels difficult, if not impossible. At rare locations of exceptional preservation, where articulated skeletons and associated soft-bodied taxa and others were found, spicular sponges are second only to arthropods in species diversity. This suggests that Cambrian sponges were much more common and more diverse than is indicated by the known fossil record. Limited information indicates that species of spicular sponges evolved slowly during the Cambrian, resulting in relatively long ranges within the stratigraphic record.

Brachiopod shells are present in many Cambrian continental-shelf deposits. In terms of the total number of species that have been described from Cambrian rocks, brachiopods are second only to trilobites. Species diversity, however, is generally low to moderate at most localities. Phosphatic shells of the class Inarticulata are normally much more common and more diverse than are calcareous shells of the class Articulata. These abundance and diversity relationships are usually reversed in post-Cambrian rocks.

The phylum Echinodermata (some present-day representatives of which are sea urchins and starfish) had a major adaptive radiation during the Cambrian Period. The number of classes increased from three early in the Cambrian to eight toward the middle of the period. Only one of these, the Eocrinoidea, is known from many species, but the described record seems to be grossly incomplete. Skeletal plates in early echinoderms were not rigidly connected, and they readily disaggregated after the death of an animal. Consequently, it is rare to find articulated skeletons that can be classified to lower taxonomic levels. In some Cambrian limestones, however, skeletal plates of echinoderms are a dominant sedimentary constituent, indicating the existence of innumerable animals and suggesting far greater diversity, especially at low taxonomic levels, than has been recorded. As in some modern echinoderm species, it is common for those in the Cambrian to show evidence of a gregarious habit and patchy distribution. Most of the Cambrian echinoderms were suspension and detritus feeders, and it was only after the Cambrian that herbivores and carnivores became common. All classes of echinoderms that were present during the Cambrian, except for the Crinoidea, subsequently became extinct.

The phylum Mollusca also underwent significant adaptive radiation during the Cambrian, with the appearance of the classes Monoplacophora, Gastropoda, Pelecypoda (synonymous with Bivalvia), Cephalopoda, Polyplacophora, Rostroconchia, Hyolitha, and Stenothecoida. (The latter three are now extinct.) The only molluscan class that appeared after the Cambrian is the Scaphopoda (tusk or tooth shells), which originated during the Ordovician. A small variety of mollusks is present in the shelly fauna of the earliest Cambrian. Mollusk shells usually are absent or rare in later Cambrian rocks, but at a few localities they are common to abundant. The small conical shells of hyoliths are the kind most commonly preserved in Cambrian rocks.

Other new Cambrian phyla largely lack biomineralization and have a poor fossil record. The Hemichordata is represented by rare sessile graptolites (order Dendroidea) of the class Graptolithina, which appeared during the middle of the Cambrian. Appearances of the more common planktonic graptolites (order Graptoloidea) have been used as informal indicators of the Cambrian-Ordovician boundary. The formal boundary stratotype coincides with the first appearance of *Iapetognathus fluctivagus*, a conodont (primitive chordate with tooth-shaped fossil remains). Cambrian worm phyla (Annelida, Priapulida, and probable Pogonophora) are mainly known from localities where preservation was extraordinary. Other rarely represented phyla include the Onychophora, with leglike lobopodia (a catchall category of Cambrian life), and the Ctenophora (comb jellies).

The origin of the phylum Chordata is unclear. If primitive conodont-like fossils (paraconodonts) are included, as argued by some paleontologists, the phylum appeared during the late Precambrian. Rare soft-bodied possible chordates have been described from Lower Cambrian rocks. The oldest unequivocal chordate remains come from the Lower Cambrian of south China, where small jawless fish similar to present-day lamprey and hagfish occur as part of the Chengjiang Biota. The fossils from this Lagerstätte (a fossil-rich deposit of sedimentary rock) preserve the remains of different soft body tissues — traces of gill pouches, dorsal fins, and likely the notochord itself.

Trace fossils, as discussed above, provide independent evidence of accelerated animal diversification and a distinct increase in the complexity of animal behaviour near the beginning of the Cambrian Period. Other evidence from trace fossils indicates changes in Cambrian bioturbation, the churning and stirring of seafloor sediment by animal forms. Late Precambrian (Ediacaran) trace fossils from around the world are essentially surface trails that show little evidence of sediment burrowing. Quantitative study in the western United States has shown that a significant increase in bioturbation occurs between pretrilobite (Tommotian) and trilobite-bearing (Atdabanian) Lower Cambrian rocks. Throughout the Cambrian, bioturbation was more intensive in nearshore and inner-shelf environments than in more offshore settings. The depth of bioturbation in carbonate environments of the inner shelf was consistently less than a few centimetres throughout Cambrian time.

Deposits with Soft-Bodied Organisms

Modern biota are largely dominated by soft-bodied organisms, whereas the fossil record is overwhelmingly dominated by the hard parts of organisms. Rare deposits of fossils with soft parts are therefore of great importance in helping to establish the original diversity and ecology of ancient communities. Among the most famous soft-bodied biota are those found in the Burgess Shale of western Canada (British Columbia), which was formed during the middle of the period, and the Chengjian Biota from southern China (Yunnan), which was formed earlier in the period. In the case of the Burgess Shale, tens of thousands of complete specimens, many with soft parts preserved in remarkable detail, were apparently buried by submarine slumping of sediment on the continental shelf of Laurentia. Fossils from the Burgess Shale have been used to demonstrate the presence of a complex community as diverse in habit, structure, and adaptation as many modern communities. If isolated, fossils with hard parts would constitute a typical Cambrian fauna, but they represent only about 40 percent of the genera in the Burgess Shale,

The largest predator to swim the Cambrian seas, the Anomalocaris *flexes its mighty appendages to feed on the hapless* Opabinia. De Agostini Picture Library/Getty Images

a proportion similar to that in modern faunas on continental shelves. Approximately 15 percent of the genera known from the Burgess Shale also occur in the older Chengjian deposit. Mollusks and echinoderms appear to be the only major groups absent in the Chengjian Biota that occur in the Burgess Shale.

The most celebrated invertebrate from the Burgess Shale is attributed to the genus *Anomalocaris*. This creature was the largest predator that swam in Cambrian seas. It was outfitted with a pair of giant flexible appendages that could grasp and move prey toward a peculiar mouth structure consisting of armoured plates arranged in a circular pattern. The articulated mouth of *Anomalocaris* has been described as resembling a pineapple ring with the center cut out. Trilobites with telltale scars on their carapace are believed to represent the cookie-cutter bite of *Anomalocaris*.

In the Canadian Rockies, a photographer zooms in on the famous Burgess Shale fossil formation, formed by Middle Cambrian mudslides that buried and preserved in startling detail more than 60,000 soft-bodied specimens. Michael Melford/National Geographic/Getty Images

A smaller relative of *Anomalocaris* is the bizarre *Opabinia*, with its five eyes mounted on an arthropod-like body and a long nozzlelike structure fitted with a single pair of claws that protrudes forward from the head. It is thought that *Opabinia* moved across the seafloor, using its flexible nozzle to stir up bottom sediment and grasp hidden prey with extended claws.

Other less-diverse Cambrian deposits with soft-bodied organisms have been discovered in places such as South Australia, northern Greenland, Sweden, and the United States (Utah and Pennsylvania). Some of these are important in demonstrating that the biota of the Burgess Shale is unusual only in preservation and not in composition. They also demonstrate that some of the soft-bodied taxa have substantial geologic ranges and wide geographic distributions. Extraordinary preservation of arthropods dating to the later parts of the Cambrian Period in Sweden is especially notable, as the bodies and appendages remain largely uncrushed. The integument retains many fine structures, including setae (bristly hairs or organs) and pores.

CAMBRIAN EXTINCTION EVENTS

Minor extinction events occurred sporadically throughout the Cambrian Period. One near the middle of the Cambrian was apparently related to global marine regression. At least three later Cambrian events primarily affected low-latitude shelf communities and have been used in North America to define biostratigraphic units called biomeres. (Such units are bounded by sudden nonevolutionary changes in the dominant elements of a phylum.) Each of the Cambrian biomere events eliminated several trilobite families, which collectively contained most of the genera and species that were living on the continental shelves. Less attention has been paid to extinction patterns among other inverte-brates, but some evidence of corresponding extinctions among brachiopods and conodonts is available.

Geochemical evidence suggests that the biomere extinctions were probably caused by abrupt drops in water temperature. Oxygen isotopes from the skeletons of bot-tom-dwelling trilobites associated with one biomere boundary in Texas indicate a drop in water temperature of about 5°C (9°F) at the boundary. A comparable decrease in temperature would kill the larvae of many modern marine invertebrates that live in warm oceans. Following each Cambrian extinction, shelf environments were repopu-lated by low-diversity trilobite faunas of relatively simple form, which apparently emigrated from deeper and cooler off-shelf environments. In effect, every one of the bio-mere events was followed by an adaptive radiation of new taxa, especially among the trilobites.

SIGNIFICANT CAMBRIAN LIFE-FORMS

Several different kinds of life emerged during the period, and much of what is known about Cambrian life comes from the Burgess Shale formation of western Canada. Some organisms, such as the conodonts, trilobites, and graptolites, have been useful in the global correlation of Cambrian rocks and those of subsequent geologic peri-ods. The brachiopods, or lamp shells, which is a group that can also be used in geologic correlation, have modern liv-ing representatives.

BURGESS SHALE

The celebrated Burgess Shale, as mentioned previously, is a fossil formation containing remarkably detailed traces of soft-bodied biota of the Middle Cambrian Epoch (520 to 512 million years ago). Collected from a fossil bed in the Burgess Pass of the Canadian Rockies, the Burgess Shale is one of the best preserved and most important fossil formations in the world. Since it was discovered in 1909, over 60,000 specimens have been retrieved from the bed.

The Burgess Shale captures a complex marine environment containing a rich diversity of arthropods, miscellaneous worms, sponges, lophophorates, echinoderms, mollusks, priapulids, chordates, hemichordates, annelids, and coelenterates. The fossil bed is likely the result of mud slides from the Laurentian shelf that rapidly buried the fauna, preserving great morphological detail. While many of the fossils clearly belong to established phyla and reveal important information about phylogenetic development, there are many other genera that do not fit so easily into modern phyla. Such unusual fossils as *Hallucigenia,* a creature with a long tubular body and two rows of tall dorsal spines; *Wiwaxia,* an oval creature with two rows of spines down its plated back; and *Opabinia,* which had five eyes and a long nozzle, have led many scientists to conclude that the Cambrian Period may have produced many unique phyla. However, deposits discovered in China, Greenland, and elsewhere have demonstrated that at least some of the shale's oddities (including *Hallucigenia* and *Wiwaxia*) belong to known groups of animals—though they were members of lineages that diverged early from the others and soon became extinct—and that the Burgess Shale is unique in preservation, but probably not in composition.

CONODONTS

Conodonts are among the most frequently occurring fossils in marine sedimentary rocks of Paleozoic age. These minute toothlike fossils are composed of the mineral apatite (calcium phosphate). Between 0.2 millimetres (0.008

inch) and 6 millimetres (.236 inch) in length, they are known as microfossils and come from rocks ranging in age from the Cambrian Period to the end of the Triassic Period. They are thus the remains of animals that lived during the interval of time from 542 million to 200 million years ago and that are believed to have been small marine invertebrates living in the open oceans and coastal waters throughout the tropical and temperate realms. Only recently has the conodont-bearing animal been found, preserved in fine-grained rock from North America. Conodont shapes are commonly described as either simple cones (like sharp teeth), bar types (a thin bent shaft with needlelike cusps or fangs along one edge), blade types (flattened rows of cones of ranging size), or platform types (like blades, with broad flanges on each side making a small ledge or platform around the blade). Well over 1,000 different species or shapes of conodonts are now known.

Some conodonts exist in two forms, "right" and "left." They are known to have occurred in bilaterally symmetrical pair assemblages in the animal, like teeth but more delicate and fragile. The few assemblages discovered so far appear to contain as many as nine different species, or forms, of conodonts. Bars, blades, and platforms may all be present in a single assemblage or apparatus. How single cones fitted into assemblages is uncertain. The conodont apparatus seems to have been placed at the entrance to the gut and to have assisted in food-particle movement. The relationship of this little animal (30–40 mm long) to the known wormlike animal groups is still debatable, and no exactly compatible creature is known to exist today.

Conodonts are very useful fossils in the identification and correlation of strata, as they evolved rapidly, changing many details of their shapes as geologic time passed. Each successive group of strata thus may be characterized by distinctive conodont assemblages or faunas.

Moreover, conodonts are very widespread, and identical or similar species occur in many parts of the world. Black shales and limestones are especially rich in conodonts, but other sedimentary rock types may also be productive. In some parts of the world assemblages of conodonts, regarded as those of animals living out in the open ocean, can be distinguished from others thought to belong to inshore communities.

The oldest conodonts are from Lower Cambrian rocks. They are largely single cones. Compound types appeared in the Ordovician Period, and by Silurian time there were many different species of cones, bars, and blade types. The greatest abundance and diversity of conodont shape was in the Devonian Period, wherein more than 50 species and subspecies of the conodont *Palmatolepis* are known to have existed. Other platform types were also common. After this time they began to decline in variety and abundance. By Permian time the conodont animals had almost died out, but they made something of a recovery in the Triassic. By the end of that period they became extinct.

Conodonts are most commonly obtained by dissolving the limestones in which they occur in 15 percent acetic acid. In this acid, they are insoluble and are collected in the residue, which is then washed, dried, and put into a heavy liquid such as bromoform through which the conodonts sink (the common acid-insoluble mineral grains float). The conodonts are studied under high magnification by using a binocular microscope. Work on these fossils is now carried out in many countries. Originally discovered in Russia in the middle of the 19th century, they were recognized as being very useful in rock dating and correlation in the United States and Germany about 100 years later. Perhaps the most detailed correlations by means of these microfaunas have been made in the

Devonian System of rocks. Thick continuous sequences of limestones in which they occur have been especially studied in North America, Europe, and Morocco, and the succession of conodonts there serve as reference standards. The conodonts obtained from similar rocks elsewhere can then be compared with these, and correlations can be made. Strata distinguished by special conodont assemblages are termed zones. There are 10 generally recognized conodont zones in the Ordovician, 12 zones in the Silurian, 30 in the Devonian, 12 in the Carboniferous, 8 in the Permian, and 22 in the Triassic. Refinements and variations of these zonal schemes are made from time to time as knowledge increases.

The extinction of the conodont animal remains an unsolved mystery. It does not seem to have coincided with a particular geologic event, nor were there extinctions of other groups of marine creatures at the same time. Records of conodonts from younger strata have all proved to be of fossils derived from older rocks and reburied at the later date.

DENTICLES

Denticles are parts of a conodont. Although they resemble cusps, denticles are generally smaller than distinct cusps and vary greatly in shape and structure. Denticles may be spaced closely to each other or separated by gaps of varying size. In addition, they may be distinctly formed or partially fused to each other. In shape, denticles may be needlelike, spiny, or saw-toothed. In some conodonts, denticles are completely absent, and the major part of the conodont consists of a single cusp. The form, number, and arrangement of denticles are frequently distinctive and characteristic of particular kinds of conodonts. In some forms, denticles are present as single straight, or almost straight, rows. In others, the denticles may be curved or even split into several branches. The earlier conodont forms that possess denticles generally consist of a main bar that supports the denticle row and the main cusp. In later forms, the main cusp and denticle row are flanked by a platform on either side.

GRAPTOLITES

Graptolites belong to an extinct group of small, aquatic colonial animals that first became apparent during the Cambrian Period (542 million to 488 million years ago) and that persisted into the Early Carboniferous Period (359 million to 318 million years ago). Graptolites were floating animals that have been most frequently preserved as carbonaceous impressions on black shales, but their fossils have been found in a relatively uncompressed state in limestones. They possessed a chitinous (fingernail-like) outer covering and lacked mineralized hard parts. When found as impressions, the specimens are flattened, and much detail is lost.

The graptolite animal was bilaterally symmetrical and tentacled. It has been suggested that graptolites are related to the hemichordates, a primitive group of invertebrates. Graptolites have proved to be very useful for the stratigraphic correlation of widely separated rock units and for the finer division of Lower Paleozoic rock units (Cambrian to Devonian). Examples include the genera Climacograptus, Clonograptus, Didymograptus, Diplograptus, Monograptus, Phyllograptus, and Tetragraptus. Graptolites show a gradual development through time, and evolutionary relationships between different graptolite groups have been discovered and analyzed.

LAMP SHELLS

Lamp shells, also known as brachiopods, belong to the phylum Brachiopoda, a group of bottom-dwelling marine invertebrates. They are covered by two valves, or shells. One valve covers the dorsal, or top, side, and the other covers the ventral, or bottom, side. The valves, of unequal size, are bilaterally symmetrical—i.e., the right and left sides are mirror images of one another. Brachiopods (from the Greek words meaning "arm" and "foot") are commonly known as lamp shells because they resemble early Roman oil lamps.

Brachiopods occur in all oceans. Although no longer numerous, they were once one of the most abundant forms of life.

Members of this phylum first appeared rather early in zoological history. It is possible, by means of fossil representatives, to survey their evolution from the Cambrian Period (about 542 million years ago) to the present. Although some of the evolutionary development is revealed, it is still imperfectly understood. Other than their usefulness in dating geological periods, members of this phylum have no economic value, except as curios and museum pieces.

General Features

Lamp shells are generally small and their modern forms exhibit little diversity. They are found in polar regions as well as tropical ones. Relatively large concentrations of species occur along parts of the South American, Australian, and Japanese coasts.

Size Range and Diversity of Structure

Most brachiopods are small, 2.5 centimetres (about one inch) or less in length or width. Some are minute, measuring 1 millimetre (more than 130 of an inch) or slightly more, while some fossil forms are relative giants—about 38 centimetres (15 inches) wide. The largest modern brachiopod is about 10 centimetres (4 inches) in length.

Great diversity existed among brachiopods in the past; modern brachiopods, however, exhibit little variety. They are commonly tongue-shaped and oval lengthwise and in cross section. The surface may be smooth, spiny, covered with platelike structures, or ridged. Most modern brachiopods are yellowish or white, but some have red stripes or spots. Others are pink, brown, or dark gray. The tongue-shaped shells (*Lingula*) are brown with dark-green splotches. Rarely, they are cream yellow and green.

Distribution and Abundance

Today, brachiopods, numbering about 300 species representing 80 genera, are abundant only locally. In parts of the Antarctic, they outnumber all other large invertebrates. As mentioned previously, they are common in the waters around Japan, southern Australia, and New Zealand. Although rare in the Indian Ocean, some unusual types are common along the coast of South Africa. In Caribbean and West Indian waters, 12 species occur. The east and west coasts of the North Atlantic Ocean are sparsely occupied by brachiopods. The waters around the British Isles contain a few species, and a few genera live in the Mediterranean Sea. The West Coast of the United States and Hawaii have a number of brachiopod species, and the coasts of Chile and Argentina have a considerable variety, including the largest living species. Some live in the polar regions, and a few are abyssal—i.e., they inhabit deep parts of the ocean.

Natural History

Although the bulk of lamp shell species occur in shallow water, many species are found in the ocean depths. Before becoming sessile filter-feeders as adults, lamp shell eggs mature into a motile larval stage.

Reproduction

Not much is known about the reproduction of brachiopods. Except in three genera, the sexes are separate. Eggs and sperm are discharged into the mantle cavity through funnel-shaped nephridia, or excretory organs, on each side of the mouth. Fertilization takes place outside the shell. In a few genera the young develop inside the female in brood pouches formed by a fold of the mantle, a soft extension of the body wall. Some fossil forms had internal cavities that may have served as brood chambers. The egg develops into a free-swimming larva that settles to the bottom. The free-swimming stage of the articulate brachiopods (whose valves articulate by means of teeth and sockets) lasts only a few days, but that of the inarticulates may last a month or six weeks. In inarticulate larvae the pedicle, a stalklike organ, develops from a so-called mantle fold along the valve margin. In articulates it develops from the caudal, or hind, region.

Behaviour and Ecology

About 60 percent of brachiopods live in shallow water (less than 100 fathoms—about 180 metres [600 feet]) on the shelf areas around the continents. More than 35 percent occupy waters deeper than 100 fathoms, and a few live in the abyss down to more than 6,000 metres (about 20,000 feet). *Lingula* lives from the tidal zone to 23 fathoms (about 42 metres [138 feet]). Most modern branchiopods anchor by the pedicle to pebbles, to the undersides of stones, or to other hard objects. They prefer quiet water and protected surroundings. *Lingula* lives in mud or sand and is attached at the bottom of its burrow.

Brachiopods feed by opening the shell and bringing in food-bearing currents by lashing of the cilia (hairlike structures) attached to the filaments of the lophophore, a horseshoe-shaped organ that filters food particles from the seawater. Cilia in lophophore grooves bring food particles, often trapped in mucus, to the mouth. Brachiopods feed on minute organisms or organic particles. Articulate brachiopods, which have a blind intestine, may depend partly on dissolved nutrients.

Shells of some articulate brachiopods have a fold, which forms a trilobed anterior that helps keep lateral, incoming food-bearing currents separated from outgoing, waste-bearing currents. When feeding, *Lingula* protrudes its anterior (front) end above the mud and arranges its setae (bristle-like structures) into three tubes. These channel the water into lateral incoming and medial, or central, outgoing currents. Some coralliform brachiopods of the Permian Period (299 million to 251 million years ago) are thought to have fed by rapid beating of the dorsal valve, causing a sucking in and expulsion of food-bearing water. Some ostreiform (oyster-shaped) types of the same period are believed to have fed by gentle pulsation of the dorsal valve.

Form and Function

Two major groups of brachiopods are recognized, based on the presence or absence of articulation of the valves by teeth and sockets. The valves of inarticulate brachiopods are held together by muscles. *Lingula*, with its elongated, tonguelike shell, is an example. Its convex valves bulge outward at the middle and taper posteriorly, or away from the hinge. A long, fleshy pedicle protrudes between the valves at the tapered end. The pedicle of *Lingula* differs from that of most other brachiopods in being flexible and capable of movement—an aid in burrowing and in attaching the animal in its burrow. The shell interior is divided into posterior coelomic (internal-body) and anterior mantle cavities. The internal organs are located in the coelom. The digestive system consists of mouth, gullet, stomach, intestine, and anus, all surrounded by a liver, or digestive gland. A complex set of muscles opens the valves and slides them laterally, or sideways, when feeding. The mantle cavity is occupied by the lophophore. *Lingula* lives in a burrow in mud or sand with the tip of its pedicle attached in mucus at the bottom of the burrow. The contractile pedicle permits extension of the shell when feeding or retraction if the animal is startled.

The articulate-brachiopod shell is typified by *Waltonia*, which is small (about 2 centimetres [3/4 inch]) and red in colour, with a smooth or slightly ridged shell. This type of shell is more highly specialized than that of most inarticulate species and is composed of three layers. The outer layer, called periostracum, is made of organic substance and is seldom seen in fossils. A middle layer consists of calcium carbonate (calcite). The inner layer is composed of calcite fibres and may be punctate—i.e., perforated by minute pits—or it may be pseudopunctate, with rods (taleolae) of calcite vertical to the surface. Impunctate shells have neither pits nor taleolae.

Many hinged brachiopods attach to the substrate, or surface, by a tough, fibrous pedicle; but some specialized forms are cemented to the substrate by the beak of the ventral valve. Cemented forms are commonly distorted, scalelike, or oyster shaped or resemble a cup coral. The pedicle of some brachiopods is atrophied; their shells lie loose on the seafloor.

The shell of an articulate brachiopod tapers posteriorly to a beak. The ventral valve is usually the larger. The hinge may be narrow or wide. Many hinged genera have a flat or curved shelf, called the palintrope, between the beak and the hinge line. The ventral palintrope is divided at the middle by the delthyrium, a triangular opening for the pedicle. The delthyrium may remain open or be wholly or partly closed by small plates growing from its margins. In some families the delthyrium is closed completely or partly by one plate, the pseudodeltidium, anchored to the delthyrial margins. The articulating teeth occur at the angles of the delthyrium and may or may not be supported by vertical dental plates, which may be separate or united to form a so-called spondylium. Teeth are of two types, deltidiodont and cyrtomatodont. Deltidiodont teeth grow anteriorly with the palintrope and leave a growth path along the delthyrial edge. Cyrtomatodont teeth are knoblike and occur in shells without a hinge line. They grow anteriorly but are kept knoblike by posterior resorption.

The dorsal valve contains structures called crura that diverge from the beak. In some fossil forms the crural bases (brachiophores) bound a triangular cavity, the notothyrium, in which the diductor, or opening, muscles are attached onto the floor or to a ridge, or boss, called the cardinal process at the apex. The notothyrium may be closed by a solid plate, the chilidium. In more highly developed genera a hinge plate bearing the pedicle or dorsal adjustor muscles occurs between the crural bases. The hinge plate is said to be divided when it is incomplete but undivided when it forms a flat or concave structure. The hinge plate is often supported by a median septum, or wall. The hinge sockets are located between the inside shell wall and a socket ridge to which the hinge plate is attached. In many specialized genera the crura support calcareous loops or spires (brachidia), the inner skeleton of the lophophore. Structures corresponding in function but of different origin and with different names occur in the pedicle region of some inarticulate brachiopods.

The fleshy body of the articulate brachiopod is divided transversely by the body wall into a posterior visceral cavity filled with coelomic fluid and an anterior mantle cavity filled with seawater. The visceral cavity contains the U-shaped digestive canal, four reproductive glands, and a liver, or digestive gland, held in place by mesenteries (sheets of tissue). Extensions of the coelom into the mantle hold the eggs and sperm. The mouth leads into a saclike stomach that ends in an intestine. There is no anus. The liver surrounds the stomach. Waste is excreted through the mouth. The nervous system, which consists of two principal ganglia, or nerve centres, encircles the esophagus and sends branches to other parts of the body. One pair of excretory organs (nephridia) occurs in most brachiopods, but two pairs may be present.

The mantle cavity is lined by the thin, shell-secreting mantle that is fringed by setae at its edges. Within the mantle cavity is the lophophore, which may be a simple or complicated loop, often horseshoe-shaped. Ciliated filaments along the loop direct food-bearing currents to the mouth, which is located on the body wall between the branches of the lophophore and crura.

The shell opens by contraction of diductor muscles that extend from near the centre of the ventral valve to the process under the dorsal beak. These muscles pull the dorsal beak forward, rotating it on a line joining the hinge teeth. Contraction of the adductor muscles closes the valves. In the ventral valve the adductors are located between the diductors. Pedicle muscles or adjustors extending from the pedicle to the hinge plate of the dorsal valve rotate the shell on the pedicle. In places where the muscles are attached to the shell there are scars, which are helpful in the identification of genera.

Paleontology

Brachiopods were among the first animals to appear at the beginning of the Cambrian Period (542 million years ago). Their evolution and distribution was wide and rapid. More than 35,000 species in more than 2,500 genera are known, and the number of described species increases yearly. Articulate and inarticulate brachiopods appeared at the same time in a relatively advanced state of development, indicating a long evolution from forms without shells, an evolution apparently lost or unrecorded in Precambrian times.

The Inarticulata, the most abundant brachiopods of the Cambrian, soon gave way to the Articulata and declined greatly in number and variety toward the end of the Cambrian. They were represented in the Ordovician (488 million to 444 million years ago) but decreased thereafter. In the Cretaceous (146 million to 66 million years ago) the punctate calcareous Inarticulata proliferated, but this trend soon ended. The Inarticulata dwindled through the Cenozoic (66 million years ago) to the Recent (last 10,000 years). Only nine genera are known during the Recent Epoch. Inarticulate genera represent about 6.5 percent of all brachiopod genera.

The Articulata, diverse and most numerous from Ordovician times to the present, were, in the Cambrian, represented by several specialized forms. Articulate evolution tended toward shell elaboration for bottom dwelling and perfection of feeding mechanisms from the simple looped lophophore to the elaborate lobate and spiral forms. The Orthida, the most common articulate brachiopods of the Cambrian and Ordovician, decreased in numbers after the Ordovician, and the impunctate Orthida became extinct in the Early Devonian (416 million to 398 million years ago). The punctate Orthida lingered into the Permian Period (299 million to 251 million years ago). The Strophomenida appeared in the Early Ordovician and increased rapidly. They were abundant and varied in the Devonian, becoming even more so by Permian times. This large order became greatly reduced at the end of the Permian Period. The Pentamerida, never prolific, flourished in the Ordovician. An evolutional burst of huge forms occurred in the Silurian (444 million to 416 million years ago), but after that the pentamerids decreased into the Devonian (416 million to 359 million years ago) and became extinct early in the late part of that period. The Spiriferida are conspicuous for the great elaboration of the spiral brachidium. They appeared in the Ordovician, were widely distributed into the Permian, and survived into the Jurassic, which began about 200 million years ago. The Rhynchonellida were abundant from mid-Ordovician throughout the Paleozoic. They survived into the Triassic (251 million to 200 million years ago) and had a rebirth in the Jurassic, after which they declined into the Cenozoic. They now number only 14 genera.

The Terebratulida, now the dominant group, appeared in the early Devonian and rapidly expanded in the mid-Devonian to produce a number of gigantic forms. A few long-looped and short-looped genera persisted into the Permian. The Terebratulida survived the Permian and were widely distributed in the Triassic and evolved into a great variety of forms in the Jurassic, especially the short-looped types. Decline of the short-looped terebratulids began in the Late Cretaceous (100 million to 66 million years ago). They have continued to dwindle into the present and are now outnumbered by the long-looped terebratulids.

Classification

Brachiopods possess a lophophore (a feeding structure that filters food from seawater), excretory organs

CLASSIFICATION OF INVERTEBRATES

The classification below is based on that proposed by A. Williams and A.J. Rowell in 1965 in *Treatise on Invertebrate Paleontology*.

Phylum Brachiopoda (lamp shells)

Marine invertebrates with two valves, or shells; lophophore horseshoe-shaped; about 300 living species known; more than 30,000 extinct species described; occur in all oceans.

Class Inarticulata

Shell does not articulate, is usually composed of chitinophosphatic material; shell muscles complex; pedicle (stalk) develops from ventral mantle, a soft extension of the body wall; intestine with anal opening.

Order Lingulida

Shell usually contains phosphate, rarely calcareous, biconvex (i.e., both valves convex), beak for attachment to surface apical, or located at the tip, in both valves; fleshy pedicle emerging between the valves at the tapered end; about 51 genera; Cambrian to Recent.

Order Acrotretida

Usually circular in outline; shell either contains phosphate or is punctate calcareous; pedicle opening confined to the ventral valve; 62 genera; Early Cambrian to Recent.

Order Obolellida

Mostly calcareous, biconvex, shape nearly circular to elongated; position of pedicle opening variable; dorsal valve with marginal beak; 5 genera; Early to mid-Cambrian.

Order Paterinida

Shell with phosphate, rounded or elliptical; pedicle opening partly closed by cover called homeodeltidium; dorsal valve similar to the ventral but with a convex homeochilidium; 7 genera; Early Cambrian to mid-Ordovician.

Class Articulata

Shells articulate by means of teeth and sockets; shells always calcareous; musculature less complicated than in Inarticulata; larval pedicle develops from rear region; no outside opening from intestine.

Order Kutorginida

Calcareous, biconvex interarea (smooth surface in area between beak and hinge line) present; delthyrium (opening in the pedicle) closed by a plate, the pseudodeltidium; dorsal valve with interarea; muscle area narrow and elongated in both valves; 3 genera; Early to mid-Cambrian.

Order Orthida

Usually biconvex, wide-hinged, with interareas in both valves; teeth deltidiodont (leave a growth path along margin of pedicle opening); hinge structures consist of brachiophores (supporting structures), shell substance punctate or impunctate—i.e., with or without pits; more than 200 genera; Early Cambrian through Permian.

Order Strophomenida

Teeth deltidiodont when present; ventral muscles large; shell substance pseudopunctate (with rods of calcite), rarely impunctate; more than 400 genera; mid-Ordovician to Early Jurassic.

Order Pentamerida

Biconvex, ventral valve usually with a spondylium (united dental plates); delthyrium usually open; dorsal-valve brachiophores supported by bracing plates; impunctate; nearly 100 genera; mid-Cambrian to Late Devonian.

Order Rhynchonellida

Narrow-hinged with functional pedicle; dorsal valve with or without a median septum; lophophore (of Recent genera) dorsally spiral and attached to crura (supporting structures); spondylia rare; nearly 300 genera; Ordovician to Recent.

Order Spiriferida

Lophophore supported by a calcareous spiral structure (brachidium); punctate or impunctate, usually biconvex; delthyrium open or closed; more than 300 genera; mid-Ordovician to Jurassic.

Order Terebratulida

Pedicle functional, cyrtomatodont teeth; lophophore supported wholly or in part by a calcareous loop, short or long and free or attached to a median septum; more than 300 genera; Early Devonian to Recent.

(nephridia), and simple circulatory, nervous, and reproductive systems. Brachiopods have usually been divided into two classes, Articulata and Inarticulata, as introduced above.

Critical Appraisal

The classes Articulata and Inarticulata were first proposed by T. H. Huxley in 1869. Before 1932 they were further subdivided into four orders based on the imperfectly known larval development and formation of the shell around the pedicle opening. In 1927 a fifth order was proposed, and it was suggested that a classification be based on the pedicle development of the larvae.

Most brachiopods are extinct, and larval development can only be conjectured. Because of this, the early classification schemes have been abandoned. Eleven orders distributed in Huxley's classes have been retained in the present classification, which is still being modified. On the basis of hinge and tooth types some systematists have divided the Articulata into two subclasses: Protremata and Telotremata. The Protremata are wide-hinged forms with deltidiodont teeth. The Telotremata are narrow-hinged brachiopods with cyrtomatodont teeth.

LINGULIDS

Lingulids belong to a group of brachiopods, or lamp shells, that include ancient extinct forms as well as surviving representatives. First known from Cambrian rocks (about 500 million to 570 million years old), they probably originated during Precambrian time. The lingulids are small, inarticulate brachiopods. Their shells are unhinged and consist of chitinous (fingernail-like) material. A modern genus, *Lingula,* is found in normal marine environments but is most common in muddy, brackish water that is poor in oxygen and generally unsuited to most organisms. The genus *Lingulella* is a fossil form known from the Cambrian and was similar in appearance and structure to the modern *Lingula. Lingulepis,* a related genus more or less restricted to the Late Cambrian, differs from other lingulids in appearance. It is more teardrop in form. The lingulids are useful fossils for the environmental information that they provide. They are of little use for stratigraphic correlations. The lingulids were an important component of Cambrian brachiopod faunas.

OBOLUS

This genus of extinct brachiopod lived during the Cambrian Period (from 542 million to 488 million years ago). *Obolus* was a small animal with a spherical shape. One valve, or shell, was larger than the other. Unlike the shells of its relatives, the lingulids, the obolus shells were composed of calcium carbonate. *Obolus* inhabited shallow marine waters.

STROMATOPORIDA

Stromatoporida is the name of an extinct order of corals found as fossils in marine rocks of Cambrian to Cretaceous age (542 million to 65.5 million years ago). The stromatoporidian corals were colonial forms that consisted of dense laminated masses of calcium carbonate. Some forms constructed reeflike masses.

TRILOBITES

Extinct fossil arthropods easily recognized by their distinctive three-lobed, three-segmented form, trilobites were exclusively marine animals. They first appeared at the beginning of the Cambrian Period, about 542 million years ago, and they dominated the seas. Although they became less abundant in succeeding geologic periods, a few forms persisted into the Permian Period, which ended about 251 million years ago.

Because trilobites appear fully developed in the Cambrian Period,

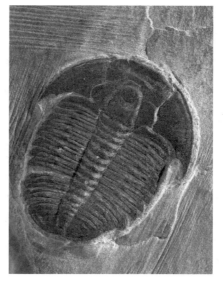

Trilobites, which appeared fully developed at the beginning of the Cambrian Period, exhibit three distinct segments: head, thorax, and tail. ©www.istockphoto.com / Russell Shively

it appears likely that the ancestral trilobites originated during the Ediacaran Period (630 million to 542 million years ago) of Precambrian times. An organism that may be ancestral to the trilobites, as well as to other arthropods, may be represented by *Spriggina,* which is known from Precambrian shallow-water marine deposits in Australia. Trilobites are frequently used for stratigraphic correlations.

Trilobites had three body lobes, as indicated above, two of which lay on each side of a longitudinal axial lobe. The trilobite body was segmented and divided into three regions from head to tail: the cephalon, or head region, separated from the thorax, which was followed in turn by the pygidium, or tail region. Trilobites, like other arthropods, had an external skeleton, called exoskeleton, composed of chitinous material. For the animal to grow, the exoskeleton had to be shed, and shed trilobite exoskeletons, or portions of them, are fossils that are relatively common.

Each trilobite body segment bore a pair of jointed appendages. The forwardmost appendages were modified into sense and feeding organs. Most trilobites had a pair of compound eyes. Some of them, however, were eyeless.

Some trilobites were active predators, whereas others were scavengers, and still others probably ate plankton. Some trilobites grew to large size. *Paradoxides harlani,* which has been found near Boston in rocks of the Middle Cambrian Epoch (521 million to 501 million years ago), grew to be more than 45 centimetres (18 inches) in length and may have weighed as much as 4.5 kilograms (10 pounds). Others were small.

Some important trilobite genera of the Cambrian are listed next.

Bathyuriscus

This genus of trilobites provides a useful index fossil for the Middle Cambrian Epoch of North America (520 to 512 million years ago). In *Bathyuriscus* the head segment is well developed and marginal spines are present. The tail region is large and has many well-developed segments. Several species of *Bathyuriscus* are recognized.

Cedaria

Cedaria is another genus of trilobites that is a useful index fossil for Cambrian rocks and time (about 542 million to 488 million years ago). *Cedaria* was small, with a well-developed tail section and a prominent head section.

Crepicephalus

This genus of trilobites serves as an index fossil for Upper Cambrian rocks in North America (dating 512 to 505 million years ago). It is a relatively common fossil and occurs over a wide geographic range but within a relatively narrow time span. *Crepicephalus* is recognized by the prominent spines at the lateral margins of the tail section. Smaller spines occur at the margins of the head shield.

Dikelocephalus

A genus of trilobites that is a useful guide fossil for the Late Cambrian rocks (512 to 505 million years ago) of Europe and North America, *Dikelocephalus* is distinguished by its broad head, its large and relatively well-developed tail, and its pair of short spines at the end of the tail. The eyes of *Dikelocephalus* are large and crescentic in shape.

Olenellus

This trilobite genus was common in but restricted to Early Cambrian rocks (540 to 520 million years ago) and thus a useful guide fossil for the Early Cambrian. *Olenellus* had a well-developed head, large and crescentic eyes, and a poorly developed, small tail.

Paradoxides

Paradoxides, a genus of trilobites (an extinct group of arthropods) found as fossils in Middle Cambrian rocks of North America and western Europe (the Cambrian Period lasted from 540 to 505 million years ago), possessed a well-developed head region terminating laterally in pointed spines that vary in development from species to species. The tail region is poorly developed. The body is well-segmented, and the axial lobe tapers to the minuscule pygidium (tail). Some species of *Paradoxides* attained a large size of 45 centimetres (18 inches). *Paradoxides* is useful in correlating Middle Cambrian rocks and time.

CAMBRIAN GEOLOGY

Cambrian rocks are primarily known for the fossils they contain and thus are useful in correlating the ages of rocks in different parts of the world. However, Cambrian rocks are also economically valuable. In some locations they contain ores such as gold. In others, Cambrian carbonate rocks may be made into fertilizers or provide the raw materials for building and road construction.

TYPES AND DISTRIBUTION

Cambrian rocks have a special biological significance, because they are the earliest to contain diverse fossils of

Quartzite slope breccia of Cambrian age from Ardennes, Belg. Courtesy of Ernst ten Haaf

animals. These rocks also include the first appearances of most animal phyla that have fossil records. It is because the Cambrian evolution produced such an extraordinary array of new body plans that this event has been referred to as the Cambrian explosion. The beginning of this remarkable adaptive radiation has been used to divide the history of life on Earth into two unequal eons. The older, approximately three-billion-year-old Cryptozoic Eon began with the appearance of life on Earth, and it is represented by rocks with mainly bacteria, algae, and similar primitive organisms. The younger, approximately half-billion-year-old Phanerozoic Eon, which began with the Cambrian explosion and continues to the present, is characterized by rocks with conspicuous animal fossils.

Rocks of Cambrian age occur on all of the continents, and individual sections may range up to thousands of metres thick. The most fossiliferous and best-studied deposits are principally from marine continental-shelf environments. Among the thicker and better-documented sections are those in the Cordilleran region of western North America, the Siberian Platform of eastern Russia, and areas of central and southern China. Other well-documented fossiliferous but thinner sections are located in Australia (especially in western Queensland), the Appalachian Mountains of eastern North America, Kazakhstan, and the Baltic region (most notably in Sweden).

Lateral changes in the composition of Cambrian rocks resulted from regional differences in environments of deposition. Nearshore deposits are commonly composed of siliceous sandstone. This usually grades seaward into siltstone and shale, which formed by accumulation of finer-grained sediment in deeper water where the seafloor was less affected by wave action. Extensive carbonate platforms, analogous to the present-day Bahama Banks, developed along some continental shelves that were in low latitudes during Cambrian time. Rapid production of carbonate sediment in this warm, shallow-water environment resulted in massive deposits of Cambrian limestone and dolomite. Examples are exposed in the Cordilleran region of North America, in north central Australia, along the Yangtze River in central China, and along the Lena River in Siberia. Few Cambrian rocks from land environments have been documented, and most of those are of limited areal extent. They mainly represent deposits of floodplains and windblown sand. Without plants or animals, the desolation of Cambrian landscapes must have rivaled that of any present-day desert. In the absence of plants with roots to hold soil in place, Cambrian lands in general probably eroded more rapidly than they do now.

Relative sea level rose significantly during the Cambrian, but with fluctuations. This is indicated by both the geographic distribution and the stratigraphic layering of sedimentary deposits. In North America, for example, marine deposits from earlier in the period covered only marginal areas, whereas later marine deposits covered much of the continent. Similar distributions of marine rocks are present on other continents. In stratigraphic sections from continental shelves that were located in low latitudes, it is common for a basal nearshore sandstone to be overlain by layers of more seaward shale and carbonate rocks deposited during times of high sea level. Shelf sections from high latitudes may be mostly or entirely sandstone, or a basal sandstone deposit may grade upward into shale, but most of these sections contain evidence of marine transgression. Exceptions to the general Cambrian sea-level pattern are commonly attributable either to local tectonism or to different rates of sediment accumulation. The most likely explanation for the general rise in Cambrian sea level seems to be increased thermal activity and related swelling of spreading ridges between lithospheric plates, which would displace vast quantities of seawater. It has been suggested that these periods of marine inundation exerted an influence on adaptive radiation (the proliferation of organic lineages) by greatly increasing the area of shallow seas where life was most abundant.

THE BOUNDARIES AND SUBDIVISIONS OF THE CAMBRIAN SYSTEM

The lower boundary of the Cambrian System is defined at a formal global stratotype section and point (GSSP), which was ratified by the International Commission on Stratigraphy (ICS) of the International Union of Geological Sciences (IUGS) in 1992. The stratotype section is located at Fortune Head on the Burin Peninsula of southeastern Newfoundland in Canada. It contains a thick and continuous marine succession of mostly shale, siltstone, and sandstone. The stratotype point, representing a moment in time, is in the lower part of the Chapel Island Formation. It coincides with the base of the remnant burrows of the fossil *Trichophycus pedum* and marks the first occurrence of well-developed, fairly complex metazoans (group of animals composed of multiple, differentiated cells). This is currently regarded as the most useful benchmark on which to characterize both the lower boundary of Cambrian time and the beginning of the Phanerozoic Eon. *T. pedum* can be found on most continents, and its chronological position puts it slightly younger than Ediacaran fossils (around 570 million years ago) and some 20 million years older than the small shelly fossils dated to the early parts of the Cambrian Period.

While there is general agreement on the point in time picked for the beginning of the Cambrian, there is little or no agreement on how to subdivide the remaining 53 million years of Cambrian time. In most regions of the world, Cambrian rocks have been divided into lower, middle, and upper series according to regional standards and practices, but these distinctions are neither uniform nor internationally recognized. Furthermore, regional series boundaries are not necessarily synchronous with one another, owing to differences in definition and problems in correlation. Some series have been further divided into stages, but these are mostly identifiable only within individual regions. Many supplementary sections were investigated at boundary localities around the world before the stratotype was selected in Newfoundland. All these supplementary sections are important references for reconstructing the physical and biological histories of the boundary interval. Among the more thoroughly studied supplementary sections are those along the Aldan River of eastern Siberia and near the city of Kunming in the Yunnan province of southern China.

The lower boundary of the Ordovician System indirectly defines the upper boundary of the Cambrian System. A formal boundary stratotype coincides with the first appearance of the conodont *Iapetognathus fluctivagus*. This boundary marks the base of the Tremadoc Series in the Ordovician System. British geologists have traditionally assigned rocks and fossils of Tremadoc age to the Cambrian, whereas many others have assigned them to the Ordovician.

Rocks in the Cambrian-type area in Wales are so poorly exposed, structurally complicated, and sparsely fossiliferous that they have had little influence on development of modern concepts of the Cambrian and its subdivisions. In fact, many rocks in the Cambrian-type area have been reassigned to either the Precambrian or the Ordovician. Rocks in Wales that are now assigned to the Cambrian System roughly correspond to Sedgwick's Lower Cambrian.

THE ECONOMIC SIGNIFICANCE OF CAMBRIAN DEPOSITS

Cambrian rocks are of moderate economic importance, as they provide a variety of resources. For example, ore bodies rich in such metals as lead, zinc, silver, gold, and tungsten have secondarily replaced Cambrian carbonate rocks, especially in parts of North America and Australia.

Other carbonate rocks have been widely used as building stone and for making lime and portland cement. Large Cambrian phosphorite deposits are major sources of agricultural fertilizer in northern Australia, southwestern China, and southern Kazakhstan. Other Cambrian resources in China are mercury, uranium, and salt. Eastern Russia also has salt deposits of Cambrian age, as well as those of bauxite, the chief commercial source of aluminum. Some oil fields in southern Siberia produce oil from Lower Cambrian rocks.

THE CORRELATION OF CAMBRIAN STRATA

Time correlation of Cambrian rocks has been based almost entirely on fossils. The most common fossils in Cambrian rocks are trilobites, which evolved rapidly and are the principal guide fossils for biostratigraphic zonation in all but rocks below the Atdabanian Stage or those of equivalent age. Until the mid-1900s, almost all trilobite zones were based on members of the order Polymerida. Such trilobites usually have more than five segments in the thorax, and the order includes about 95 percent of all trilobite species. Most polymeroids, however, lived on the seafloor, and genera and species were mostly endemic to the shelves of individual Cambrian continents. Therefore, polymeroid trilobites are useful for regional correlation but have limited value for intercontinental correlation, which has been difficult and subject to significant differences in interpretation.

From the 1960s, investigators began to recognize that many species of the trilobite order Agnostida have intercontinental distributions in open-marine strata. These trilobites are small, rarely exceeding a few millimetres in length, and they have only two thoracic segments.

Specialized appendages, which were probably useful for swimming but unsuitable for walking on the seafloor, suggest that they were pelagic (living in the open sea). Agnostoids make up less than 5 percent of all trilobite species, but individuals of some agnostoid species are abundant. This fact, together with their wide geographic distribution and rapid evolution, makes them valuable for refined intercontinental correlation. Agnostoids first appear in upper Lower Cambrian rocks but did not become common or diversify significantly until the middle of the Cambrian. Therefore, agnostoids have their greatest biostratigraphic value in the upper half of the Cambrian System. A comprehensive trilobite zonation in Sweden has frequently been cited as a standard for correlation.

Other kinds of fossils have had more limited use in Cambrian biostratigraphy and correlation. Among them are the archaeocyathan sponges in the Lower Cambrian and brachiopods (moss animals) throughout the Cambrian, but use of both groups has been hampered by problems of endemism. Small mollusks and other small shelly fossils, mostly of problematic affinities, have been employed for biostratigraphy in the Tommotian Stage (a Russian designation for the pretrilobite portion of the Cambrian explosion), but their utility is also limited by endemism. Conodonts appear in the uppermost Precambrian but are rare in most Cambrian rocks except those of latest Cambrian age, when adaptive radiation of conodont animals accelerated. Wide species distributions, rapid evolution, and abundance make conodonts excellent indexes for global biostratigraphy in uppermost Cambrian to uppermost Triassic rocks.

Since roughly the 1980s, trace fossils have been used with limited precision to correlate uppermost Precambrian and basal Cambrian strata. Although the biostratigraphic use of such fossils has many problems, they nevertheless demonstrate progressively more complex and diverse patterns of locomotion and feeding by benthic (bottom-dwelling) marine animals. *T. pedum*, which initially appears in Cambrian deposits and marks the base of the period, demonstrates the first regularly branching burrow pattern.

STAGES OF THE CAMBRIAN PERIOD

The Cambrian Period is divided into 10 stages. However, only four of them are named. This situation is attributed to the difficulty in finding markers that adequately correlate rocks from different parts of the world. As a result of this challenge, the bases of all stages but the Fortunian are approximations.

FORTUNIAN STAGE

This interval is the first of two internationally defined stages of the Terreneuvian Series, encompassing all rocks deposited during the Fortunian Age (542 million to approximately 528 million years ago) of the Cambrian Period. The name of this interval is derived from the town of Fortune, Newfoundland, Can.

In 1992 the ICS established the Global Stratotype Section and Point (GSSP) defining the base of this unit in the sandstone and mudstone of the Chapel Island Formation, located on the Burin Peninsula near Fortune. The GSSP marks the first appearance of the trace fossil *Trichophycus pedum* in the fossil record. The base of the Fortunian Stage also serves as the base of the Cambrian System, the Paleozoic Erathem, and the Phanerozoic Eonothem. The stage follows the Ediacaran System of the

Proterozoic Eonothem and precedes Stage 2 of the Terreneuvian Series of the Cambrian System.

DRUMIAN STAGE

The Drumian Stage is the second of three internationally defined stages of the Series 3 epoch of the Cambrian Period, encompassing all rocks deposited during the Drumian Age (approximately 506.5 million to 503 million years ago). The name of this interval is derived from the Drum Mountains of western Utah, U.S.

In 2006 the ICS established the Global Stratotype Section and Point (GSSP) defining the base of this unit in the calcareous shales of the Wheeler Formation, a rock formation located in Utah's Drum Mountains. It marks the first appearance of the trilobite *Ptychagnostus atavus* in the fossil record. The Drumian Stage follows Stage 5 and precedes the Guzhangian Stage, all three stages making up Series 3 of the Cambrian System.

GUZHANGIAN STAGE

The Guzhangian Stage is the final internationally defined stage of the Series 3 epoch of the Cambrian Period, encompassing all rocks deposited during the Guzhangian Age (approximately 503 million to 499 million years ago).

In 2008 the ICS established the Global Stratotype Section and Point (GSSP) defining the base of this unit in the carbonate rock beds of the Huaqiao Formation in the Wuling Mountains of Hunan, China. The GSSP marks the first appearance of the trilobite *Lejopyge laevigata* in the fossil record. The Guzhangian Stage follows the Drumian Stage of Series 3 and precedes the Paibian Stage of the Furongian Series.

PAIBIAN STAGE

The first of three internationally defined stages of the Furongian Series is the Paibian Stage. This interval encompasses all rocks deposited during the Paibian Age (approximately 499 million to 496 million years ago) of the Cambrian Period. The name of this interval is derived from the village of Paibi, Huayan county, Hunan, China.

In 2006 the ICS established the Global Stratotype Section and Point (GSSP) defining the base of this unit in Huaqiao Formation in the Wuling Mountains of Hunan, China. The GSSP marks the first appearance of the trilobite *Glyptagnostus reticulatus* in the fossil record. The Paibian Stage underlies Stage 9 of the Furongian Series and overlies the Guzhangian Stage of Series 3.

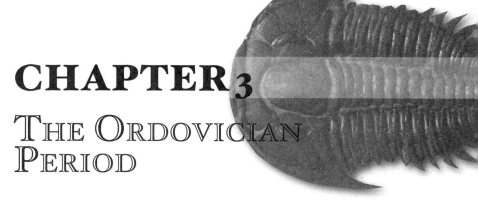

CHAPTER 3

THE ORDOVICIAN PERIOD

The second period of the Paleozoic Era, the Ordovician began 488.3 million years ago, following the Cambrian Period, and ended 443.7 million years ago. Ordovician rocks have the distinction of occurring at the highest elevation on Earth—the top of Mount Everest.

The Ordovician Period ushered in significant changes in plate tectonics, climate, and biological systems. Rapid seafloor spreading at oceanic ridges fostered some of the highest global sea levels in the Phanerozoic Eon. As a result, continents were flooded to an unprecedented level, with North America almost entirely underwater at times. These seas deposited widespread blankets of sediment that preserved the extraordinarily abundant fossil remains of marine animals. Numerical models of the Ordovician atmosphere estimate that levels of carbon dioxide were several times higher than today. This would have created warm climates from the Equator to the poles. However, extensive glaciation did occur for a brief time over much of the Southern Hemisphere at the end of the period.

THE ORDOVICIAN ENVIRONMENT

The Ordovician Period was characterized by the intense diversification (an increase in the number of species) of marine animal life in what became known as the Ordovician radiation. This event precipitated the appearance of almost every modern phylum (a group of organisms

This New Zealand calcite marble outcrop was likely formed in the Ordovician Period when all the major tectonic plates were in motion. G. R. "Dick" Roberts/NSIL/Visuals Unlimited/Getty Images

having the same body plan) of marine invertebrate by the end of the period, as well as the rise of fish. Ordovician seas were filled with a diverse assemblage of invertebrates, dominated by brachiopods (lamp shells), bryozoans (small colonial animals that produce a skeletal framework of calcium carbonate), trilobites, mollusks, echinoderms (a group of spiny-skinned marine invertebrates), and graptolites (small, colonial, planktonic animals). On land the first plants appeared, as well as possibly the first invasion of terrestrial arthropods. The end of the Ordovician was heralded by a mass extinction, the second largest in Earth history. The largest mass extinction took place at the end of the Permian Period and resulted in the loss of about 90 percent of then-existing species.

The Ordovician was demarcated in the late 19th century as a compromise in a dispute over the boundaries of the Cambrian and Silurian systems. Studying the rock succession from northwest to southeast within Wales, English geologist Adam Sedgwick named the Cambrian System in 1835. At the same time and working in the opposite direction, Scottish geologist Roderick Murchison named the Silurian System. Both geologists expanded their systems until they overlapped, triggering a scientific feud. English geologist Charles Lapworth proposed the Ordovician System (named for an ancient Celtic tribe of northern Wales called the Ordovices) in 1879 to define the disputed overlapping interval. Lapworth's proposal was resisted in Britain into the 1890s and, despite subsequent widespread international usage, was not officially adopted there until 1960.

The Ordovician is divided into three epochs: Early Ordovician (488.3–471.8 million years ago), Middle Ordovician (471.8–460.9 million years ago), and Late Ordovician (460.9–443.7 million years ago).

PALEOGEOGRAPHY

During the Ordovician Period, four major continents were present and separated by three major oceans. Although the positions of these continents are frequently updated with new evidence, current understanding of their position is based on paleomagnetic evidence, fossil markers, and climatically sensitive sediments, such as evaporite minerals. The craton (stable interior portion of a continent) of Laurentia—made up of most of present-day North America, Greenland, and part of Scotland—straddled the Equator and was rotated approximately 45° clockwise from its present orientation. The craton of Siberia-Kazakhstan lay east of Laurentia, along and slightly north of the Equator. The Iapetus Ocean separated these two landmasses on the south from the Baltica craton, which included present-day Scandinavia and north-central Europe. The microcontinent of Avalonia— made up of England, New England, and maritime Canada—was positioned to the west of Baltica and also faced Laurentia across the Iapetus Ocean. The Paleotethys Sea separated England, Baltica, and Kazakhstan from the supercontinent of Gondwana, which consisted of Africa, South America, India, Arabia, China, Australia, Antarctica, Western Europe, the southeastern United States, and the Yucatán Peninsula of Mexico. This immense supercontinent straddled both the South Pole, located then in what is now northwest Africa, and the Equator, which then crossed present-day Australia and Antarctica. In this position, Africa and South America were rotated nearly 180° from their present orientation. A single body of water, the Panthalassic Ocean, covered almost the entire Northern Hemisphere and was as wide at the Equator as the modern Pacific Ocean.

SEA LEVEL

Following the breakup of the supercontinent Rodinia during the Cambrian Period, the rate of seafloor spreading reached a maximum during the Ordovician Period. Tall oceanic ridges produced by this activity raised the average elevation of the seafloor and flooded parts of many continents, creating vast shallow seas within their interiors and at their margins. During the Early and Late Ordovician epochs, almost all of North America was submerged under these epicontinental seas.

Sea level fluctuated continuously throughout the Ordovician. At the broadest scale, sea level was highest during the Early and Late Ordovician epochs and may have been up to 200 metres (about 660 feet) lower during the Middle Ordovician Epoch. Numerous shorter-term fluctuations were superimposed on this broad rise and fall, with each fluctuation typically lasting one to five million years. Additional minor fluctuations of a few metres or less, occurring on the order of tens to hundreds of thousands of years, have also been identified. The causes of all of these changes in sea level are difficult to identify. Some may have been driven by variations in the rates of plate motion, some by glaciation, some by local tectonic uplift or subsidence, and some by changes in groundwater storage capacity. The end of the Ordovician Period is marked by a pronounced fall in sea level of nearly 160 metres (525 feet), which was triggered by the rapid expansion of continental ice sheets on Gondwana.

THE CIRCULATION OF THE OCEAN

Although it is impossible to observe Ordovician oceanic currents directly, major circulation patterns can be inferred from basic oceanographic principles. Circulation within the Panthalassic Ocean was unimpeded by continents and followed a relatively simple zonal system, with westward circumpolar flow north of 60° N. The northward projections of Laurentia and Gondwana into the Panthalassic Ocean would have created two large clockwise-spinning gyres (eddies) between the equator and 60° N. In the Southern Hemisphere, Gondwana blocked this zonal flow by spanning the area from the South Pole to the equator. Smaller gyres were set up within the Paleotethys Sea and Iapetus Ocean, with generally counterclockwise flow south of 60° S and clockwise flow between the equator and 60° S. The tectonic movements of small continents and oceanic islands considerably modified these relatively simple gyres. Monsoonal circulation, characterized by seasonal alterations in ocean currents, would have been fostered in subtropical latitudes, particularly along the margins of Gondwana.

Upwelling (the movement of colder, nutrient-rich water from the depths to the surface) would have developed along the west coasts of continents, along the equator and 60° S. Unlike the present time, in which the water in the deep ocean is generated from the sinking of cold, dense water at the poles, bottom water in the Ordovician would have originated in the warm, saline conditions of tropical epicontinental seas. Relatively rapid evaporation in these warm locations would have increased the density of a volume of water because of the high concentrations of dissolved salts. Similar conditions also existed during the Cretaceous Period and led in both cases to sluggish ocean circulation and resulting anoxia (lack of dissolved oxygen) in deep marine environments. The widespread black shales found in deepwater settings in the Ordovician are evidence of anoxic conditions. Only at the very end of Ordovician times during the extended glacial period would ocean circulation patterns accelerate. Chilled by continental glaciation, surface waters would have descended and displaced the warmer, deep ocean water. Because the sinking of cold polar water occurs at a faster rate than the sinking of warm, saline tropical water, the strength of cold ocean currents, and thus upwelling, would have increased.

PLATE TECTONICS

Following the breakup of the Rodinia supercontinent in the Cambrian, extensive oceanic ridges were established, circling the globe and creating the Paleotethys Sea and Iapetus and Panthalassic oceans. The production of oceanic lithosphere at these ridges was accommodated through its destruction at subduction zones. The Panthalassic Ocean was apparently bordered on all sides by subduction zones, much like the Pacific Ocean is today. A subduction zone also separated Laurentia from both Siberia and Baltica.

All of the major tectonic plates were in motion during the Ordovician Period. Laurentia gradually rotated counterclockwise as Siberia-Kazakhstan approached it from the east. Baltica drew toward Laurentia from the southeast, gradually closing the Iapetus Ocean and ultimately colliding with Laurentia in the Silurian Period. The Paleotethys Sea also gradually narrowed as a subduction zone on the west side of Gondwana consumed the ocean floor. Gondwana itself underwent a gradual clockwise rotation in the Ordovician, bringing Africa over the South Pole and Australia and North China across the equator and into the Northern Hemisphere.

Ordovician volcanism was extensive and was primarily generated at subduction zones and oceanic ridges. Globally, volcanism appears to have peaked twice during the early Paleozoic Era, first near the end of the Cambrian Period through earliest parts of the Ordovician Period and later within the Middle to Late Ordovician epochs. The progressive closing of ocean basins as continents collided during the Middle Paleozoic is thought to reflect an overall slowing of rates of plate motion and therefore a slowdown in volcanicity, which is observed after the Ordovician. Ordovician volcanic deposits produced at subduction zones consist mostly of ashes as well as basaltic to andesitic flows, much as seen in modern subduction zones. Other Ordovician volcanic deposits record eruptions in extensional basins (rift zones) and are characterized by thick accumulations of basalt. Volcanic rocks of Ordovician origin are particularly common in Great Britain, Kazakhstan, the Baltic region and Scandinavia, eastern North America, and Argentina.

Unique mineralogical and geochemical features of many Ordovician volcanic ashes allow them to be correlated over long distances. One such ash bed, the Millbrig K-bentonite of eastern North America, has been correlated to the "Big Bentonite" of Scandinavia, which was separated from North America in the Ordovician by the 1,000-kilometre-wide (620-mile-wide) Iapetus Ocean. Reconstruction of the volume of this eruption suggests that over 1,000 cubic kilometres (about 240 cubic miles) of ash was erupted, making it one of the largest recorded ashfalls in Earth history. In contrast, the eruption of Mount St. Helens in 1980 produced a mere 0.2 cubic kilometre (about 0.05 cubic mile) of ash.

Orogenic (mountain-building) belts formed in the Ordovician wherever plates converged—at subduction zones and at collisions between continents and terranes, such as microplates (smaller fragments of continental plates), oceanic arcs (chains of volcanic islands), and oceanic plateaus. Subduction zones have been recognized along the Panthalassic margin of Tasmania, Trans-Antarctica, western South America, western North

America, Ellesmere Island, Mongolia, Kazakhstan, and the Qin (Tsinling)-Qilian ranges in China. Collisions with terranes are also well known. One well-studied example is the Taconic orogeny, which occurred during the Middle and Late Ordovician epochs in the eastern United States. This event includes at least three separate collisional events from Maine to Alabama. The Taconic orogeny created a series of deep basins along the eastern edge of Laurentia, some of which are now filled with over 3,000 metres (about 9,900 feet) of sedimentary rock. The thick accumulation of sediment filling one of these basins in present-day New York and Pennsylvania is known as the Queenston Delta.

PALEOCLIMATE

Numerical climate models as well as carbon isotope measurements from preserved Ordovician soils suggest that atmospheric levels of carbon dioxide during the period were 14 to 16 times higher than today, as previously mentioned. These high levels were driven by widespread volcanic activity, which would have released large volumes of carbon dioxide into the atmosphere. The extensive flooding of continents due to high sea levels, combined with the lack of widespread vegetation on land, would have suppressed the weathering of silicate rocks, a major mechanism for removing carbon dioxide from the atmosphere. In short, the rate at which carbon dioxide was added to the atmosphere increased during the Ordovician Period, whereas its rate of removal decreased.

Because of the greenhouse effect, high levels of atmospheric carbon dioxide would have caused temperatures to rise everywhere from the equator to the poles. Clear evidence of warm temperatures in the tropics can be seen in the extensive Ordovician limestone deposits with features similar to those found in modern tropical carbonate areas, such as the coral reefs of the Bahamas. Other evidence suggesting warm low-latitude climates in the Ordovician include bauxite deposits in Kazakhstan and evaporite minerals in North America, Australia, China, Kazakhstan, and Siberia.

Warm tropical regions would have fostered the development of tropical cyclones, or hurricanes. There is a rich record of such storms in the Ordovician. In subtropical areas of North America, sedimentary deposits from Ordovician continental shelves commonly occur in alternating beds of shale and either sandstone or limestone. These sandstone and limestone beds display evidence of erosion at their bases, become finer-grained upward within the beds, and contain distinctive sedimentary structures known to form from the combination of strong currents and large waves. These storm-driven structures and processes also occur on the continental shelves of the present day. In addition, storm deposits known as tempestites can be quite common in Ordovician rocks. For example, an interval of Late Ordovician strata near Cincinnati, Ohio, is 65 metres (213 feet) thick. This interval represents an estimated 1.5 million years of deposition and contains over 300 tempestites. Because the erosion of the seafloor during the early phases of a hurricane has the potential to remove previously deposited tempestites, the interval near Cincinnati suggests that storms left a preserved sedimentary record at least once every 5,000 years during the period.

Despite high carbon dioxide levels in the Ordovician Period, evidence of cooler climates in higher latitudes is seen by the presence of unweathered mica in sedimentary rocks from North Africa, central and southern Europe, and much of South America. Their abundance, coupled with the presence of faunas interpreted as cold-water forms, as well as paleomagnetic evidence, suggests that northwestern Africa was located over the South Pole. Furthermore, glacial deposits dating back to the Ordovician are also known from much of Africa, southern Asia, and parts of Europe. It had been thought the South Pole was glaciated for much of the Ordovician, but more-recent dating of these glacial deposits, plus isotopic evidence, suggests that major continental glaciation was limited to the last half-million years of the Late Ordovician Epoch and a shorter portion of the Early Silurian Epoch.

How continental glaciation could have formed when carbon dioxide levels were so high has been a paradox. Recently it has been proposed that the terminal Ordovician glaciation was triggered through a combination of the placement of Africa over the South Pole and a short-lived drawdown of atmospheric carbon dioxide. This drawdown was favoured by declining volcanism during the Ordovician, which would have introduced progressively less carbon dioxide into the atmosphere. Increasing orogeny and uplift during later Ordovician times would have accelerated the removal of carbon dioxide from the atmosphere through the weathering of silicate rocks. Once snow began to accumulate in North Africa, the increased albedo (surface reflectance) of the snow would have fostered lower temperatures and increased the accumulation of greater amounts of snow in Gondwana, thereby bringing about a glacial period. The cooling of the oceans may also have fostered the increased productivity of photosynthetic organisms, moving nutrients from the depths to the surface through the process of upwelling. As the populations of photosynthesizers increased, additional carbon dioxide was removed from the atmosphere. At the end of this glacial period, it is now believed, as the production of carbon dioxide from volcanoes continued, the proportion of atmospheric carbon dioxide removal due to the weathering of silicate rocks declined. The silicate rocks of Gondwana had no access to the atmosphere, because many were covered by thick layers of glacial ice.

ORDOVICIAN LIFE

Life on Earth during the Ordovician was primarily concentrated in the oceans. Although some terrestrial forms were present, such as the first land plants as evidenced by the presence of cryptospores and trilete spores in Ordovician deposits, the land was largely barren.

MARINE ORGANISMS

Ordovician marine environments harboured a complex array of plankton and invertebrates. Primitive reefs composed of simple mounds of microbes gave way to more complex structures built by stromatoporids, bryozoans, and coral. In addition, the Ordovician was the time in which the first primitive fishes emerged.

MICROFOSSILS AND PLANKTON

Ordovician seas were characterized by a rich and diverse assemblage of species. Calcified microbial mats, known as stromatolites, are found in Ordovician rocks, although they are not as common there as in strata from the Cambrian Period and the Proterozoic Eon. Chitinozoans or acritarchs, microfossils with a hollow cavity and organic walls, represent the phytoplankton (small, free-floating, photosynthetic organisms). Ordovician foraminiferans include both agglutinated (glued or cemented) and calcareous (containing calcium carbonate) forms, including the first fusulinids (single-celled, amoeba-like organisms with complex shells). The siliceous radiolarians (spherically symmetrical organisms with fine, sculptured skeletons) that lived as zooplankton (groups of small animals that feed on phytoplankton) are also found in Ordovician rocks.

INVERTEBRATES

Invertebrate life became increasingly diverse and complex through the Ordovician. Both calcareous and siliceous sponges are known. Among other types, the stromatoporoids first appeared in the Ordovician. Tabulata (platform) and rugosa (horn) corals also first appeared in the Ordovician, the solitary or horn corals being especially distinctive. Bryozoans (small colonial animals that produce a skeletal framework of calcium carbonate) and brachiopods (lamp shells) were a dominant component of many assemblages. Mollusks were also common and included the gastropods, monoplacophorans (limpet-shaped, segmented mollusks), bivalves, cephalopods, chitons, scaphopods (tusk shells), and rostroconchs (single-shelled mollusks).

The fossil record of Ordovician annelids (worms and leeches) consists chiefly of small, calcareous tubes, tiny jaws made up of phosphate material, and trace fossils. Trilobites are common and diverse in Ordovician strata but do not dominate assemblages as they did in the Cambrian Period. Ordovician arthropods are also represented by the ostracods (tiny crustaceans) as well as by much rarer forms such as branchiopods, barnacles, phyllocarid ("leaf") shrimp, aglaspids (primitive horseshoe crabs), and eurypterids (sea scorpions).

Echinoderms reached their peak diversity of 20 classes during the Ordovician, with *crinoids* (a group related to present-day sea lilies and feather stars), cystoids

Belonging to a group related to present-day sea lilies and feather stars, crinoids are among the most important Ordovician fossils for comparing ages of rock layers. Ken Lucas/Visuals Unlimited/Getty Images (spherical, stalked echinoderms), asteroids (starfishes), edrioasteroids (sessile, plate-covered echinoderms), and homalozoans (asymmetrical echinoderms) being the most common. Graptolites (small, colonial, planktonic animals) and conodonts (primitive chordates with tooth-shaped fossil remains) are among the most important fossils in the Ordovician for correlating, or demonstrating age equivalence between, different layers of rock.

EARLY FISHES

Until the discovery in 1999 of Early Cambrian vertebrates in South China, the oldest generally accepted vertebrates were known from the Ordovician. The first examples were two genera of primitive fishes, described by American geologist Charles Doolittle Walcott in the late 19th century, from the Upper Ordovician Harding Sandstone of Colorado. Subsequently, fish fragments have been described from the later part of the Early Ordovician Epoch to the early Middle Ordovician of Australia and from the first part of the Late Ordovician of Bolivia. There have been other, although unconfirmed, sightings of ancient fish remains that have been

The jawless Arandaspis *is the oldest known vertebrate, dating back to the Late Ordovician Period.* De Agostini Picture Library/Getty Images

reported from the Late Cambrian to Early Ordovician epochs of Spitsbergen, Greenland, Germany, and many localities in North America.

The complete morphology of these fishes is unknown, and only fragments and individual scales have been found. Most specimens are made up of individual bony plates covered by ridges and nodes. Enough fragmentary material has been found, however, to allow a reconstruction of these animals. Their heads appear to have been covered by densely interlocking plates and their bodies by rows of thinner plates. The tail structure is unknown.

All of these fossils are interpreted to be agnathans, or jawless fishes. The environment in which they lived continues to be disputed, although the interpreted environment at all of the localities is similar. At all three locations, sediments were laid down in very shallow marine to marginal marine environments, possibly with low salinity as found in lagoons and estuaries. The fishes are interpreted to have fed on organic matter on the seafloor.

REEFS

Reefs are known throughout the Ordovician Period, although the types of organisms that built them changed over time. Most Ordovician reefs are rather small, typically up to 5 metres (16 feet) thick, though some are up to 20 to 30 metres (65 to 100 feet) thick. Most Ordovician reefs were built on continental shelves or in shallow seas within the continental interior, although some were built at the edge of continental shelves or on the continental slopes. Earliest Ordovician reefs were most commonly mud mounds built by microbes, algae, and sponges. Microbial mounds are also known from the latest Ordovician times. Stromatoporoid and coral patch reefs first appeared in the Middle Ordovician Epoch and persisted after the close of the Ordovician Period, whereas the first appearance of bryozoan mounds and red algal reefs occurred during the Middle Ordovician Epoch. Large carbonate mud mounds containing a diverse suite of reef-building organisms first appeared in the latest part of the Early Ordovician Epoch and are notable in that they attained thicknesses exceeding 250 metres (820 feet).

TERRESTRIAL ORGANISMS

Although most of Earth's life-forms depended on Ordovician seas, a few early terrestrial pioneers gained footholds on land. The most notable of these are sporelike structures, which may have been the ancestors of both vascular and non-vascular plants. Also, some scientists contend that the first arthropods sought terrestrial habitats during this time.

EARLIEST LAND PLANTS

The Ordovician contains the oldest generally accepted remains of land plants, in the form of cuticle fragments and spores. Fragments of cuticle lack stomata and other structures and have eluded identification. The spores are more diagnostic, and two types are known. Cryptospores (sporelike structures predating land plants) first appeared in the early part of the Middle Ordovician Epoch and rapidly spread to all continents. Through this time their morphology changed little and shows minute evolution.

Trilete spores, which divide via meiosis to form a tetrad of cells, first appeared in the late Late Ordovician and form a rare, geographically isolated component in cryptospore assemblages. Although spores are known from older rocks, cryptospore and trilete spores are thought to be the direct ancestors of land plants because of their size, gross morphology, and wall structure, their abundance in nonmarine and marginal marine deposits, and their association later in the geologic record with definite land plants. Cryptospores were limited to life in damp habitats. Their distribution over a wide range of latitudes suggests their adaptability to many environments, as opposed to the much more narrowly distributed triletes.

These plant fossils suggest two phases of evolution. Cryptospores are thought to be the precursors of nonvascular plants of the liverwort or bryophyte grade of organization. Triletes are thought to be the originators of vascular plants and may have been similar to the Late Silurian and Early Devonian rhyniophytes. Both forms are thought to have arisen from green algae. Although both the cryptospore- and trilete-producing plants gave rise to other plants, both are now thought to be extinct.

Animals

Although no fossils of land animals are known from the Ordovician, burrows from the Late Ordovician of Pennsylvania have been interpreted as produced by animals similar to millipedes. A millipede-like organism is inferred because the burrows occur in discrete size classes, are bilaterally symmetrical, and were backfilled by the burrowing organism. The burrows are found in a preserved soil and are associated with carbonate concretions that precipitated within the soil, indicating that the burrows were produced at the time of soil formation. The presence of plants and possibly arthropods suggests that Ordovician terrestrial ecosystems may have been more extensive and complex than generally thought.

The Ordovician Radiation

During the Ordovician Period, life diversified to an unprecedented degree, undergoing a fourfold increase in the number of genera. This unique period, known as the Ordovician radiation, unfolded over tens of millions of years and produced organisms that would dominate marine ecosystems for the remainder of the Paleozoic Era. The Ordovician radiation was an extension of the Cambrian explosion, an event during which all modern marine phyla appeared (with the exception of the bryozoans, which emerged during the Ordovician). The Ordovician continued this diversification at lower levels of taxonomy and saw a rapid increase in the amount of habitats and ecological niches exploited by living things, as well as an increase in the complexity of biological communities.

The number of marine genera in most of the Early Ordovician Epoch was comparable to that seen in the Cambrian Period and had comparable rates of species

Graptolites belong to the extinct group of small, aquatic colonial animals that became apparent during the Cambrian Period, putting their fossils among the most crucial for correlating layers of rock. De Agostini Picture Library/ Getty Images

turnover or extinction. By the latest age of the Early Ordovician Epoch, trilobites and other organisms dominant in the Cambrian were replaced by a wide range of other marine invertebrates, including corals, bryozoans, brachiopods, mollusks, echinoderms, graptolites, and conodonts. One theory posits that diversification reached a peak by the first age of the Late Ordovician Epoch, with minor fluctuations. On the other hand, it has also been argued that this early Late Ordovician "peak" only represents a higher-quality fossil record than that of later Ordovician times. When this difference is accounted for, diversity is seen to rise to a plateau by the Middle Ordovician, after which it changes little.

The timing of diversification differs for each group of organisms and on each of the Ordovician continents. For example, graptolites reached their peak diversity in the Early Ordovician Epoch, whereas gastropods continued to diversify steadily through the entire Ordovician Period. Similarly, overall diversity on the cratons of Laurentia and Baltica peaked in the early Late Ordovician Epoch, whereas diversity peaked in South China in the Early Ordovician Epoch. These intercontinental differences suggest that global diversification was driven by changes unique to each continent rather than by a single global factor.

THE EXPLOITATION OF HABITATS

The Ordovician radiation began in shallow marine environments and proceeded into deeper water. Newer fauna intermingled with older Cambrian fauna, which was primarily made up of various trilobites and inarticulate (unjointed) brachiopods living in a wide range of environments between the shore and the continental slope. In the Early Ordovician Epoch, articulate (jointed) brachiopods, gastropods, and cephalopods appeared in shallow-water habitats as inarticulate brachiopods and trilobites declined in those habitats. Through the remainder of the Ordovician Period, articulate brachiopods and gastropods continued to spread farther offshore as trilobites and inarticulate brachiopods became rarer in all but deepwater habitats. Finally, in the Late Ordovician Epoch, bivalve communities appeared in shallow-water habitats and displaced the brachiopod-gastropod communities offshore.

Much of the increase in diversity occurring during the Ordovician Period took place within biological communities formed during the Cambrian Period. New species made use of unexploited niches within these communities. Another large portion of this new diversity came from increased provinciality—that is, the differences in the species present between one continent and another. Since most species did not expand beyond their own local regions, the species assemblages of many areas were unique, and few species were distributed globally. Diversity was also increased because of the expansion of life into new habitats not present in the Cambrian, such as reefs, hardgrounds, bryozoan thickets, and crinoid gardens.

Ordovician communities were ecologically more complicated than Cambrian ones. The Ordovician saw the rise of several new life habits, including deep-deposit feeders, mobile epifaunal (superficially attached) carnivores, and pelagic (open-water) carnivores. In contrast to Cambrian communities that lived very close to the sediment surface, Ordovician communities also grew up to 50 centimetres (1.5 feet) above the seafloor and established distinct tiers, or levels, similar to those present in modern forests. Also, invertebrates burrowed into the seafloor more intensely during the Ordovician Period than in the Cambrian Period, reaching depths of up to 1 metre (3 feet) below the seafloor.

CAUSES OF THE ORDOVICIAN RADIATION

The causes of the Ordovician radiation remain unclear. One view points to the Middle Ordovician fall in sea level, although this event has also been coupled to a global drop in diversity. Another view posits that biological interactions or an inherently higher rate of speciation in some groups fostered the diversification. Others have noted the correlation between the Ordovician diversification and the increase in global orogenic and volcanic activity. Indeed, on continents affected by orogenic activity, diversity proceeded at a faster pace than on other continents, suggesting that an increase in the supply of some nutrients, such as phosphorous and potassium, during the process of uplift may have fueled the diversification.

ORDOVICIAN EXTINCTION EVENTS

Despite the enormous biological diversity that precipitated from the Ordovician radiation, the period was also characterized by several regional diebacks and by a major global extinction. This global extinction event occurred near the period's boundary with the Silurian Period.

THE MASS EXTINCTION AT THE END OF THE ORDOVICIAN

The mass extinction that ended the Ordovician Period ranks second in severity to the one that occurred at the boundary between the Permian and Triassic periods in terms of the percentage of marine families affected, and it was almost twice as severe as the extinction event that occurred at the end of the Cretaceous Period, which is famous for bringing an end to the dinosaurs. An estimated 85 percent of all Ordovician species became extinct during the end-Ordovician extinction in the two-million-year-long Hirnantian Age and the subsequent Rhuddanian Age of the Silurian Period.

Brachiopods display the effects of this extinction well. Laurentian brachiopods were hit hard, particularly those that lived in the broad and shallow seas both within and near the continent. Many of these brachiopods were endemic (confined to a particular region) to Laurentia, as opposed to the more cosmopolitan (globally distributed) forms that lived at the edges of the continent. Following the extinction, Laurentian seas were repopulated with brachiopod genera previously found only on other continents. As a result, Silurian brachiopods were far more widely distributed than their Ordovician predecessors. Other groups of organisms—including conodonts, acritarchs (a catchall group of various small microfossils), bryozoans, and trilobites—that showed this pattern of regional, but not global, distribution were similarly affected by this extinction event. Despite the intensity of the extinction and the loss of many endemic species, Silurian ecosystems were remarkably similar to those in the Ordovician.

The extinction appears to have occurred in several phases. An early phase affecting graptolites, brachiopods, and trilobites occurred prior to the end of the Ordovician Period, before the major fall in sea level. A second phase of extinction occurred as sea levels fell because of the onset of glaciation over the African and South American portions of Gondwana. In many areas the interval of glaciation was accompanied by the invasion of cool-water brachiopod fauna, even into tropical latitudes, suggesting the onset of significant global cooling. A third phase of extinction occurred with the rise of sea level that took place during the Rhuddanian Age of the Silurian Period.

The cause of the end-Ordovician extinction is generally attributed to two factors: the first wave of extinction may be related to rapid cooling at the end of the Ordovician Period, and the second phase is widely regarded as having been caused by the sea-level fall associated with the glaciation. The drop in sea level would have drained the large epicontinental seas and reduced the available habitat for organisms that favoured those settings. No concentration of iridium has been identified near the extinction that would suggest a bolide (meteoroid or asteroid) impact like the one identified at the boundary between the Cretaceous and Tertiary periods.

REGIONAL EXTINCTIONS WITHIN THE ORDOVICIAN

In addition to this mass extinction, smaller-scale or background extinctions occurred during the Ordovician Period. Most of these are poorly understood, but one that has been studied occurred in the eastern United States during the early Late Ordovician Epoch. This extinction involved a wide range of organisms in a wide variety of life habits, including brachiopods, corals, trilobites, echinoderms, and mollusks. Especially at risk were species that were restricted to the eastern United States. Many surviving species experienced a contraction in their geographic ranges and were driven out from the eastern regions to the western United States and Canada.

This particular extinction is very closely timed with a major tectonic event that affected the North American region. The collision of a terrane with the eastern edge of the continent during the Taconic orogeny caused the continental margin to flex and the sedimentary basin to deepen. This deepening allowed cool, nutrient-rich, turbid water to spread from the Appalachians to Indiana and central Tennessee. These changes appear in the strata as a relatively rapid switch from tropical limestones with little shale to cool-water phosphatic limestones with abundant shale. Several new species adapted to these new conditions invaded the eastern United States at this time.

As this sedimentary basin filled and the source of cool, nutrient-rich water was cut off, conditions gradually returned to those prior to the extinction. Many of the organisms that had retreated from the eastern United States returned to this region later in the Ordovician and into the Silurian.

FAUNAL PROVINCES

Ordovician faunas were strikingly provincial, much more so than those in the Silurian Period. The main control on the distribution of Ordovician faunas was temperature. The planktonic graptolites are commonly divided into the Pacific and Atlantic (or European) provinces. The Pacific Province corresponds to regions that were tropical during the Ordovician, such as North America, Siberia, Kazakhstan, and parts of China. The Atlantic Province is found in more-temperate regions of the Ordovician Period, including the British Isles, the Baltic region and Scandinavia, and northern Africa. Some modern regions, such as South America, straddled both of these provinces. Acritarchs follow a distribution similar to graptolites, with their faunas limited to tropical, polar, and intermediate regions in the Ordovician.

Conodont provinces include the North American Midcontinent and the North Atlantic provinces. The North American Midcontinent Province is also found in Scotland, Siberia, and temporarily in parts of the Baltic region and Scandinavia. The North Atlantic Province is known from the Baltic region and Scandinavia, the British Isles, and the margins of North America. Australian faunas bear similarities to both of these provinces yet have some distinctive elements, suggesting that they may represent another province.

Provinces have also been recognized within single continents for other groups. Late Ordovician corals from Laurentia have been divided into a Red River–Stony Mountain Province in the western United States and Canada and a Richmond Province, extending in a narrow belt from Ontario to Michigan to central Tennessee. In addition to all these temperature-controlled provinces, Ordovician faunas are known to change with water depth, nutrient levels, and sediment type. This regional isolation of many faunas contributed to the intense pace of the Ordovician radiation, but it has also made the global correlation of Ordovician rocks difficult.

SIGNIFICANT ORDOVICIAN LIFE-FORMS

The overwhelming majority of Ordovician life-forms were relegated to marine environments. They include several genera of trilobites, graptolites, and bryozoans. Many of these genera have been useful in the correlation of Ordovician rocks. Ordovician seas also contained several types of corals and mollusks.

BELLEROPHON

This extinct genus of gastropods (snails) occurs as fossils in rocks from the Ordovician Period to the Triassic Period (251 million to 200 million years ago). *Bellerophon* is characteristic of the bellerophontids, a large group of snails. The shell of *Bellerophon* was primitive in that it was coiled with the midline in a single plane. The upper half of the shell was the mirror image of the lower half. In *Bellerophon*, growth lines angled away from a raised ridge along the midline of the shell. The anterior margins of the shell were flared outward, and they were separated by a narrow slit, called the selenizone.

BUMASTUS

A genus of trilobites found in Europe and North America as fossils in rocks of Ordovician to Silurian age, *Bumastus* is very distinctive in form. The head and tail regions are smooth and very large and have fused segments. Its elliptical body is flat on the bottom; the back and sides are strongly concave and arched. *Bumastus* was a bottom-dwelling form.

BYSSONYCHIA

Byssonychia is an extinct genus of Ordovician pelecypods (clams) that serves as a useful index fossil for the Ordovician Period. The distinctive shell of *Byssonychia,* one of the earliest clam genera known, is roughly triangular in outline, tapering sharply to a prominent beak and bearing distinct linear ribbing on the surface. Only one distinct muscle scar is present on the inside of the shell.

CALYMENE

This genus of trilobites is well known in the fossil record. *Calymene* remains have been found in which impressions or actual remains of appendages are preserved. *Calymene* and its close relative *Flexicalymene* are frequently preserved as tightly rolled fossils. The rolling may be either a death position or a defensive one that the animal assumed to protect its soft, vulnerable underside.

CERAURUS

A genus of trilobites found as fossils in rocks of Ordovician period in Europe and North America, *Ceraurus* is easily recognized by its unusual shape. Two large spines occur at the end of the tail and at the margins of the head shield.

CLIMACOGRAPTUS

Climacograptus is a genus of graptolites found as fossils in marine rocks of the Middle and Late Ordovician Period (about 472 million to 444 million years ago). *Climacograptus* is characterized by a single, serrated branch suspended from a thin stem below an irregular float. Its outline is distinctively angular. Several species are recognized, and the genus is useful for correlating smaller time divisions within the Ordovician.

CLONOGRAPTUS

Clonograptus is a genus of graptolites characterized by a frondlike form. Groups of these animals were connected by stalklike structures to a central region. Various forms or species of *Clonograptus* are important guide, or index, fossils for the correlation of Ordovician rocks.

CONSTELLARIA

This genus of extinct bryozoans (small colonial animals that produce a skeletal framework of calcium carbonate) is especially characteristic of Ordovician marine rocks. The structure of *Constellaria* is branching and generally flattened front to back with prominent bumps. *Constellaria* sometimes is found in sedimentary rocks or the shells of other animals.

CRYPTOLITHUS

Cryptolithus is a genus of trilobites found as fossils in Europe and North America in the Ordovician period. Its distinctive appearance makes the genus a useful guide fossil for Ordovician rocks and time. The head region, or cephalon, in *Cryptolithus* is large, with margins pitted in a distinctive pattern. Two long spines project back from the lateral margins. The adults lack eyes.

CRYPTOSTOMATA

This order of fossil bryozoans occurs in rocks of Ordovician to Permian age (between 488 million and 251 million years old). Many holes are exhibited, which probably contained individual animals of the colony. Cryptostome colonies consist of groups of short, individual tubes.

CYSTOIDS

Cystoids encompass any member of an extinct class (Cystoidea) of primitive echinoderms (animals with a hard, calcareous external skeleton, related to the modern sea lily and starfish) that first appeared during the Middle Ordovician epoch and persisted into the Late Devonian epoch (the Ordovician Period began about 488 million years ago, and the Devonian Period ended 359 million years ago). Once diverse and important, the cystoids had saclike bodies that were attached to a stem anchored to the seafloor. Numerous plates covered the body. Some forms are important guide, or index, fossils and thus allow the correlation of sometimes widely separated rock units.

DIDYMOGRAPTUS

This genus of graptolites is found as fossils in Early and Middle Ordovician marine rocks. The several described species of *Didymograptus*, with their wide geographic distribution and relatively narrow time ranges, are guide fossils for correlation of Early and Middle Ordovician rocks and time. The genus is characterized by its two-branched form, frequently suspended from a circular disk-shaped structure. *Didymograptus* includes some of the largest known graptolites.

DIPLOGRAPTUS

Forms or species of genus *Diplograptus* are useful index, or guide, fossils for the Ordovician period and thus allow the correlation of sometimes widely separated rock units. *Diplograptus* is characterized by a caplike float from which featherlike assemblages of graptolite organisms were suspended. It was relatively large for a graptolite. Several kinds of individuals were present in a colony.

ECHINOSPHAERITES

A genus of cystoids, an extinct group related to the sea lily and starfish, *Echinosphaerites* are found as fossils in Ordovician marine rocks. It is a useful guide, or index, fossil for Ordovician rocks and time.

FAVOSITES

An extinct genus of corals found as fossils in marine rocks from the Ordovician to the Permian periods (between 488 million and 251 million years old), *Favosites* is easily recognized by its distinctive form. The genus is colonial, and the individual structures that house each coral animal are closely packed together as long, narrow tubes. In cross section, the structure has a distinctive honeycomb appearance.

HALLOPORA

Hallopora is a genus of extinct bryozoans (small colonial animals that produce a skeletal framework of calcium carbonate) found as fossils in Ordovician to Silurian marine rocks (from 488 to 416 million years old). *Hallopora* is distinguished by the large size of its pores and by its internal structure. Various species of *Hallopora* are known, some of them useful for stratigraphic correlation.

HALYSITES

Corals of genus *Halysites* are found as fossils in marine rocks from the Late Ordovician Period to the end of the Silurian Period (461 million to 416 million years ago). *Halysites* is also known as the chain coral from the manner of growth observed in fossilized specimens. The genus is colonial, and individual members of the colony construct an elliptical tube next to each other in the manner of chain links.

HESPERORTHIS

Hesperorthis is an extinct genus of brachiopods, or lamp shells, which as fossils are especially characteristic of Ordovician marine rocks. The plano-convex shell of *Hesperorthis* consists of two units (or valves), the brachial valve being flat and the pedicle valve convex. The shell has a radiating pattern of ribs and a relatively broad, triangular area at the dorsal shell margin.

HORN CORALS

All horn corals belong to the order Rugosa, which first appeared in the geologic record during the Ordovician Period. The Rugosa persisted through the Permian Period, which ended 251 million years ago. Horn corals, which are named for the hornlike shape of the individual structures built by the coral animal, were either solitary or colonial forms. Of the many forms known, some are important as index, or guide, fossils for specific spans of geologic time and serve to correlate sometimes widely separated rock units. Because of their mode of growth, some horn corals have been employed as biological clocks to determine the length of the day and year in the distant geologic past.

ISOTELUS

A genus of trilobites restricted to Europe and North America during the Ordovician Period, *Isotelus* was relatively large for a trilobite and was characterized by its distinctive flat shape. The head and the tail were well developed and large relative to the whole animal. The number of thoracic segments was small, and the eyes were large and crescentic in shape.

LEPTAENA

Leptaena is a genus of extinct brachiopods (lamp shells) commonly found as fossils in Ordovician to Lower Carboniferous sedimentary rocks (between 488 million and 318 million years old). The very distinctive shell of *Leptaena* is characterized by its wrinkled ornamentation and fine linear markings.

LITUITES

A genus of extinct cephalopods (animals related to the modern pearly nautilus) found as fossils in marine rocks of the Ordovician Period, the distinctive shell of *Lituites* is composed of serially arranged chambers. The shell begins with a tightly coiled portion that gradually straightens out after a few whorls. The anterior portion of the shell, the largest part, is straight in form and expands toward the front. The sutures between the chambers appear as simple lines around the shell.

LOPHOSPIRA

Lophospira is a genus of extinct gastropods (snails) found as fossils in marine rocks of Ordovician to Devonian age (488 million to 359 million years old). The shell consists of a series of whorls arranged much like a series of ascending steps, each successive whorl smaller than the one below it. The apex of the shell is closed by a small cone-shaped whorl.

LOXONEMA

This genus of extinct gastropods (snails) is found as fossils in rocks of Ordovician to Early Carboniferous age (488 million to 318 million years ago). *Loxonema* has a distinctive high-spired, slender shell with fine axial ornamentational lines. A distinct lip is present at the base of the aperture of the main whorl.

MACLURITES

Maclurites is an extinct genus of Ordovician gastropods (snails) found as fossils and useful for stratigraphic correlations. The shell is distinctively coiled and easily recognized. The animal also had an operculum, or second shell, that covered the aperture of the larger body shell. *Maclurites* is characteristic of a group of early gastropods that first appeared in the Late Cambrian and became extinct at the end of the Ordovician.

MODIOLOPSIS

An extinct genus of pelecypods (clams) found as fossils in Ordovician rocks, the form and structure of *Modiolopsis* is distinct, with a shell roughly elliptical in outline and broader at the margins. Markings on the shell consist of prominent growth lines in an arcuate or concentric pattern. *Modiolopsis* is a useful guide fossil for Ordovician rocks.

NEOPRIONIODIFORM

This conodont, or small toothlike phosphatic fossil of uncertain affinity, is characterized by a main terminal cusp, varying numbers of subsidiary cusps or denticles that may be completely fused, and an underside region that is deeply grooved. Several genera are included in the neoprioniodiforms, including excellent guide fossils for the Ordovician Period.

PHYLLOGRAPTUS

Phyllograptus is a genus of graptolites readily distinguished by its characteristic leaflike form and structure. Various species of *Phyllograptus* are excellent guide, or index, fossils for Ordovician rocks and time and allow the correlation of sometimes widely separated rock units.

PLATYSTROPHIA

Platystrophia is a genus of extinct brachiopods (lamp shells) that occurs as fossils in marine rocks of the Middle Ordovician epoch to about the middle of the Silurian period (i.e., from about 472 million to 423 million years ago). Each valve of the shell is convex in profile, and the hinge line between the valves is wide. Surface markings on the shell include prominent angular ridges and intervening linear depressions. *Platystrophia* is a common Late Ordovician fossil that is very useful for stratigraphic correlations.

PLECTOCERAS

Members of this extinct genus of small marine nautiloid cephalopods had a coiled shell composed of a series of chambers. *Plectoceras* was active in the Ordovician Period. The junctures between successive chambers of *Plectoceras* were simple in character.

PRASOPORA

This extinct genus of bryozoans was especially characteristic of the Ordovician Period. *Prasopora* generally is characterized by caplike colonies domed on top and flat on the bottom. The hard framework of the colony is composed of calcium carbonate, which formed the closely packed tubelike structures that housed the individual animals in the *Prasopora* colony.

RESSERELLA

An extinct genus of brachiopods that occurs as fossils in marine rocks of Middle Ordovician to Lower Silurian age (478 to 421 million years old), *Resserella* has a dorsal shell whose margin is horizontal, and a distal, or upper, shell with an arcuate (bow-shaped) margin. Both valves are often gently convex. Surface markings consist of fine lines, and the internal structure of *Resserella* is very distinctive.

RHYNCHOTREMA

Rhynchotrema is an extinct genus of brachiopods, or lamp shells, found as fossils in Middle and Late Ordovician rocks. The shell is small and distinctive for its strongly developed ribbing. *Rhynchotrema* is a useful Ordovician index, or guide, fossil.

STREPTELASMA

Streptelasma is an extinct genus of corals found as fossils in marine rocks of Ordovician to Devonian age (488 million to 359 million years old). Each horn-shaped specimen represents a single individual. The hard, and thus preserved, parts of the animal consist of a carbonate skeletal structure distinctive in form and construction.

STROPHOMENA

Members of this genus of extinct brachiopods are found as fossils in Middle and Upper Ordovician marine rocks. The shell consists of two parts, or valves, dissimilar in shape—one strongly convex, the other concave. A distinctive laminated pattern occurs at the margins of the shell, along with fine, arcuate (bowlike) growth lines. *Strophomena* is representative of an important group of fossil brachiopods, the strophomenids.

Tabulata

A major division of extinct coral animals found as fossils in Ordovician to Jurassic marine rocks (488 million to 146 million years old), Tabulata is characterized by the presence of interior platforms, or tabulae, and by a general lack of vertical walls, or septa. Colonial masses of these tabulate corals sometimes comprised sizable structures.

Tetragraptus

Tetragraptus is a genus of extinct graptolites that occur as fossils in marine rocks of the Early Ordovician Epoch (488.3 to 471.8 million years ago). The genus is a useful guide, or index, fossil for the Early Ordovician. Long-distance correlations between rock units are possible employing the many known *Tetragraptus* species. As its name implies, *Tetragraptus* is distinguished by its four branches, which are suspended from a thin filamentous support.

Trepostomata

Members of an extinct order of bryozoans found as fossils in marine rocks of Ordovician to Triassic age (488 million to 200 million years old), the trepostomes are characterized by colonies in long, curved calcareous tubes, the interiors of which are intersected by partitions. The order includes several common and well-known genera, including the Ordovician forms *Prasopora* and *Dekayella*.

Trochonema

Members of *Trochonema*, a genus of extinct gastropods, are found as fossils in rocks dating from the Ordovician Period to the Devonian Period (488.3 to 359.2 million years ago). The shell of Trochonema consists of a series of turretlike whorls, each ornamented by slight lines. The aperture is large, conspicuous, and roughly circular.

ORDOVICIAN GEOLOGY

Rocks laid down during the period range from carbonate types, such as dolomite, limestone, and sandstones from sedimentary processes, to igneous types produced by volcanism. Ordovician carbonate rocks have been sources of fossil fuels in North America as well as in Estonia. In addition, phosphate rocks dating to Ordovician times are useful as fertilizers.

SIGNIFICANT GEOLOGIC EVENTS

A wide variety of rock types is found in the Ordovician System. Limestone and dolomite are the predominant rock types from the tropical epicontinental sea regions in the Ordovician, such as Laurentia, Siberia, Kazakhstan, and South China. These limestones formed principally from the accumulation of calcareous skeletons of organisms, from carbonate mud, and from ooids (a type of seafloor sand) and peloids (small sand-sized grains formed from fecal matter, algae, and mud). Reefs are also commonly found in these limestone regions.

Ordovician evaporite deposits, such as anhydrite, are found in areas that were situated in arid belts near 30° N and 30° S. Anhydrite is known from the Early and Late Ordovician epochs of Laurentia and Kazakhstan.

Ordovician siliciclastic (made from broken parts of silica rocks) rocks can be divided into coarse-grained and fine-grained types. Relatively coarse-grained siliciclastic rocks such as sandstones and conglomerates tended to accumulate in high latitudes where significant carbonate accumulation was precluded and in low latitudes where orogenic uplift supplied abundant sediment. In North America, thick accumulations of coarse siliciclastic sediment can be found in the Appalachians. The Ordovician Taconic orogeny supplied voluminous amounts of sediment to the Queenston Delta, which spread from the Appalachians westward to Ontario and Ohio. Many of these sandstones are resistant to weathering and form the tops of ridges in the Ridge and Valley Province of the Appalachians. Additional thick sandstones are known from the Middle Ordovician Saint Peter Sandstone, which accumulated as a vast coastal sand dune system spread across much of North America. On other continents, thick successions of sandstones may be found in the Gondwana-associated regions of Antarctica, Australia, Great Britain, southern Europe, South America, and Africa. Coarse siliciclastic rocks also occur as glacial deposits in the late Late Ordovician of Africa and South America. These deposits consist of tilloids (gravity-driven sediments) and dropstones (rocks dropped into fine-grained sediments as they melted out of floating glacial ice).

Fine-grained siliciclastic rocks, represented by mudstones and shales, accumulated for the most part in deepwater settings of the Ordovician Period. As a result, thick accumulations of shale tend to occur around the margins of Ordovician continents and in the deepwater portions of epicontinental seas. Finely laminated black shales record deposition in anoxic water, whereas burrowed gray or red mudstones indicate oxygenated conditions. Bedded chert is sometimes associated with these basinal shales, as in China.

Volcanic ashes are known from many regions in the Ordovician Period, attesting to the widespread volcanism of the times. These ashes are commonly weathered to form K-bentonites (a type of clay useful in correlation because its particles are easily dated) that are interbedded with other rock types, such as limestone, shale, and sandstone. Other volcanic and igneous rocks are found principally near Ordovician subduction zones and back-arc basins (marine basins that form behind subduction zones), as in the British Isles, Kazakhstan, and China. Rock types include volcanic breccia, tuff, basalt, andesite, and rhyolite.

THE ECONOMIC SIGNIFICANCE OF ORDOVICIAN DEPOSITS

Several types of Ordovician deposits are economically important. Petroleum and natural gas have been extracted from Middle and Upper Ordovician carbonates from the United States and Canada. Oil was first produced from a well that was drilled into Ordovician limestone in western Pennsylvania. Oil and natural gas continue to be produced from Middle and Upper Ordovician limestone and dolomite in the United States and Canada. Unusual oil-rich shales called kukersites are major sources of petroleum in Estonia. Limestone deposits in the Mississippi valley, central Tennessee, and the southern Appalachians are an important source of lead and zinc. Limestone itself is quarried in many places as a building stone, for use in roads, and for use in reducing sulfur emissions from coal-burning power plants. Phosphates have been mined for fertilizer from Ordovician limestones, particularly where weathering has concentrated the phosphate, as in central Tennessee. Ordovician sandstones, such as the Saint Peter Sandstone in the Midwestern United States, are important for glassmaking. Ordovician shales have been used to manufacture bricks. Black cephalopod-bearing limestones from Africa are widely sold as decorative pieces and tabletops.

THE MAJOR SUBDIVISIONS OF THE ORDOVICIAN SYSTEM

The rocks that originated during the Ordovician compose the Ordovician System. The Ordovician Period is divided into seven stages—two each in the early and middle epochs and three in the late epoch. The intense provincialism of Ordovician faunas has long hindered the establishment of a single global succession of stages and zones. Existing names and descriptions useful at regional levels are inconsistent and do not correlate well at the global level.

The International Commission on Stratigraphy (ICS) has formed several working groups to define new stages based on a more accurate global correlation of stratigraphic and fossil markers. Thus far, all seven stages have been named: the Tremadocian (Stage 1), Floian (Stage 2), Dapingian (Stage 3), Darriwilian (Stage 4), Sandbian (Stage 5), Katian (Stage 6), and Hirnantian (Stage 7). Both the Tremadocian and Floian stages date to the Early Ordovician Epoch, which occurred between 488.3 and 471.8 million years ago; the Dapingian and the Darriwilian Stage date to the Middle Ordovician Epoch, which occurred between 471.8 and 460.9 million years ago; and the Sandbian, Katian, and Hirnantian stages date to the Late Ordovician Epoch, which occurred between 460.9 and 443.7 million years ago.

THE CORRELATION OF ORDOVICIAN STRATA

Correlation, or the demonstration of the age equivalence, of strata in the Ordovician System has traditionally relied on fossils. Shelly fossils, such as brachiopods (lamp shells) and trilobites, have proved most useful for correlation within individual continents because of their tendency to be endemic. Other shelly groups, including bryozoans (small colonial animals that produce a skeletal framework of calcium carbonate), crinoids, and corals, have also been used for correlation but to a lesser extent. The Cambrian-Ordovician boundary is marked by the first appearance of the conodont *Iapetognathus fluctivagus* and the trilobites *Jujuyaspis borealis* and *Symphysurina bulbosa*.

Graptolites (small, colonial, planktonic animals) and conodonts (primitve chordates with tooth-shaped fossil remains) are the most widely used organisms for the intercontinental correlation of Ordovician strata. Graptolites in particular are now used to define most of the new global Ordovician stage boundaries. Yet, even for this purpose, the effects of provinciality can limit their geographic ranges and thus their usefulness.

More recently, packages of rocks bounded by unconformities (interruptions in the deposition of sedimentary rock) have been used for correlation within continents. The field of sequence stratigraphy recognizes these units, termed depositional sequences. Many of these units may have formed from changes in global sea level and may ultimately be useful for global correlation.

Geochemical correlation of Ordovician rocks has also been successful. Broad correlations have been achieved with oxygen and carbon isotopes. Highly precise correlations of individual volcanic ash beds have been made using their major, minor, and trace element content.

STAGES OF THE ORDOVICIAN PERIOD

The bases of six of the seven Ordovician stages correspond to the first occurrence of a graptolite. The only exception to this pattern, the Dapingian, marks its onset with the first appearance of a conodont.

TREMADOCIAN STAGE

The base of the Ordovician System, the Tremadocian Stage encompasses all rocks formed during the Tremadocian Age, which spanned the interval between 488.3 and 478.6 million years ago.

The name of this stage is derived from Tremadog, a town in North Wales. The characteristics of the stage are based on fossils found in the Tremadoc Slates. Although most non-British geologists have regarded the Tremadocian as the lowermost stage of the Ordovician System, it has only been since 1991 that the British have done so. The base of the Tremadocian Stage in Britain has been defined as the first occurrence of the graptolite *Rhabdinopora flabelliformis socialis* at Bryn-llin-fawr, North Wales. Difficulties in recognizing this graptolite globally have led an international panel to recommend defining the base of the Tremadocian at the first appearance of the conodont *Iapetognathus fluctivagus*. The Tremadocian Stage overlies Stage 10 of the Cambrian Period and underlies the Floian Stage of the Lower Ordovician Series.

FLOIAN STAGE

The last of two internationally defined stages of the Lower Ordovician Series, the Floian Stage includes all rocks deposited during the Floian Age (478.6 million to 471.8 million years ago) of the Ordovician Period.

In 2002 the ICS established the Global Stratotype Section and Point (GSSP) defining the base of this unit in the mudstone of the Tøyen Shale Formation on the northeastern slope of Hunneberg Mountain, located near the southern shore of Lake Väner in southwestern Sweden. The GSSP marks the first appearance of the graptolite *Tetragraptus approximatus* in the fossil record, and it

is placed very close to the first appearance of the graptolite *T. phyllograptoides* and the trilobite *Megistaspis
planilimbata*. The Floian Stage overlies the Tremadocian
Stage and precedes the Dapingian Stage of the Middle
Ordovician Series.

DAPINGIAN STAGE

The first of two internationally defined stages of the Middle
Ordovician Series, the Dapingian Stage was the last to be
named. It is made up of all rocks deposited during the
Dapingian Age (471.8 million to 468.1 million years ago) of
the Ordovician Period.

In 2007 the ICS established the Global Stratotype
Section and Point (GSSP) defining the base of this unit in
the shale of the Dawan Formation at the centre of the
Ordovician Geopark near Huanghuachang, Hubei, China.
The GSSP marks the first appearance of the conodont
Baltoniodus triangularis in the fossil record. In addition, the
first appearance of the chitinozoan (a type of marine
plankton) believed to be *Belonechitina
henryi* is nearly coincident with the GSSP. The
Dapingian Stage follows the Floian Stage of the Lower
Ordovician Series and precedes the Darriwilian Stage.

DARRIWILIAN STAGE

The Darriwilian Stage is the second (in ascending order)
of two main divisions in the Middle Ordovician Series,
representing rocks deposited worldwide during the
Darriwilian Age, which occurred between 468.1 million
and 460.9 million years ago during the Ordovician
Period. Rocks of the Darriwilian Stage overlie those of
the Dapingian Stage and underlie rocks of the Sandbian
Stage. The Darriwilian is distinguished by the presence of

a graptolite fossil fauna composed of two species of the genus *Undulograptus* and a single species of the genus *Arienigraptus* found in the Ningkuo Formation in Zhejiang province, China.

SANDBIAN STAGE

The first of three internationally defined stages of the Upper Ordovician Series, the Sandbian Stage consists of all rocks deposited during the Sandbian Age (460.9 million to 455.8 million years ago) of the Ordovician Period.

In 2002 the ICS established the Global Stratotype Section and Point (GSSP) defining the base of this unit in a deposit of shale and mudstone along a section of the Sularp Brook at Fåglesång near Lund, Skåne, Swed. The GSSP is set about 1.4 metres (4.6 feet) below a thin phosphorite deposit and marks the first appearance of the graptolite *Nemagraptus gracilis* in the fossil record. The Sandbian Stage follows the Darriwilian Stage of the Middle Ordovician Series and precedes the Katian Stage.

KATIAN STAGE

The Katian Stage is the second of three internationally defined stages of the Upper Ordovician Series. It includes all rocks deposited during the Katian Age (455.8 million to 445.6 million years ago) of the Ordovician Period.

In 2006 the ICS established the Global Stratotype Section and Point (GSSP) defining the base of this unit in the chert of the Bigfork Chert Formation on Black Knob Ridge near Atoka, Okla., U.S. The GSSP marks the first appearance of the graptolite *Diplacanthograptus caudatus* in the fossil record. Other graptolites such as *Orthograptus pageanus* and *Neurograptus margaritatus* also make their first appearance very close to that of *D. caudatus* and are used as secondary markers. The Katian Stage follows the Sandbian Stage and precedes the Hirnantian Stage.

HIRNANTIAN STAGE

The Hirnantian Stage is the last of three internationally defined stages of the Upper Ordovician Series. It covers all rocks deposited during the Hirnantian Age (445.6 million to 443.7 million years ago) of the Ordovician Period. The name of this interval is derived from the Hirnant Beds in Wales, which served as the site marking the Hirnantian subdivision of Britain's Ashgill regional stage.

In 2006 the ICS established the Global Stratotype Section and Point (GSSP) defining the base of this unit in the dark brown shales of the Wufeng Formation near the village of Wangijiawan, Hubei, China. It marks the first appearance of the graptolite *Normalograptus extraordinarius* in the fossil record. Other important fossils characteristic of this interval include the graptolite *N. ojsuensis*, the trilobite *Dalmanitina yichangensis*, and several brachiopods (*Dalmanella testudinaria*, *Hirnantia sagitifera*, *Kinella kielanae*, *Eostropheodonta parvicostellata*, and *Plectothyrella crassicosta*). The top of the Hirnantian, and thus the boundary between the Ordovician and Silurian periods, has been demarcated by a GSSP placed at Dob's Linn near Moffat, Scot. This GSSP was ratified by the ICS in 1984. The Hirnantian Stage follows the Katian Stage of the Ordovician System and precedes the Rhuddanian Stage of the Silurian System.

CHAPTER 4
THE SILURIAN PERIOD

The third period of the Paleozoic Era, the Silurian Period began 443.7 million years ago and ended 416 million years ago, extending from the close of the Ordovician Period to the beginning of the Devonian Period.

During the Silurian, continental elevations were generally much lower than in the present day, and global sea level was much higher. Sea level rose dramatically as the extensive glaciers from the Late Ordovician ice age melted. This rising prompted changes in climatic conditions that allowed many faunal groups to recover from the extinctions of Late Ordovician times. Large expanses of several continents became flooded with shallow seas, and mound-type coral reefs were very common. Fishes were widespread. Vascular plants began to colonize coastal lowlands during the Silurian Period, whereas continental interiors remained essentially barren of life.

The name of this period is derived from work done by Scottish geologist Roderick I. Murchison, who in 1835 named a sequence of rocks in Wales and its borderland with England in honour of a native people called the Silures. The Silures, under the leadership of Caratacus, resisted Roman conquest for 30 years until 78 CE, when they were finally overcome.

THE SILURIAN ENVIRONMENT

The high sea level conditions of the Ordovician Period carried into the Silurian. As a result, significant parts of

Scottish geologist Roderick I. Murchison named the Silurian System and vehemently argued over the definition and placement of the Cambrian-Silurian boundary, firing up an acrimonious controversy between many biologists, most notably Adam Sedgwick. SSPL via Getty Images

the low-lying continents became flooded with shallow seas. Seafloor flatness and constancy during this time is thought to have contributed to species with global, rather than regional, distributions. In contrast to the Northern Hemisphere, which was all but covered by a vast ocean, the climate of the Southern Hemisphere depended on a complex interplay between land and water.

PALEOGEOGRAPHY

During most of the Silurian Period, the vast Panthalassic Ocean covered the northern polar regions, the super-continent of Gondwana stretched over the southern polar region, and a ring of at least six continents spanned the Equator and middle latitudes. The approximate orientations and locations of Silurian continents can be reconstructed using a combination of paleomagnetic, paleoclimatic, and biogeographic data. The Earth's magnetic field leaves its signature on volcanic rocks and certain sedimentary rocks rich in such iron-bearing minerals as magnetite. As rocks capable of being magnetized are cooled or otherwise lithified, their component crystals (grains) are lined up with the Earth's magnetic field. Unless the rocks are remelted by the heat from the planet's interior or reworked by erosion, they retain this signature regardless of whether they change position or not. The Earth's zonal climate also has an effect on global patterns of sedimentation.

The most unusual features of the Silurian that distinguish it from the present-day physical environment relate to conditions of low continental elevations combined with a much higher global stand in sea level. Extensive continental regions were flooded by shallow seas ranging in water depth from a few to little more than 100 metres

(330 feet). Where these seas occupied a tropical to sub-tropical climatic zone, coral mound reefs with associated carbonate sediments were very common. Strata forming in arid regions differ from those formed in inundated areas or other regions with high annual rainfall. The deposition of evaporites (salts) was periodically set in motion as a result of reduced ocean circulation occurring in geographically restricted places such as shallow embayments.

The strong faunal endemism (the restriction or limiting of species to specific continents or isolated regions) present during the Ordovician Period was replaced during the Silurian Period by a situation where some species were distributed globally. Seafloor topography was muted over large areas of flooded continental platforms, and faunas of shelly invertebrates in different regions were remarkably consistent with one another. This has allowed geologists and stratigraphers to correlate layers of Silurian rock found on different present-day continents.

The geographic summary that follows is based on a global reconstruction specific to the Wenlock Epoch which spans the middle of the Silurian Period.

LAURENTIA

Much of North America (including Greenland), north-western Ireland, Scotland, and the Chukotskiy Peninsula of northeastern Russia belonged to the paleocontinent Laurentia. With respect to the present-day Great Lakes and Hudson Bay, Laurentia was rotated clockwise during Wenlock time to fit fully between the latitudes 30° N and 30° S of the paleoequator. The present south shore of Hudson Bay was at the centre of Laurentia, with the Wenlock paleoequator crossing near Southampton Island. The microcontinent of Barentsia, which included Norway's island of Svalbard, was likely appended to

Laurentia off eastern Greenland. Island arcs and highland areas, such as Taconica (a landmass that would become part of eastern North America) and Pearya (a landmass that would become the northern part of Ellesmere Island), rimmed the flooded continent. During the Llandovery and Wenlock epochs, more than 65 percent of Laurentia was flooded by shallow seas.

BALTICA

The narrow, north-south Iapetus Ocean still separated Laurentia from another paleocontinent, Baltica, during Wenlock time. The Uralian and Variscan-Hercynian sutures—regions where earlier orogenies (mountain-building events) had welded landmasses together—marked the eastern and southern margins of this paleocontinent. The northern tip of Scandinavia was situated just below the paleoequator during the Wenlock Epoch, but the islands of Novaya Zemlya extended well to the north. The most prominent features were the Caledonian highlands of Norway, although a lowland attributed to the Fennoscandian Shield (rocks of Precambrian origin underlying the present-day Baltic Sea, the Kola Peninsula of Russia, and the countries of Norway, Sweden, and Finland) existed in the vicinity of Finland. Another lowland within Baltica is related to the Sarmatian Shield, in the region between the Vistula and Volga rivers in Poland and adjacent Russia. The microcontinent of Avalonia—its name derived from the Avalon Peninsula of eastern Newfoundland—was appended to Baltica by the end of Ordovician time. It included what are now England, Wales, southeastern Ireland, the Belgian Ardennes, northern France, eastern Newfoundland, part of Nova Scotia, southern New Brunswick, and coastal New England.

SIBERIA, KAZAKHSTANIA, AND OTHER CONTINENTS

Separated from Baltica by the Pleionic Ocean (essentially the northwestern arm of the Paleotethys Sea), the paleocontinent of Siberia assumed an orientation rotated 180° from its present alignment (as recognized by the inverted position of Lake Baikal). A huge Siberian platform sea extended southward. Similarly, Kazakhstania was a neighbouring continent to the east in the same northern middle latitudes. North China (including Manchuria and Korea) and South China (the Yangtze platform) were two separate continents situated in a more equatorial position. In contrast to Siberia and Kazakhstania, most of North and South China were elevated above sea level during Wenlock time.

GONDWANA

The vast supercontinent of Gondwana was centred over the South Pole. In addition to Australia, Antarctica, India, Arabia, Africa, and South America, Silurian Gondwana also included smaller pieces of Florida, southern Europe, and the Cimmerian terranes—namely, Turkey, Iran, Afghanistan, Tibet, and the Malay Peninsula—on its outer fringes. Either present-day Brazil or contiguous West Africa was stationed directly over the South Pole, buried by an ice cap likely comparable in size to the one capping Antarctica today. During Wenlock time, India, Tibet, the Malay Peninsula, and Australia projected into subtropical or tropical latitudes. The east-west ocean separating the southern European sector of Gondwana from northern Europe (Baltica) is called the Rheic Ocean and was essentially a southwestern extension of the Paleotethys Sea. The flooded margin of eastern Australia had a more-varied seafloor topography than the other shallow seas because of the extensive volcanism occurring there during Silurian time, but it shared many of the same faunal elements because of its tropical latitude.

PALEOCLIMATE

Broad-scale Silurian climatic conditions can be inferred by determining the positions and orientations of the pale-ocontinents and assuming that atmospheric circulation functioned according to the same basic principles during Silurian times as it does today. The global paleoclimate was effectively driven by major contrast in the propor-tions of land and water between the Northern and Southern hemispheres. A zonally uniform climate would be expected in the Northern Hemisphere during the Silurian, because it was dominated by a North Polar ocean. Wind patterns must have included strong polar easterlies at high northern latitudes, prevailing westerlies at mid-latitudes, and northeast trade winds in the tropics. In contrast, with Gondwana centred over the South Pole, climate in the Southern Hemisphere must have been dominated by the interaction of cellular air masses over land and water. The large continent would have experi-enced wide temperature variations due to summer heating and winter cooling.

Atmospheric circulation patterns interpreted for an early Silurian summer in the Northern Hemisphere indi-cate high pressure over the polar ocean with a zone of low pressure around 60° N latitude. Distinct high-pressure cells formed above subtropical oceans, much like the per-sistent Bermuda high-pressure centre over the present subtropical North Atlantic. Another zone of low pressure formed above the thermal equator, or the region of most intense solar warming. This somewhat migratory zone was the Silurian intertropical convergence zone (ITCZ), where the convergence of Northern and Southern Hemispheric trade winds caused the warm tropical air to rise, which in turn produced regular cloud cover and precipitation.

Mostly, the ITCZ remained near the Equator, but it may have migrated slightly to the north in response to strong summer heating on Laurentia, Baltica, and possibly Kazakhstania. This tendency would have been strongest along the eastern margins of tropical continents, where anticyclonic circulation around subtropical highs pulled warm, moisture-laden air northwestward from equatorial oceans. Subtropical high pressure probably spread onto Gondwana, particularly the Australian and Antarctic sectors. A pressure ridge may have merged with these subtropical highs to form a massive cold cell penetrating to higher latitudes over the continental interior of Gondwana. Low-pressure systems over Gondwana's mid-latitude shelf were not unlike the Aleutian and Icelandic lows of today.

Pressure systems should have moved somewhat southward during the Northern Hemispheric winter—particularly the ITCZ, which generally follows the region of maximum heating to the Southern Hemisphere during this season. A low-pressure system between Laurentia and Baltica is consistent with the erosion of thick clastic rocks (sedimentary rock composed of fragments of older rocks) derived from the Taconic and Caledonian highlands. The most significant seasonal variation surely occurred in the eastern Australian and Antarctic sectors of Gondwana, where summer heating abolished winter high-pressure cells and pulled the ITCZ more poleward. This is comparable to today's monsoons, which pull the ITCZ in the opposite direction over the subcontinent of India during the Northern Hemispheric summer. Subtropical highs intensified over the ocean waters of the Southern Hemisphere and probably insulated the arid climate of Western Australia.

The broadly flooded shelf of Gondwana had a circumference of at least 28,000 kilometres (17,400 miles), most of which sat in the belt of persistent westerly winds. This had the effect of producing intense surface upwelling of oceanic waters along the margins of the supercontinent and significantly boosting biological productivity. After the organisms living in these waters died, their remains sank into a bottom layer of water characterized by low levels of dissolved oxygen. This dearth of oxygen (anoxia) significantly decelerated the decomposition process, thereby providing the right conditions for the development of black shales. Today, black shale deposits are widespread around the perimeter areas of the former supercontinent, as evidenced by the rich source rocks yielding concentrations of Silurian oil in present-day Algeria and Saudi Arabia.

SILURIAN LIFE

Marine benthic (bottom-dwelling) invertebrates of the Silurian Period belonged to persistent assemblages, or communities, that commonly conformed to ecological zonation. One way in which zonation expresses itself is through bathymetric gradients (changes in light, temperature, salinity, and pressure with depth).Paleoecologists studying in Wales, Norway, Estonia, Siberia, South China, and North America have used very similar models to explain the geographic distribution of Silurian communities. Some of these communities were adapted to life under conditions of stronger sunlight and more vigorous wave energy in shallow nearshore waters. Others were restricted to darker, quieter environments in deeper offshore waters.

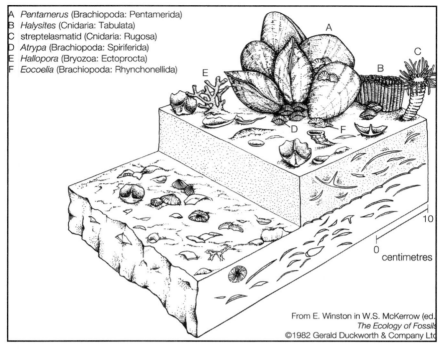

A Pentamerus (Brachiopoda: Pentamerida)
B Halysites (Cnidaria: Tabulata)
C streptelasmatid (Cnidaria: Rugosa)
D Atrypa (Brachiopoda: Spiriferida)
E Hallopora (Bryozoa: Ectoprocta)
F Eocoelia (Brachiopoda: Rhynchonellida)

10

0
centimetres

From E. Winston in W.S. McKerrow (ed.
The Ecology of Fossils
©1982 Gerald Duckworth & Company Ltd

An early Silurian Pentamerus *community.*

Pentamerid Communities

The *Pentamerus* community was an early Silurian community dominated by the large-shelled brachiopod (lamp
shell) of the species *Pentamerus oblongus*. The community
often included 5 to 20 associated species, although enormous populations of only one species sometimes are found
preserved in growth position. The *Pentamerus* community
and its slightly older and younger equivalents dominated
by similar pentamerid species in the genera *Virgiana*,
Borealis, *Pentameroides*, and *Kirkidium* all occupied a bathymetric zone of medium water depth. These pentamerid
communities are known to have lived in sunlit waters
because they are associated with robust, calcareous green
algae. The waters were not too shallow, however, because

pentamerid brachiopods lost their pedicle (the fleshy appendage that tethers the shell to the seafloor) as they matured, and thus unsecured populations were vulnerable to disruption by steady wave activity. The pentamerid communities thrived within depths of perhaps 30 to 60 metres (100 to 200 feet). This was below the level of normal (fair weather) wave activity but still in reach of storm waves. At their lower depth limit, the pentamerid communities were out of reach of all but the most intense and infrequent storms.

In regions such as Wales that are characterized by clastic rock deposition, an onshore-offshore array of five brachiopod-dominated communities may be mapped in belts running parallel to the ancient shoreline. Listed in order from shallowest to deepest position, they are the *Lingula*, *Eocoelia*, *Pentamerus*, *Stricklandia*, and *Clorinda* communities. Below a relatively steep gradient, the centre of the Welsh Basin was filled by graptolitic shales.

Other areas, such as the Laurentian and Siberian platforms, characterized by carbonate deposition, typically developed a continuum of coral-stromatoporoid, *Pentamerus*, and *Stricklandia* communities. (Stromatoporoids are large colonial marine organisms similar to hydrozoans.) *Clorinda* communities were rare in this setting. *Stricklandia* communities sometimes included smaller, less-robust individuals of calcareous green algae, indicating a slightly deeper-water environment than that occupied by the *Pentamerus* community. Coral-stromatoporoid communities, which sometimes formed reef mounds, preferred wave-agitated waters shallower than 30 metres (100 feet). Much like the reef communities of today, they could not tolerate the more excessive rates of sedimentation typical of clastic settings. Bathymetric relief on carbonate platforms was very gentle. The full spectrum of available communities was likely often expressed over a gradient hundreds of kilometres (miles) long. In contrast, the bathymetric gradient on the Welsh shelf was no more than a few tens of kilometres (miles) long. Like the *Pentamerus* community, the other early Silurian communities have ecological equivalents that took their place in later Silurian time.

REEF MOUNDS AND CORAL BIOSTROMES

Reef mounds (bioherms) provided the Silurian seafloor with an organically constructed microtopography featuring zonations of segregated brachiopods, gastropods (class of mollusk containing present-day snails and slugs), crinoids (class of echinoderm containing present-day sea lilies and feather stars), and trilobites. The Thornton Reef Complex outside Chicago is an example of a well-zoned Wenlock complex more than 1 kilometre (0.6 mile) in diameter. Others are well known from the Silurian of Manitoulin Island (Ontario, Can.), northern Greenland, Shropshire (Eng.), Gotland (Swed.), Estonia, the central and southern Urals of Russia, and Siberia. The most spectacular complex is a barrier reef 350 kilometres (215 miles) long of late Llandovery–early Wenlock age in northern Greenland.

Reefs of all Silurian ages are known, but their development probably reached a climax during Wenlock time. Several thousand bioherms have been recognized from outcrop and subsurface evidence across a tract of 800,000 square kilometres (309,000 square miles) surrounding the Great Lakes region of North America. Quite distinct from the Silurian reef mounds are concentrations of tabulate corals and lamellar stromatoporoids that lived in shallow water on a level seafloor. The resulting accumulations are flat-layered (biostromal) in design. The tabulate corals are often dominated by species belonging to the genera *Favosites* (honeycomb corals) and *Halysites* (chain corals) and by tabulate corals of the genera *Syringopora* and *Heliolites*. The associated stromatoporoids are essentially armoured sponges, the lamellar construction of which commonly lends them a pancake shape.

The creation of global biozones of different organisms is also evident in Silurian sedimentary deposits. The rich benthic faunas just described were tropical to subtropical in distribution. The southern temperate zone, sometimes called the Malvinokaffric Realm, is represented by the low-diversity *Clarkeia* (brachiopod) fauna from Gondwanan Africa and South America. A northern temperate zone is represented by the low-diversity *Tuvaella* (brachiopod) fauna mostly restricted to Mongolia and adjacent parts of Siberia. The *Tuvaella* fauna also has been discovered in northwestern China, which apparently represents a more southern extension, since it straddled the paleoequator during the Silurian Period.

FISHES

Fishes representative of all Silurian ages were widely distributed in marine environments (carbonate and clastic) in a broad belt within the latitudes 40° N and 40° S of the paleoequator. They are known from fossils of individual scales as well as from rare body molds. A wide variety of agnatha (jawless) fishes are represented by species belonging to the orders Thelodonti, Heterostraci, Osteostraci, and Anaspida. Fishes with a primitive jaw apparatus are represented by members of the subclasses Acanthodii, Elasmobranchii, and Actinopterygii. Different endemic groups developed in Laurentia (known widely from sites in the Canadian Arctic, the Yukon, Pennsylvania, New York, and especially Scotland), Baltica (especially Norway and Estonia), and Siberia (including adjacent Mongolia).

VASCULAR LAND PLANTS

Land colonization by vascular plants was under way during most of the Silurian Period, although activity clearly was restricted to coastal lowlands—the remainder of the land being essentially barren. These plants were small (about 6 centimetres, or 2.4 inches, in height), with smooth, simply branched stems bearing spore sacs at their tips. Photosynthesis took place entirely within the leafless stems. Plant megafossils preserved as coalified impressions are fragmentary. Their known distribution includes most of the Silurian continents with limited representation on Laurentia (New York and northern Greenland), Baltica (Avalonian Wales and England, as well as Podolia in what is now southwestern Ukraine), the Siberian corner of Sinkiang (northwestern China), and some Australian and North African sectors of Gondwana (Victoria and Libya, respectively). Latitudinal distribution apparently ranged from about 45° N (Siberia) to 30° S (Libya). Species belonging to the genus *Cooksonia* were among the first and most successful vascular land plants found in all the above-cited areas except for northern Greenland and Australia. A distinctly endemic group is represented by the genus *Baragwanathia* during Ludlow times in Victoria, Austl.

SILURIAN EXTINCTION EVENTS

Early Silurian marine faunas recovered from a mass extinction brought on during late Ordovician times by climatic change and lowered sea levels. This mass extinction claimed 26 percent of all marine invertebrate families and 60 percent of all marine invertebrate genera. Only 17 percent of late Ordovician brachiopod genera survived the start of the Silurian Period, but 20 out of 70 tabulate and heliolitoid coral genera (29 percent) and 45 out of 71 trilobite genera (63 percent) successfully made the same transition.

During the Silurian, several small extinction and radiation events in the evolution of nektonic (free-swimming) and pelagic (free-floating) organisms appear to be linked to fluctuations in sea level. Ten individual extinction events for graptolites alone are recorded in the rock layers of the Silurian Period, during which time 52 to 79 percent of these planktonic animals disappeared. Most of these events correspond to drops in sea level. Among conodonts (primitive chordates with tooth-shaped fossil remains), a significant radiation was indicated by species within the *Pterospathodus amorphognathoides* biozone, which straddles the Llandovery-Wenlock boundary and includes the late Telychian Age (Llandovery Epoch) highstand. Extinction of key species followed by the emergence of several new species during early Sheinwoodian time (Wenlock Epoch) was one of the most drastic changes in Silurian conodont succession.

Acritarchs are a catchall group of various small microfossils that may represent the pelagically dispersed spore cases of benthic algae. Four major turnovers in Silurian acritarch species are recognized. Among those coinciding with highstands in sea level, the turnovers of the mid-Aeronian Age (Llandovery Epoch) and early Gorstian Age (Ludlow Epoch) are the most extensive. The various nektonic and pelagic organisms may have been affected by changes in water temperature related to minor episodes of glaciation.

SIGNIFICANT SILURIAN LIFE-FORMS

In Silurian times, the first land plants gained footholds near the coasts of islands and continents. Lycopsids such as *Baragwanathia* were the first plants to grow to large sizes. As far as animals were concerned, brachiopods and graptolites continue to be well-represented in Silurian marine faunas worldwide. Other animals that lived in Silurian seas included trilobites, several groups of mollusks, and monstrous predatory arthropods called giant water scorpions.

ATRYPA

Atrypa is a genus of extinct brachiopods, or lamp shells, that has a broad time range and occurs abundantly as fossils in marine rocks from the Silurian through the Early Carboniferous (444 million to 318 million years ago). Many species of *Atrypa* have been described. The genus is easily recognized by its distinctive concentric growth lines and peculiar outgrowths of the shell. It is unusual that in some Devonian exposures the abundant remains of only the pedicle (foot) valves of *Atrypa* occur. The brachial (upper) valves are rare or absent—apparently because of some sort of selective ocean current action.

BARAGWANATHIA

This genus of early lycopsid plants had true leaves bearing a single strand of vascular tissue and kidney-bean-shaped sporangia arranged in zones along the stem. These features relate it to both ancient and modern club mosses. The first confirmed occurrence of *Baragwanathia* is in Australian rocks that date from Late Silurian times (about 420 million years ago). This discovery suggests that the lycopsids were the first lineage of land plants to evolve tracheids, true leaves, and a large stature. It also implies that the evolutionary split between lycopsids and all other vascular plants occurred very early in their colonization of terrestrial environments. This genus is also known from the Early Devonian Epoch (about 416 to 398 million years ago) of Australia and the Late Devonian Epoch of Canada (about 385 to 360 million years ago). *Baragwanathia* grew up to 28 centimetres (11 inches) long.

BIRKENIA

A genus of extinct early fishlike vertebrates found in Late Silurian and Early Devonian rocks in Europe (from about 421 to 387 million years ago), *Birkenia* was a primitive jaw-less vertebrate that attained a length of only about 10 centimetres (4 inches). *Birkenia* was adapted for active swimming, and its sucking mouth was in a terminal rather than a ventral position. The head of *Birkenia* was covered by small scales rather than by the fused bony shield of some of its relatives.

CHONETES

A genus of extinct brachiopods, or lamp shells, found as fossils in marine rocks of Silurian to Permian age (about 444 million to 299 million years old), *Chonetes* and closely related forms were the longest lived group of the productid brachiopods. The shell is small, one half concave in form and the other moderately convex. The horizontal margin of the shell bears short, angled spines that the animal used in anchoring or attaching itself. The internal structure of the shell of *Chonetes* is distinctive.

CONCHIDIUM

Conchidium, a genus of extinct brachiopods, is a valuable index fossil in marine rocks of the Lower and Middle Silurian. Both portions of the moderately large shell are strongly convex, and prominent linear ridges or markings, costae, are developed. Beaks may be present at the dorsal ends of the shell.

CYATHOCRINITES

An extinct genus of crinoids, or sea lilies, *Cyathocrinites* is found as fossils in Silurian to Permian marine rocks (between 444 million and 251 million years old). The genus is especially well represented in the Early Carboniferous Epoch (359 million to 318 million years ago), a time that saw an abundance of many crinoids. More than 100 species of *Cyathocrinites* have been described.

CYSTIPHYLLUM

Members of *Cystiphyllum*, an extinct genus of solitary corals, are found as fossils in Silurian and Devonian marine rocks (the Silurian Period preceded the Devonian Period and ended 416 million years ago). *Cystiphyllum* was one of the horn corals, so named for their hornlike shape. Like other corals, it had specialized requirements, and thus its fossils are important environmental indicators.

DEIPHON

The trilobite genus *Deiphon* is easily recognized in fossil form in Silurian rocks in North America because of its highly unusual shape. The pleural lobes (at the sides of the body axis) are reduced except for the development of spiny segments. Strongly developed spines occur at the margins of the anterior region as well as at the posterior margin of the small tail region. The head region is strongly globose, with many small nodes on its surface.

EOSPIRIFER

Members of this genus of extinct brachiopods are found as fossils in Middle Silurian to Lower Devonian marine rocks (the Silurian Period ended and the following Devonian Period began about 416 million years ago). The genus *Eospirifer* is closely related to other genera included in the brachiopod group known as the spiriferids, a formerly important group of animals. *Eospirifer* has a moderate-sized shell bearing fine, radiating ribs (costae). Arcuate (bow-shaped) growth lines are also present.

GIANT WATER SCORPIONS

Also called sea scorpions, these creatures were members of the extinct subclass Eurypterida of the arthropod group Merostomata, a lineage of large, scorpionlike, aquatic invertebrates that flourished during the Silurian Period. Well over 200 species have been identified and divided into 18 families. They include the largest arthropod species known, *Jaekelopterus rhenaniae* (also called *Pterygotus rhenanius* or *P. buffaloenis*), which measures nearly 2.5 metres (8 feet) in length. Several other eurypterid forms were almost as large. The fossils of giant water scorpions

Sea scorpions are a lineage of large, scorpion-like, aquatic invertebrates that flourished during the Silurian Period, patrolling brackish and freshwater deposits with large, fearsome pincers to prey on early vertebrates and sundry shelled animals. Ken Lucas/Visuals Unlimited, Inc.

are usually found in brackish and freshwater deposits, but the animals probably first lived in shallow coastal areas and estuaries and moved into freshwater environments later. Only a few species appear to have been good swimmers. They are presumed to have been fearsome predators, with large grasping pincers that may have entrapped early vertebrates and various shelled animals. Their distant relative, the horseshoe crab of the order Xiphosura, has survived to the present day.

GONIOPHORA

This extinct genus of clams appears in Silurian to Devonian rocks. *Goniophora* is characterized by a distinctive shell that is sharply angular. A prominent ridge extends the length of the shell; from it the shell flanks taper away. Fine growth lines extend about the shell.

LEPTODESMA

Leptodesma is an extinct genus of pelecypods (clams) found as fossils in Silurian to Lower Carboniferous rocks (between 438 and 320 million years old). Its distinct shell, roughly oval except for a sharp outgrowth that extends posteriorly, makes *Leptodesma* easy to identify. A troughlike flange connects the spinous outgrowth to the main body of the shell. Concentric growth lines are also present.

MONOGRAPTUS

An extinct genus of graptolites (small, colonial, planktonic animals), *Monograptus* fossils occur in Silurian marine rocks (formed 438 to 408 million years ago). The most common Silurian graptolite genus, *Monograptus* is characterized by a single branch, or stipe, in which distinctive features of the structure occur. *Monograptus* descended from the genus *Diplograptus,* a two-branched form. Several forms or species are known and are useful for correlating Silurian rocks in widely separated areas and for further subdividing Silurian time.

NUCULANA

Nuculana is a very long-lived genus of mollusks (clams) that first appeared during the Silurian Period and may still be found along beaches today. *Nuculana* is typical of a group of clams characterized by a small, teardrop-shaped shell that is globous anteriorly and pointed in the back. The hinge region is characterized by the presence of many small pits and ridges, sockets and teeth. *Nuculana* has an interior shell with two roughened areas at both ends where the muscles for closing the shell are located. *Nuculana* is active and moves about on the substrate.

OZARKODINIFORMS

Members of the conodont group called Ozarkodiniforms had a prominent, centrally located denticle flanked on either side by smaller, less pointed denticles. In some forms the row of denticles may be straight, whereas in others it is curved. Ozarkodiniforms are especially useful as index, or guide, fossils in studies of the Silurian Period.

PHACOPS

Fossils of *Phacops,* a trilobite genus, appear in Silurian and Devonian rocks (between 359 million and 444 million years old) in Europe and North America. *Phacops* is a common and easily recognizable form, with its rounded rather than angular outline, globose head region, and large compound eyes. A common form is the species *Phacops rana.*

PLATYCERAS

Members of *Platyceras*, a genus of extinct gastropods (snails), occur as fossils in rocks of Silurian to Permian age

(444 million to 251 million years ago). Its distinctive shape is easily recognized. The caplike shell is high and broad anteriorly. The posterior portion of the shell, at the apex, is slightly coiled in an asymmetrical fashion. Frequently, the front portions of the shells are broken, though the posterior sections are relatively well preserved. *Platyceras* is particularly abundant in Devonian deposits (359 million to 416 million years old).

PREFERNS

Prefern is a name is given to a group of extinct plants considered transitional between the first land plants, the psilophytes, of the Silurian and Devonian periods (438 to 360 million years ago), and the ferns and seed-ferns that were common land plants later in time. The preferns appeared in Middle Devonian times (about 380 million years ago) and lasted into the Early Permian Epoch (about 280 million years ago). The preferns are difficult to classify because they retained certain primitive features of psilophytes and only manifested some of the traits characteristic of true ferns. They had, however, advanced beyond the stage of psilophytes, which had only scalelike leaves or none at all and no distinct roots. The orders usually included in the prefern group are the Protopteridales and Coenopteridales.

The Protopteridales had leaves and reproduced by spores as ferns do but had true wood similar to that of gymnosperms (cone-bearing plants that include pine, spruce, and fir trees), representing an advance for fluid conduction. Their members include *Protopteridium,* which, like certain psilophytes, had leafless lower branches, and *Aneurophyton,* which was a fernlike tree at least 6 metres (20 feet) tall. The Coenopteridales were a large group of ferns or fernlike plants that displayed a variety of growth forms, such as creeping stems and erect trunks resembling those of trees. Some were vines that lived on other plants. In certain classifications many of the Protopteridales are called progymnosperms, and the Coenopteridales are categorized with the ferns.

Rhynchotreta

An extinct genus of brachiopods, *Rhynchotreta* fossils are commonly found in Silurian marine rocks. Its small, roughly triangular shell is prominently ornamented by distinct ridges that run lengthwise to the shell margin. Because of its limited time range, *Rhynchotreta* is a good guide, or index, fossil for Silurian rocks and time.

SILURIAN GEOLOGY

Silurian formations widely scattered around the world display a wealth of natural beauty. Niagara Falls and the 11-kilometre (7-mile) Niagara Gorge on the Canadian-U.S. border are products of erosion that continue to be sculpted by rushing waters undercutting the soft shale beneath a ledge of more-resistant Silurian dolomite.

The Niagara Escarpment is a curved ridge of resistant Silurian dolomite stretching more than 1,000 kilometres (about 600 miles) from Niagara Falls through Michigan's Upper Peninsula to Wisconsin's Door Peninsula and beyond. This resistant feature stands as much as 125 metres (400 feet) above the Great Lakes, which were shaped by the excavation of soft shales during the glaciations of the Pleistocene Epoch. In Ontario the Niagara Escarpment fringes the eastern and northern sides of Lake Huron, and it is recognized by the United Nations Educational, Scientific and Cultural Organization (UNESCO) as a biosphere reserve. A continuous footpath follows the Niagara Escarpment for 800 kilometres (about 500 miles) from

Queenston Heights, Ont., in the Niagara Falls area to the tip of the Bruce Peninsula at Tobermory, Ont.

Other notable manifestations of Silurian rock include the rolling hills of eastern Iowa and central and southern Indiana, as well as similar rounded hills, called klintar, that dot the island landscape of Gotland, Swed., where Silurian mound reefs reach the surface. These ancient reef deposits have been eroded into remarkable shapes where they surface near the modern seacoast. The renowned naturalist Carolus Linnaeus sketched in his field notebook the bizarre shapes of "stone giants"—large limestone sea stacks, 8 to 10 metres (about 26 to 33 feet) high, which still stand in ranks along the shores of Gotland at Kyllej.

Some of Norway's beautiful inland fjords, such as Tyrifjorden, northwest of Oslo, are lined by Silurian shales and limestones. Long, graceful curves made by the Dniester River in Ukraine and the Moiero (Moyyero) River in Siberia cut through high bluffs of Silurian limestone and marl. Picturesque sea cliffs formed by Silurian clastic rocks guard the coasts of Ireland's Dingle Peninsula. Australia's Kalbarri National Park features gorges on the Murchison River, which winds to bold sea cliffs on the Indian Ocean, all set in Silurian Tumblagooda Sandstone. The partly Silurian Tabuk Formation forms vast desert stretches in Saudi Arabia. At an elevation of 6,000 metres (19,700 feet), the Spiti River valley in India's Himalayan region is lined partly by limestone and quartzite belonging to the Muth Formation.

THE ECONOMIC SIGNIFICANCE OF SILURIAN DEPOSITS

Petroleum and natural gas are the most notable resources found in Silurian strata. The organic material buried in Silurian source rocks constituted about 9 percent of the world's known reserves in oil and gas when last surveyed in the 1990s. The most important fields that yield oil traceable to Silurian source rocks are located in Saudi Arabia, accounting for 74 percent of Silurian stock. In particular, the Qalibah Formation, which reaches a subsurface thickness of 955 metres (3,133 feet) in central Saudi Arabia, is believed to be the source of the low-sulfur, high-gravity oil pumped from younger reservoir rocks in that part of the world. The Erg Oriental and Erg Occidental in southern Algeria are the location of additional fields related to Silurian source rocks, accounting for an additional 20 percent of Silurian petroleum stock. A minor amount of petroleum is associated with Silurian reef structures in the Michigan Basin of the north-central United States.

A substantial quantity of Silurian salt is mined. Silurian limestones or dolomites (the later altered from limestone by partial secondary substitution of magnesium for calcium) are widely quarried for crushed rock.

Aside from oil and gas, the economic significance of Silurian raw materials is mostly of historical relevance. Industrial iron production first began in the Severn River valley in Shropshire, Eng., where the necessary mineral ore, coal, and limestone were all available. Limestone provided the fluxing agent necessary for the manufacture of iron and was locally quarried from Wenlock strata. The construction in 1779 of the world's first iron bridge, on the River Severn, is regarded as the starting point of the Industrial Revolution, and Ironbridge Gorge was named in 1986 as a UNESCO World Heritage Site.

The English iron industry later shifted to the Birmingham area, where the Wenlock Limestone continued to be exploited for this purpose. A major underground canal system was built at Dudley in order to facilitate limestone mining.

A similar juxtaposition of raw materials led to the industrial development of Birmingham, Ala., in the southeastern United States. Again, Silurian rocks provided one of the key ingredients—this time, hematite ore from the Llandovery Red Mountain Formation, which was mined from 1862 to 1971. A third unusual site in this regard is the ghost town of Fayette in Michigan's Upper Peninsula. It was founded as a company town in 1867 because local resources offered an abundance of Silurian dolomite for use in iron smelting. At the opposite end of the Upper Peninsula, on Drummond Island, dolomite from the Wenlock Engadine Group is still quarried on a large scale for this specialized industrial use.

THE MAJOR SUBDIVISIONS OF THE SILURIAN SYSTEM

The rocks that originated during the Silurian Period make up the Silurian System, which is divided into four rock series corresponding to four epochs of time. The Llandovery Series (443.7–428.2 million years ago) is made up of the Rhuddanian (443.7–439 million years ago), Aeronian (439–436 million years ago), and Telychian (436–428.2 million years ago) stages. The Wenlock Series (428.2–422.9 million years ago) is made up of the Sheinwoodian (428.2–426.2 million years ago) and Homerian (426.2–422.9 million years ago) stages. The Ludlow Series (422.9–418.7 million years ago) is made up of the Gorstian (422.9–421.3 million years ago) and Ludfordian (421.3–418.7 million years ago) stages. And finally there is the Pridoli Series (418.7–416 million years ago), which has not been divided into stages. The names of the Llandovery, Wenlock, and Ludlow series correspond to historical units originally proposed by Murchison.

They are now rigorously defined in terms of basal stratotypes (assemblages of certain fossils whose first occurrence in the stratigraphic column defines the beginning of a particular time interval). For example, the upper boundary of the Wenlock Series occurs where specific index fossils signifying the base of the Ludlow Series first appear. The last of the four series, the Pridoli, takes its name from an area outside Prague.

SIGNIFICANT GEOLOGIC EVENTS

Many Silurian rock formations were influenced by events taking place in the Late Ordovician Period. Decreasing sea levels resulting from a Late Ordovician glaciation exposed many rock formations to the air for the first time early in the Silurian. Later sea-level fluctuations altered ocean circulation patterns and promoted the production of evaporites near some continents.

THE EFFECTS OF LATE ORDOVICIAN GLACIATION

Dramatic unconformities (interruptions in the deposition of sedimentary rock) between the Silurian and Ordovician systems indicate how extreme the glacially induced drawdown in late Ordovician sea level had been. The maximum global fall in sea level was on the order of 70 metres (about 230 feet) and drained immense areas of former marine habitat. River valleys were eroded into Upper Ordovician marine shales stretching across Iowa, Wisconsin, and Illinois on the Laurentian platform. On Baltica, carbonate reef mounds in Sweden were transformed into karst surfaces through subareal exposure. A network of extensive tidal channels was developed across a formerly much deeper shelf in Wales. Close to the edge of the Gondwanan ice sheet in Saudi Arabia, the Jabal Sarah paleovalley was deeply cut into by glacial outwash streams eroding through Ordovician shales to a depth of 275 metres (900 feet). Ordovician-Silurian paleovalleys in the Middle East show much more topographic relief than their counterparts in Laurentia and Baltica away from the ice cap. Ice loading and isostatic rebound during the melting period near the end of the glacial event were the contributing factors to excessive erosion around the margins of the Gondwanan supercontinent.

Coastal valleys and rocky shores on all paleocontinents were eventually filled and buried with the return of marine sedimentation in early Silurian time. Basal Silurian strata virtually everywhere record a rapid rise in the level of the sea, which reflooded vast continental platforms.

SILURIAN SEA LEVEL

Smaller fluctuations in sea level, between 30 and 50 metres (about 100 and 165 feet) in magnitude, continued to occur on a global basis throughout the Silurian. In contrast to the Late Ordovician event, these fluctuations did not strongly affect the shelly bottom-dwelling invertebrates perched on continental platforms. Benthic faunas adapted to their changing living conditions at particular bathymetric levels by simply shifting upslope or downslope. The amount of available habitat space was not drastically altered as a result of these sea level fluctuations.

Data from three or more different paleocontinents indicate that at least four global highstands (intervals where sea level lies above the continental shelf edge) took place during Llandovery time. Sea level fluctuations are reconstructed by studying biological community replacement patterns through well-exposed stratigraphic sequences and then comparing the timing of trends on an interregional to intercontinental basis. These cycles of rising and falling sea levels had an average duration of about 2.5 million years during the Llandovery Epoch. The first event probably corresponds to the maximum rise in sea level achieved as the extensive Late Ordovician glaciers melted. This highstand occurred during the transition between the Rhuddanian and Aeronian Stages of Llandovery time. A second highstand is mid-Aeronian in age, the third early Telychian, and the fourth late Telychian.

Present data are not as complete for the rest of the Silurian, but a highstand in sea level has been identified during the middle of the Wenlock Epoch. A mid-Ludlow lowstand in sea level separates an early Ludlow highstand from at least one subsequent Ludlow highstand. Information on sea level changes during the Pridoli Epoch is fragmentary and globally inconsistent.

Late Silurian lowstands were sufficient to downgrade ocean circulation patterns and stimulate widespread evaporite deposition in Laurentia, Baltica, Siberia, and the Australian sector of Gondwana. Some of these bathymetric changes, which were brought about by submarine volcanism or by the tectonic elevation or subsidence of the seafloor, were clearly local, rather than global, in effect. Those sea level fluctuations recorded on different paleocontinents during the same interval of geologic time may have been coordinated by minor changes in the size of the surviving Gondwanan ice cap. South American tillites interpreted as Llandovery in age lend support to this model. Global drawdown in sea level is linked directly to evidence for the onset of at least three successive glacial episodes in the Brazilian sector of Gondwana, for example.

THE OCCURRENCE AND DISTRIBUTION OF SILURIAN DEPOSITS

Excluding peat and coal, which form from vegetation, the same kinds of strata in the process of forming today were also deposited during Silurian time. Because of the high sea level coupled with the low relief of many continents, production of certain Silurian sediments was proportionately different than that in the present world, however. Chief among these are limestones, which form primarily from the carbonate detritus of coral skeletons, shells, and calcified algae. Unless such detritus is produced in great quantities or rapidly buried, it tends to dissolve in cold (temperate to polar) waters. In warm (tropical to subtropical) shallow waters, carbonates may collect more gradually to form continuous layers of limestone. The geographic locations of Laurentia, Baltica, and in part Siberia within 30° latitude on either side of the Silurian equator ensured the development of extensive platform carbonates. In North America, Silurian limestones or dolomites are found across an enormous territory stretching along one axis from northern Greenland to West Texas and along another axis from Quebec's Anticosti Island to the Great Basin of Utah and Nevada. Parts of Baltica where carbonate deposition was prevalent include Gotland in Sweden, Estonia, and the Ukrainian region of Podolia. Carbonate deposition was also prevalent over much of Siberia. Platform carbonates of this kind rarely exceed 200 to 300 metres (about 650 to 1,000 feet) in thickness. Other important limestone units that were more-restricted in Silurian time and space include the Wenlock Limestone (Shropshire, Eng.), the Ryterraker Formation (southern Norway), the Xiangshuyan Formation and lateral equivalents (South China), and the Hume Limestone (New South Wales, Austl.).

EVAPORITES

Evaporites, including salt (halite), anhydrite, and gypsum, are chemical precipitates that usually accumulate as layers through evaporation of marine waters isolated in shallow bays. This process is most effective under warm, arid climate conditions commonly found at latitudes of about 30° or less. Distributed through parts of Michigan, Ohio, and New York, strata from the Upper Silurian Salina Group laid down during the Ludlow and Pridoli Epochs is one of the world's most famous evaporite deposits. A maximum aggregate thickness of 600 metres (1,970 feet) occurs in Michigan, where one individual halite bed reaches a thickness of 165 metres (540 feet). A halite bed 2 metres (6.6 feet) thick occurs in the Interlake Formation formed during the Wenlock Epoch in North Dakota. Gypsiferous beds occur in parts of the Upper Silurian Yangadin and Holuhan formations of Siberia, as well as in comparable formations in Latvia and Lithuania. Upper Silurian evaporites from the Pridoli Epoch are characteristic of three different basins in Western Australia. Minor amounts of halite and anhydrite occur in the Dirk Hartog Formation in the Carnarvon Basin. More extensive halite or anhydrite beds or those of both have been discovered in comparable formations from the Canning and Bonaparte Gulf basins.

CLASTIC WEDGES

Clastic rocks, including conglomerates, sandstones, and shales, generally occur in wedge-shaped deposits adjacent to land areas from which terrigenous materials (items derived from the erosion of land) erode under conditions of moderate to high annual rainfall. With steady accumulation over protracted periods of time, such deposits tend to become very thick and subside under their own weight, forming troughlike structures parallel to their sediment source. In contrast to thin platform deposits, clastic wedges may be thousands of metres—more than 1 km (0.6 mile)—thick. Taconica was a long narrow highland roughly corresponding to the present position of the Appalachian Mountains in North America. During the Llandovery Epoch these highlands shed the Shawangunk Conglomerate (500 metres, or 1,640 feet, thick) near its front in southeastern New York state and distributed the Tuscarora-Clinch sandstones (150 to 250 metres, or about 490 to 820 feet, thick) throughout central Pennsylvania and western Virginia from more than 80 kilometres (about 50 miles) beyond its front. These deposits accrued from sediments carried by braided streams (a series of converging and diverging streams) crossing coastal plains to a wave-swept shore. *Arthrophycus* trails (those made by annelids tolerant of low salinity) are recorded in the more seaward portions of the Tuscarora Sandstone. Collectively attributed to the Clinton Group, a variety of Upper Llandovery rocks with high iron content subsequently were deposited from New York to Alabama. These strata often contain marine fossils, but their iron was derived from Taconica. Tiny pellets, or oolites (rock composed of small calcium grains), coated with hematite occur in seams up to 2 metres (about 6.6 feet) thick in New York; massive iron-rich sandstones are found in Pennsylvania; and oolitic ironstone beds up to 15 metres (50 feet) thick occur in Alabama (in the Red Mountain Formation).

Evidence of another Laurentian highland, called Pearya, is found in the Canadian Arctic in the vicinity of northern Ellesmere Island. Clastic sediments eroded from this source were deposited in the Hazen Trough. One Lower Silurian (Llandovery) unit called the Danish River Formation is composed of interstratified conglomerates, sandstones, and shales 1 kilometre (about 0.6 mile) thick. The Caledonian highlands dominated depositional patterns on the paleocontinent of Baltica. Much of the highland front followed approximately the present spine

of Norway and affected a broader area through genera-
tion of river-transported sandstones that gradually spread
across Sweden to Poland in one direction and through
northern England to southeastern Ireland in the other
direction. Known traditionally as the Old Red Sandstone,
these rocks date back to the Ludlow Epoch in southern
Norway, mixed with those of the Pridoli Epoch and early
Devonian times in northern England, and early Devonian
age in southeastern Ireland and Poland. This variation
in age reflects the growth of the Caledonian highlands
and their ability to shed clastic debris farther and farther
afield. In Western Australia, similar thick red sandstones
belonging to the Upper Silurian Tumblagooda Sandstone
were derived from a Precambrian massif called the
Yilgarn Block.

In contrast to sandstones that accumulated because of
river transport, eolian (wind-driven) sandstones are those
deposited under desert conditions. The Mereenie
Sandstone in central Australia (Amadeus Basin) is one of
the few examples of a possible Silurian desert sandstone.

PLATFORM MARGINS

In addition to clastic wedges closely linked to a land source,
Silurian shales also formed on continental platform margins, as in the nearly 500 metres (1,640 feet) of strata
belonging to the Road River Group in the Canadian Yukon.
Based on sections in the Mackenzie Mountains, a distance
of only one to a few kilometres (miles) separated the edge of
a shallow-water carbonate platform from the deepwater
shales of the basin. Submarine avalanches (turbidity flows)
brought the 1,200 to 1,500 metres (approximately 3,900 to
4,900 feet) of interbedded shales and fine sandstones con-
stituting the Aberystwyth Grit Formation to a deepwater
basinal setting in west-central Wales.

Less commonly, Silurian shales passively accumulated in broad platform settings. The Longmaqi Formation of the Yangtze platform in South China is one such shale body, which indicates the base of the Silurian System throughout parts of Yunnan, Sichuan, Shaanxi, Hubei, Hunan, and Guizhou provinces. As much as 500 metres (1,640 feet) thick in places, these shales developed in quiet waters with low dissolved oxygen content. Similar conditions prevailed during early Silurian times well within Baltica, including southern Sweden and Denmark. The importance of the Qalibah Formation as a widespread anoxic black shale (that is, an organic-rich shale formed under low oxygen conditions) in Saudi Arabia is tied to petroleum production.

TILLITES

Silurian sandstones and shales rest directly on Upper Ordovician tillites—masses of sedimentary rock made up of unweathered material and glacial till—in Saudi Arabia (Tabuk Formation) and throughout large parts of North Africa. In South America, which was fused with Africa during the Silurian Period, glaciation persisted well into the Wenlock Epoch. The Cancaniri Formation, including a prominent segment 60 metres (about 200 feet) thick that bears the Zapla Tillite, extends 1,500 kilometres (about 930 miles) from northern Argentina over the Andes Mountains across Bolivia to Peru. Alpine glaciers advanced from high elevations down to tidewater areas to deposit these layers, including faceted and glacially striated boulders 1.5 metres (about 5 feet) in diameter. Similarly, the widespread Lower Silurian Nhamunda Formation in the Amazon region of Brazil includes diamictite (a non-sorted conglomerate made up clastic material) beds consisting of highly diverse clastics related to tillites.

VOLCANIC ROCKS

Examples of rocks used to make absolute age determinations for the Silurian Period include a volcanic breccia dating back to the Llandovery Epoch from the Descon Formation on Esquibel Island in Alaska, ash beds (bentonites) from the Buildwas Formation at the base of the Wenlock Series and the Ludlow Elton Formation in Shropshire, Eng., and the Laidlaw Volcanics of the Ludlow Series near Canberra, Austl. Compared with other time periods, the Silurian Period was relatively quiet in terms of volcanic activity. Moderate activity in those parts of the British Isles, the Canadian Maritimes, and coastal New England is collectively attributed to the appending of Avalonia to Baltica. Approximately 1,000 metres (about 3,300 feet) of basalt flows belonging to the Skomer Volcanics in southwestern Wales are dated to the Llandovery Epoch. Rhyolite and andesite lavas were extruded in the area of the English Mendip Hills during Wenlock time. Basalts, rhyolites, and porphyritic andesites from the Newbery Volcanics in northeastern Massachusetts were formed during the Pridoli Epoch. Rhyolitic and andesitic flows of Silurian age also are known in the region of Passamaquoddy Bay in Maine, as are volcanic flows and breccias in adjacent New Brunswick. A Silurian chain of volcanic islands stood off the Laurentian craton, stretching from the Klamath Mountains of northern California to Alaska. Likewise, andesitic and basaltic sites of volcanism stretched along the edge of Baltica, as framed by the Ural Mountains.

The most extensive Silurian volcanism occurred in eastern Australia, principally in New South Wales but also in Victoria and Queensland. Activity was initiated during early Wenlock time with the Paddys River and Uriarra volcanic events. This was expanded during the Ludlow Epoch with the Laidlaw, Mineral Hill, Bennetts Creek, Mullions Range, and Bells Creek volcanics and concluded during Pridoli time with the Bombay Creek and Woodlawn volcanics and the Currawan Basalt event. Most of this volcanic activity took place in terrestrial environments. In New South Wales more than 200 intrusive granitic bodies of the late Silurian or early Devonian are geochemically linked to these silica-rich volcanics, but their precise age is difficult to establish.

THE CORRELATION OF SILURIAN STRATA

The most-challenging goal in stratigraphy is to identify on a global basis all those rocks formed during the shortest possible interval of geologic time. Correlation of Silurian strata within limits more refined than a stage (or its corresponding age) traditionally is achieved through the recovery of fossils belonging to shaley and shelly facies.

GRAPTOLITES

Shaley facies generally represent deeper-water environments, such as those under which the Road River Group in the Yukon, the Aberystwyth Grit Formation in Wales, and the Longmaqi Formation of southern China accumulated. Fossils of graptolites (small, colonial, planktonic animals) are abundant in these dark Silurian shales. Graptolites were colonial hemichordates that secreted a protein exoskeleton commonly preserved as a carbon film in shales. An individual lived within a cuplike structure called a theca. Multiple cups were spaced along one or more branches called stipes, and the entire colony sometimes was connected, by a threadlike structure known as a nema, to a central float.

Some graptolites were bottom-dwellers, but the free-floating (or pelagic) species were geographically more cosmopolitan. They make excellent index fossils because they underwent rapid evolution and attained a broad distribution. The genera *Pristiograptus* and *Cyrtograptus* are pelagic graptolites characteristic of the Wenlock Series. As many as 42 graptolite biozones have been defined for the Silurian System. Each biozone takes the name of one particular species but is usually based on several coeval species. The span of time represented by each graptolite biozone probably is not perfectly uniform, but the zonation allows the correlation of strata in depositional units of one million years or less. Superb as it is, this level of precision is restricted to regions rich in graptolitic shales. It is easier to correlate the deepwater shales of Wales and the Yukon with each other, for example, than it is to correlate either with nearby shallow-water shelf deposits.

BRACHIOPODS

In contrast to shaley facies, shelly facies are represented by relatively shallow platform carbonates and clastic wedges with a retinue of mostly bottom-dwelling invertebrates. Among these, Silurian brachiopods were especially abundant, diverse, and widely distributed, making them effective index fossils. A still-extant group, the brachiopods possess a pair of bilaterally symmetrical shells and are tethered to the seafloor by a fleshy appendage usually protruding through one of the shells (thus, the shells are typically unequal in shape). Biostratigraphic zonations based on brachiopod lineages are well suited to the correlation of Llandovery and Wenlock strata. Those most frequently used are the *Stricklandia-Costistricklandia*, the *Borealis-Pentamerus-Pentameroides*, and the *Eocoelia* lineages. Excluding most of Gondwana save for eastern Australia, these brachiopods attained a broad tropical-to-subtropical distribution. Lineage members (including four subspecies of *Stricklandia*) may be employed for independent correlation but are more effective when they are used in combination with one another as overlapping taxon zones. Thus, *Pentameroides subrectus* alone may indicate a late Llandovery (Telychian) age or an early Wenlock (Sheinwoodian) age. In association with *Stricklandia laevis* or *Eocoelia curtisi*, however, a Telychian age is certain. Single-taxon zones also are helpful in characterizing Ludlow and Pridoli times. Only in unusual cases where brachiopod-bearing layers are interbedded with graptolite-rich shales (at the narrow transition between shelly and shaley facies) may the temporal relationships between the two kinds of index fossils be established. Most of the projected correlations between graptolite and brachiopod biozones are approximate.

CONODONTS

Conodonts constitute a third group of index fossils important for Silurian correlation. These phosphatic microfossils with the shape of conelike teeth (as the name implies) are the remains of an apparatus from the mouth cavity of a small, bilaterally symmetrical, free-swimming (nektonic) animal extinct since Triassic time. Rare body fossils suggest some affinities with surviving cephalochordates, such as *Amphioxus*, or the chaetognaths (arrowworms). The individual elements comprising the conodont apparatus are very common in Silurian rocks that accumulated under a wide range of marine environments. Hydrochloric acid (HCl), which has no effect on phosphatic material, is used to dissolve limestone or lime-cemented sediments from which the conodonts may be recovered. Graptolite and brachiopod zonations have a long history of use in the Silurian, but the first conodont zonation based on material collected at Mount Cellon in the Carnic Alps of Austria was not proposed until the early 1960s. Different kinds of conodont-bearing animals lived in shallow nearshore environments (as opposed to deeper, more-offshore environments), and some were more conservative in their evolutionary development than others. Global correlation is based on 1212 conodont biozones for the complete Silurian. The base of each zone is defined by the first occurrence of the taxon. All are characteristic of open marine environments. The zonation is not applicable to strata that accumulated in restricted nearshore or deep-basin facies.

ISOTOPE STRATIGRAPHY

An alternative method gaining increased attention for the correlation of Silurian rocks is by means of isotope stratigraphy, which heretofore has found greater application to rocks of much younger age in the Cenozoic Era. Variations in oxygen, carbon, and strontium isotopes through sequences of layered limestone beds on Anticosti Island, Quebec, and in several localities in northern Europe, including the island of Gotland in Sweden, indicate changes in climate and long-term patterns of erosion. Samples for geochemical analysis are taken by the whole-rock method or by the retrieval of fossils with unaltered shells composed of calcium carbonate. Implicit in these methods is the assumption that the shells of some marine invertebrates, and the carbonate sediments derived thereof, are able to pick up and hold isotopic markers showing changes in the chemistry of Silurian seawater. High ratios of the oxygen isotopes ^{18}O to ^{16}O or of the carbon isotopes ^{13}C to ^{14}C, for example, are indicative of colder intervals during times of low sea level. Low ratios are interpreted as indicative of warmer intervals during times of high sea level. Particularly through the lower

Silurian stages, patterns in the variation of carbon and oxygen isotopes tend to corroborate the sequence of minor glacial and interglacial episodes using the succession of tillites and diamictites from the South American sector of Gondwana. Likewise, high ratios of the strontium isotopes ^{87}Sr to ^{86}Sr typically indicate periods of increased erosion as radiogenic strontium was transferred from the continents to the ocean during warmer intervals of climate. The strontium isotope curve shows a distinct inflection point near the base of the Wenlock Series, which may be used to widely correlate the Llandovery-Wenlock boundary.

ESTABLISHING SILURIAN BOUNDARIES

The delineation of the Silurian Period, which began with the work of a group of 19th-century geologists and paleontologists, relies heavily on results of radioisotope and fossil studies. Despite disagreements over the boundaries between the Silurian System and others, over time the international community came together to develop a system of standardized type references that could apply to all intervals of geologic time. The first such Global Standard Section and Point (GSSP) marker was placed in rocks that specified the boundary between the Silurian and Devonian Periods.

THE WORK OF RODERICK MURCHISON AND OTHER RESEARCHERS

Scottish geologist Roderick I. Murchison began in 1831 to study rocks from the early Paleozoic Era in South Wales. In 1835, as mentioned previously, he named a sequence of rocks found in Wales and its border region with England for a native people called the Silures, who had resisted Roman conquest. Murchison published his findings in his classic work, *The Silurian System* (1839), illustrating 656 fossils, most of which were defined as characteristic of Silurian time. In this way, the formal groundwork was laid for recognition of Silurian rocks elsewhere around the world.

Murchison's genius for military-style organization promoted the rapid adoption of his Silurian System throughout the British Isles, Scandinavia, and Europe. He was an active traveler who conceived of his field studies in terms of "campaigns." Local guides and fossil collectors were considered "aides-de-camp" in his service.

Murchison's original concept grew in his lifetime to embrace what is now differentiated into the Cambrian, Ordovician, and Silurian systems. Claims for a monolithic system began to weaken in 1854 with discovery of the famous unconformity on the River Onny in Shropshire, Eng., which indicates a natural break within the classic Silurian on its own home territory. Major unconformities exhibiting a sustained pause in sedimentation subsequently were recognized between the Ordovician and Silurian systems in many other places around the world where the boundary beds are exposed.

While the absolute limits of Silurian time remained imprecise, Murchison's triumph was the identification of successive fossil types with broad geographic distributions that always follow in the same relative stratigraphic order wherever they occur. Exposed fossiliferous strata are now classified as belonging to a particular Silurian time interval so long as they correlate with fossils diagnostic of the appropriate stratotype in the United Kingdom or the Czech Republic.

Some years earlier (1822), English geologist and minister William Buckland of Oxford University had observed that fossil brachiopods and corals collected by British army officers stationed on Drummond Island (Michigan Upper Peninsula) and by fur traders working at Cumberland House (east-central Saskatchewan) in North America were equivalent to fossils from Dudley, Eng., as well as to those from the Swedish island of Gotland and the Baltic countryside (Estonia) neighbouring St. Petersburg. Each of these sites rests on Silurian bedrock, as now strictly delimited.

Contemporaries who undertook research on Silurian strata and fossils with equal vigour were the French paleontologist Joachim Barrande in the Prague Basin of Bohemia and the American geologist and paleontologist James Hall in the states of New York, Michigan, Wisconsin, and Iowa. Other investigators who circulated to the distant territories of the British Empire lost little time in recording the worldwide distribution of Silurian fossils. The first report of Silurian fossils in Australia, for example, was made (erroneously) in 1838, prior to the publication of *The Silurian System*.

GEOCHEMICAL ANALYSES

As stated above, absolute dates in geologic time are calculated using radioisotopes (radioactive isotopes), which must be analyzed geochemically from samples of igneous rock. The radioisotopes decay at an exponential rate starting with the crystallization of the host rock from a magmatic source. Reheating of the host rock due to metamorphism, however, has the effect of resetting the radioisotope clock.

Igneous rocks associated with sedimentary layers bearing fossils defined as Silurian are the desired targets for geochemical analysis, but few have remained untouched by metamorphism during their long existence. Typically, no more than four or five igneous localities are selected by teams of geochronologists to establish Silurian dates.

Because igneous bodies are seldom found near the defined boundaries between geologic systems, the boundary ages for the Silurian Period must be extrapolated, taking into account a limited number of data points from older Ordovician and younger Devonian rocks.

Competing groups of geochronologists disagree on precisely when and for how long the Silurian Period occurred. The oldest suggested age is 445 million years. The youngest is 395 million years. Some researchers believe the Silurian was as brief as 18 million years, while others argue for a span of 40 million years. In any case, the Silurian qualifies as one of the shortest geologic time periods—many others are approximately twice as long.

SILURIAN BOUNDARIES

Much work has been done to determine exactly where the starting and ending points of Silurian life occur in the stratigraphic record and how the Silurian System may be broken into smaller chronostratigraphic units. Boundaries for subdivisions for the entire period have been internationally recognized and indicated with a GSSP marker, or "golden spike." This work is being done by The International Commission on Stratigraphy (ICS) and its committees or working groups, which are under the International Union of Geological Sciences (IUGS).

The Ordovician-Silurian Boundary

The GSSP marker for the Ordovician-Silurian boundary is not associated with any unusual climatic changes or other physical phenomena that might have left a stratigraphic signature. Instead, in 1985 the working group on the Ordovician-Silurian boundary ratified its decision to use the base of the *Parakidograptus acuminatus* biozone (a group of concurrent graptolite species) as the base of the

Silurian System. The stratotype was fixed at a horizon in Dob's Linn near Moff in the Southern Uplands of Scotland. The effect on sea level of Late Ordovician glaciation, combined with increasing deglaciation during the early Silurian, accounts for widespread stratigraphic unconformities at the Ordovician-Silurian boundary that usually omit the *P. acuminatus* biozone. In earliest Silurian time the Dob's Linn locality was situated environmentally in marine waters deep enough to remain unaffected by these changes.

The Silurian-Devonian Boundary

The results of lengthy deliberations by the working group on the Silurian-Devonian boundary were published in 1977, fixing the base of the *Monograptus uniformis* biozone (a single graptolite taxon but reinforced by associated conodont and trilobite taxa) as the base of the Devonian System. The top of the Silurian System is constrained by this golden spike, which has its stratotype at a designated horizon in a cliff section near Klonk in the Czech Republic. Thus, the Silurian-Devonian boundary is anchored to the first occurrence of specific index fossils. The Klonk section acts as a kind of standard reference section with which other stratigraphic sections, potentially involving the Silurian-Devonian boundary beds, may be compared. This agreement, arrived at by a committee of specialists, represents the first time that the concept of the golden spike was put into effect internationally.

STAGES OF THE SILURIAN PERIOD

Silurian rocks are divided into eight divisions that span four series. Although the rocks of most Paleozoic series are subdivided into stages, the Silurian is unique in that its uppermost series, the Pridoli, stands alone. Together the earlier Silurian rocks (that is, those of the Llandovery, Wenlock, and Ludlow Series) are divided into seven stages.

RHUDDANIAN STAGE

The Rhuddanian Stage is the base of the Silurian System. It is the first of three stages of the Llandovery Series and includes all rocks deposited during the Rhuddanian Age (443.7 million to 439 million years ago) of the Silurian Period. It forms the base of the Silurian System. The name of the interval is derived from the Cefn-Rhuddan Farm near Llandovery, Powys, Wales.

In 1984 the ICS established the Global Stratotype Section and Point (GSSP) defining the base of the Rhuddanian Stage within the shale of the Birkhill Shale Formation in Dob's Linn near Moffat, Scot. The GSSP marks the first appearance of the graptolites *Akidograptus ascensus* and *Parakidograptus praematurus*. The Rhuddanian Stage overlies the Hirnantian Stage of the Ordovician System and precedes the Aeronian Stage.

AERONIAN STAGE

The second of three stages of the Llandovery Series, the Aeronian Stage consists of all rocks deposited during the Aeronian Age (439 million to 436 million years ago) of the Silurian Period. The name of the interval is derived from the Cemcoed-Aeron Farm near Llandovery, Powys, Wales.

In 1984 the ICS established the Global Stratotype Section and Point (GSSP) defining the base of the Aeronian Stage within the block-shaped mudstones of the Trefawr Formation near Llandovery. The GSSP marks the first appearance of the graptolite *Monograptus triangulatus*. The

Aeronian Stage follows the Rhuddanian Stage and precedes the Telychian Stage.

Telychian Stage

The Telychian Stage is the last of three stages of the Llandovery Series. It is made up of all rocks deposited during the Telychian Age (436 million to 428.2 million years ago) of the Silurian Period. The name of the interval is derived from the Pen-lan-Telych Farm near Llandovery, Powys, Wales.

In 1984 the ICS established the Global Stratotype Section and Point (GSSP) defining the base of the Telychian Stage within the sandstone and siltstone of the Wormwood Formation. The GSSP marker, located in an unused quarry bordering the Cefn-Cerig Road near Llandovery, is placed just above the highest strata within which the brachiopod *Eocoelia intermedia* appears and below the strata recording the emergence of *E. curtisi*. The Telychian Stage follows the Aeronian Stage. It precedes the Sheinwoodian Stage of the Wenlock Series.

Sheinwoodian Stage

The Sheinwoodian Stage is the first of two stages of the Wenlock Series, encompassing all rocks deposited during the Sheinwoodian Age (428.2 million to 426.2 million years ago) of the Silurian Period.

The ICS established the Global Stratotype Section and Point (GSSP) defining the base of the Sheinwoodian Stage in 1980. The GSSP is located at the intersection of the top of the Purple Shale Formation and the base of the Buildwas Formation on the north bank of Hughley Brook near Hughley, Shropshire, Eng. The marker approximates the position of the first appearance of the graptolite *Cyrtograptus centrifugus*, but these fossils and the base of the Buildwas Formation do not coincide. Some geologists suggest that other index fossils such as the graptolite *C. murchisoni* may be better suited for correlation. However, the ICS has not made a decision regarding this issue. The Sheinwoodian Stage precedes the Homerian Stage and follows the Telychian Stage of the Llandovery Series.

HOMERIAN STAGE

The second of two stages of the Wenlock Series, the Homerian Stage includes all rocks laid down during the Homerian Age (426.2 million to 422.9 million years ago) of the Silurian Period. The name of this interval is derived from the town of Homer, Shropshire, Eng.

The ICS established the Global Stratotype Section and Point (GSSP) defining the base of the Homerian Stage in 1980. The GSSP is located in Whitwell Coppice near Homer, on the northern bank of a small stream that flows into a tributary of Sheinton Brook. It has been set into the mudstone of the Coalbrookdale Formation where the graptolite *Cyrtograptus lundgreni* first appears. The Homerian Stage precedes the Gorstian Stage of the Ludlow Series and follows the Sheinwoodian Stage.

GORSTIAN STAGE

The Gorstian Stage is the first of two stages of the Ludlow Series. It is made up of all rocks deposited during the Gorstian Age (422.9 million to 421.3 million years ago) of the Silurian Period.

In 1980 the ICS established the Global Stratotype Section and Point (GSSP) defining the base of the Gorstian Stage in Pitch Coppice Quarry, near the town of

Ludlow, Shropshire, Eng. The GSSP has been placed at the boundary between the older limestone of the Much Wenlock Formation and the younger siltstone of the Lower Elton Formation. The marker is close to the first appearance of the graptolite *Saetograptus (Colonograptus) varians* in the fossil record. These fossils occur about 0.03 metre (1 inch) above the marker. Rocks of the Gorstian Stage are overlain by those of the Ludfordian Stage and overlay those of the Homerian Stage.

LUDFORDIAN STAGE

The Ludfordian Stage is the second of two stages of the Ludlow Series, made up of all rocks deposited during the Ludfordian Age (421.3 million to 418.7 million years ago) of the Silurian Period.

In 1980 the ICS established the Global Stratotype Section and Point (GSSP) defining the base of the Ludfordian Stage in Sunnyhill Quarry, a silty limestone quarry near the town of Ludlow, Shropshire, Eng. The GSSP has been placed in a thin shale seam amid the limestone, which marks the base of the Lower Leintwardine Formation. The marker is close to the first appearance of the graptolite *Saetograptus leintwardinensis leintwardinensis* in the fossil record. However, it is not coincident with it. Rocks of the Ludfordian Stage are overlain by those of the Pridoli Series and rest upon those of the Gorstian Stage.

PRIDOLI SERIES

The uppermost of four main divisions of the Silurian System, the Pridoli Series represents those rocks deposited worldwide during the Pridoli Epoch (418.7–416 million years ago). The series name is derived from the Pridoli area of the Daleje Valley on the outskirts of Prague in the Czech Republic, where about 20 to 50 metres (about 65 to 165 feet) of platy limestone strata rich in cephalopods and bivalves are well-developed.

By international agreement, the base of the Pridoli Series is defined by the first occurrence of the graptolite species *Monograptus parultimus* in rock exposures at the entrance to the Pozary Quarries, which lie about 1.5 kilometres (about 1 mile) east of Reporyje, outside of southwestern Prague. The *M. parultimus* biozone, in short, constitutes the global stratotype section and point (GSSP) for the base of the series. In addition, two species of chitinozoans (a type of marine plankton), *Urnochitina urna* and *Fungochitina kosovensis*, first occur at or just above the base of the series. The earliest known simple vascular land plants, of the genus *Cooksonia*, typically occur in the lower portions of the Pridoli Series in many parts of the world. The Pridoli Series is overlain by the Lochkovian Stage, the first stage of the Devonian System. The base of the Lochkovian and the base of the Devonian System automatically define the top of the Pridoli and thus the top of the Silurian System. The Pridoli Series has not been divided into stages and is underlain by the Ludlow Series.

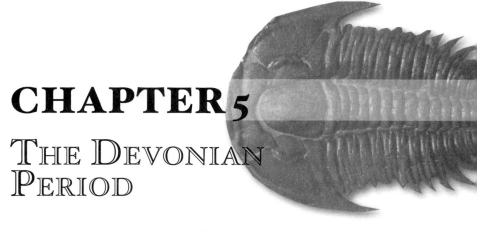

CHAPTER 5

THE DEVONIAN PERIOD

The Devonian Period followed the Silurian Period in geologic time and spanned the interval between about 416 million and 359.2 million years ago. The Devonian Period is sometimes called the Age of Fishes because of the diverse, abundant, and, in some cases, bizarre types of these creatures that swam Devonian seas. Forests and the coiled shell-bearing marine organisms known as ammonites first appeared early in the Devonian. Late in the period the first four-legged amphibians appeared, indicating the colonization of land by vertebrates.

During most of the Devonian Period, North America, Greenland, and Europe were united into a single Northern Hemisphere landmass, a minor supercontinent called Laurussia or Euramerica. This union of the paleocontinents of Laurentia (comprising much of North America, Greenland, northwestern Ireland, Scotland, and the Chukotsk Peninsula of northeastern Russia) and Baltica (now most of northern Europe and Scandinavia) occurred near the beginning of the Devonian Period. Extensive terrestrial deposits known as the Old Red Sandstone covered much of its northern area, while widespread marine deposits accumulated on its southern portion. The paleoequator (the site of the equator at a point in the geological past) passed through North America and through China, which was at that time a separate landmass. South America, Africa, India,

Australia, and Antarctica were joined into the Southern Hemisphere continent of Gondwana. Parts of this continent were also often covered by seawater.

An ocean covered approximately 85 percent of the Devonian globe. There is limited evidence of ice caps, and the climate is thought to have been warm and equitable. The oceans experienced episodes of reduced dissolved oxygen levels, which likely caused the extinction of many species, especially marine animals. These extinctions were followed by periods of species diversification, as the descendants of surviving organisms filled in abandoned habitats.

The name of the Devonian Period is derived from the county of Devon, Eng. The English geologist Adam Sedgwick and the Scottish geologist Roderick Murchison proposed the designation in 1839 for the marine rocks they encountered in southwestern England, following the recognition by another British geologist, William Lonsdale, that fossil corals from Torquay in Devon seemed intermediate in type between those of the Silurian System below and those of the Lower Carboniferous System above. This led to the conclusion that the fossil corals were marine equivalents of the terrestrial Old Red Sandstone rocks already known in Wales and Scotland. The recognition that such major paleogeographic differences existed was a great scientific advance, and it was soon confirmed when Sedgwick and Murchison visited Germany and again when Murchison discovered an intercalation of Devonian marine fossils and Old Red Sandstone fishes near St. Petersburg, Russia. By 1843 American geologist and paleontologist James Hall was able to describe equivalent rocks in eastern North America, but precise correlation with European rocks was not achieved until some years later.

Adam Sedgwick was the English geologist who named the Cambrian System in 1835 and took Roderick Murchison to task regarding the Cambrian-Silurian debate. Kilburn/Hulton Archive/Getty Images

THE DEVONIAN ENVIRONMENT

The Panthalassa, or world ocean, continued to cover the Northern Hemisphere during the Devonian, whereas the supercontinent of Gondwana covered much of the Southern Hemisphere. Between them lay smaller continents (Laurussia, Kazakhstania, and others). The Devonian Period is generally regarded to be an interval of relatively warm temperatures. Evidence of warm conditions includes rocks characteristic of salt deposits, fossils and rocks associated with extensive reef development, and the suspected absence of glacial deposits.

PALEOGEOGRAPHY

The physical geography of the Devonian can be reconstructed using evidence from paleomagnetism, paleoclimate, paleobiogeography, and tectonic events. Because the paleomagnetic data for the Devonian is conflicting, recent efforts to describe the positions of the continents have concentrated on the rock types associated with particular environments. Such methods focus on the distribution of evaporites, shelf carbonates, and corals because present-day deposits of these types have specific, well-known climatic constraints. Faunal distributions are also employed but to a lesser extent.

The distribution of nonmarine fish and marine invertebrate fossils demonstrates that Europe, Siberia, and the Canadian Arctic islands were linked and formed the bulk of Laurussia. During the Devonian, Asia was composed of many separate microplates that are now joined together. Of these, Siberia and Kazakhstania began fusing during the late Devonian and later joined Laurussia, forming the Ural Mountains along the junction.

There is general agreement that the paleoequator crossed the northern part of Laurussia during the Devonian. Paleomagnetic evidence, however, is not clear, and various positions for the exact placement of the paleoequator have been proposed. Though Laurussia was essentially tropical or subtropical, its climatic zones changed somewhat through the course of the Devonian as this landmass migrated northward during Late Devonian and Early Carboniferous times. Evidence for this movement includes the reduction in evaporitic environments in western Canada and the onset of humid and moist conditions in the area of New York.

The southern continents of today were united into the supercontinent of Gondwana during the Devonian approximately along the lines of their present-day continental shelf boundaries. Establishing the position of Gondwana is more difficult than for Laurussia. Some interpretations favour a wide ocean separating these two large landmasses, but this arrangement is thought to be unlikely because of the remarkable occurrences of similar corals, brachiopods, and ammonites in eastern North America, Morocco, and Spain. Yet, even if these areas were close together, their precise positioning is not certain. Based on the similarity in fossils, some researchers would place North Africa adjacent to the eastern North American seaboard during this period. The late Devonian reef developments in Western Australia suggest a near tropical site for this portion of the southern landmass. The positions of the microcontinents that later came together to form Asia are rather uncertain, but many of them probably were either attached or adjacent to the northern margin of Gondwana and migrated north to fuse with the growing area of Asia at several junctures during the later Phanerozoic Eon.

Paleomagnetic evidence is inconsistent regarding the position of the South Pole. Though some researchers postulate a location in central South America, most favour a position south of central Africa or off its southeast coast. The North Pole was in the ocean.

PALEOCLIMATE

Though most environments present today were represented during the Devonian, evidence of glacial deposits is questionable. It is clear that if polar ice caps did exist, they were very much smaller than they are today. It is thus concluded that Earth was warmer during Devonian time than at present.

Warm and equable climates were common, as shown by the wide distribution of evaporite basins in the Northern Hemisphere, by coal deposits in Arctic Canada and Spitsbergen, and by widespread desert conditions and carbonate reefs. Devonian salt deposits indicative of high evaporation rates, and thus of high temperatures, range from western Canada to Ukraine and Siberia and are found locally in Australia. Evidence of cooler average temperatures is provided by annual tree rings in *Archaeopteris* trunks from New York state that record seasonal growth patterns characteristic of higher latitudes.

Studies of growth lines on Devonian corals indicate that the Devonian year was longer, about 400 days. The lunar cycle, about 3012 days, was one day longer than it is now.

DEVONIAN LIFE

A highly varied invertebrate fauna that originated in the preceding Silurian Period continued in the Devonian, and most ecological niches of shallow and deep marine water were exploited. The remarkable proliferation of primitive fishes during the Age of Fishes occurred in both fresh and marine waters. Derivation of carnivorous fishes from mud-eating forms occurred early in the period, and tetrapods (four-legged land animals) were derived from fishes near the middle of the period. Also remarkable is the rise to dominance of vascular plants. Though groves of trees must have arisen earlier to provide the widespread plant debris noted in Devonian deposits, the first known evidence of in-place forests dates from the Middle Devonian.

INVERTEBRATES

The Devonian invertebrates are essentially of the type established during the Ordovician Period. In nearshore sandy and silty environments, bivalves, burrowing organisms, brachiopods (lamp shells), and simple corals abounded. In offshore environments free from land detritus, biostromes and bioherms flourished, rich in corals, stromatoporoids (large colonial marine organisms similar to hydrozoans), crinoids, brachiopods, trilobites, gastropods, and other forms. In deeper waters, goniatite ammonites (a form of cephalopod), which were one of the few new groups to appear, were abundant. Surface waters were occupied by small dacryoconarids (a shelled marine invertebrate) and by ostracods (mussel shrimp) later in the period. Among the Protozoa, both Foraminifera and Radiolaria were well represented, and sponges were locally abundant.

The corals and stromatoporoids were extremely important for building reef facies. The limestone-reef and forereef facies and biostromal limestones are known in many areas of the world. The corals include tabulate corals, such as *Favosites* and *Alveolites*, but especially rugose corals (horn corals), which have been used to establish correlations. Stromatoporoids (a type of sponge with a layered skeleton composed of calcium carbonates) such as *Amphipora* were common rock builders in the mid-Devonian of the Northern Hemisphere. The twiglike form of *Amphipora* produces a "spaghetti" or "vermicelli" rock. Elsewhere, only simple corals are frequently found.

Bryozoans (marine moss animals superficially similar to corals) were especially common in shallow shelf seas of the period. Both stony and netted forms occurred, but only the latter, the fenestellids, became important during the period.

The brachiopods (lamp shells) are a group of marine filter-feeding species that bear a resemblance to clams but are not mollusks. Brachiopods were present in a multitude of diverse forms during the Devonian Period. The spire-bearing spiriferoids were perhaps the most common and have been used as index fossils. Two groups of importance emerged: the loop-bearing terebratulids and the spiny mud-dwelling productids. At the same time, a number of groups became extinct, including various orthids and the pentamerids.

Molluscan groups were well represented. The marine clams (bivalves) diversified greatly during the period, especially in the nearshore environments. The earliest freshwater bivalves appeared in the Late Devonian. The gastropods were well diversified, particularly in calcareous (calcium carbonate or limestone) environments, and became even more diversified in later periods. The Scaphopoda (tusk shells) first appeared in the Devonian Period. Another significant Devonian event was the emergence of the ammonites from their still-extant nautiloid ancestors. In the chambered shell of the ammonites, internal septa create elaborate patterns where they join the outer shell. The complexity of these suture patterns culminated in the ammonites of the Mesozoic Era. From their origin (probably in the Emsian Age) the evolution of goniatite ammonites, as well as other ammonites, allows detailed zonal subdivisions to be established until the end of the Cretaceous Period. Devonian goniatites have been found on all continents except Antarctica.

Among the arthropods, the giant eurypterids (sea scorpions) are found in the Old Red Sandstone facies. Some were predatory carnivores and probably lived on fish. The first insect, most likely a collembolan (apterygote), from a group of wingless insects that feed on leaf litter and soil, has been recorded from the Devonian Period of Russia and other areas of Asia. Ostracods (a type of crustacean) were locally very abundant. Benthic (bottom-dwelling) forms occur in continental shelf sea deposits, and planktonic (floating) forms occur in the Upper Devonian, where their remains form widespread ostracod-slate facies. Trilobites were well developed in size (some up to 61 centimetres, or 24 inches, long), variety, and distribution. Nearly all have clearly established Silurian ancestors. The most common were the phacopids, which exhibit a curious trend toward blindness in the Late Devonian. Almost all the diverse Lower Paleozoic trilobite stocks that entered the period were extinct before the close, and only the proetaceans survived into the Carboniferous Period.

Among echinoderms, the holothureans, asteroids, and ophiuroids are known, but they are rare. Crinoids were abundant, including free-living types with grapnel-shaped anchors. The blastoids diversified considerably, but the cystoids did not survive the period.

Vertebrates

Conodonts (primitive chordates with tooth-shaped fossil remains) are abundant in many Devonian marine facies. Conodonts had perhaps their greatest diversification during the Late Devonian and are of major importance for the correlation of rock layers. More than 40 conodont zones are recognized within the Devonian, and these provide a high-resolution biostraphic framework for the period.

Many groups of Devonian fishes were heavily armoured, and this has led to their good representation in the fossil record. Fish remains are widespread in the Old Red Sandstone rocks of Europe, especially in the Welsh borderland and Scottish areas of Britain. These are mostly associated with freshwater or estuarine deposits. In other areas marine fishes are known, and some of these, such as *Dunkleosteus* (*Dinichthys*) from the Upper Devonian Period of Ohio, U.S., may have reached 9 metres (30 feet) in length.

Dr. John Long presents Gogo, a well-preserved fossil of Gogonasus *from Western Australia that could indicate how fish evolved into land animals.* William West/AFP/Getty Images

The earliest fishes, comprising the agnathans, were without jaws and presumably were mud eaters and scavengers. These types are usually called ostracoderms. Some, such as the osteostracan cephalaspids, had broad, plate-like armour of varied form. The brain and nerve structures in some of these are well known. The anaspids also were covered with armour in the form of scales. The heterostracans, which include the oldest known fishes, have an anterior armour basically of upper (dorsal) and lower (ventral) plates. *Pteraspis* is an example. The Early Devonian saw the entry of jawed forms or gnathostomes, and the armoured forms of these, the placoderms, characterize the epoch. The arthrodires, which had a hinged frontal armour in two portions, and the grotesque antiarchs belong here. The close of the Devonian saw the diminution and extinction of most of these groups, but several other groups continued and have a significant later history.

Sharklike fishes, the chondrichthians, have been found in the Middle Devonian. The bony fishes, or osteichthians of current classification, include the climatioid acanthodeans, which had appeared before the period began, but the lungfishes (Dipnoi), the coelacanths, and the rhipidistians made their first appearance during this time. The last group is thought to have given rise to the four-footed amphibians as well as to all other higher groups of vertebrates.

PLANTS

It is now known that some supposedly Silurian plants, such as those at Baragwanath, Vic., Australia, are actually from the Early Devonian. The Late Silurian record of *Cooksonia* fossils of the Czech Republic seems to be the earliest unquestionable evidence of vascular plants. Information on spores provided by palynologists would help determine the antecedents of the Devonian plants.

There was a remarkable initiation of diverse types of vascular plants during the Devonian, and a varied flora was established early in the period. Evidence of algae is common. Indeed, it is during this period that bryophytes first appear, and charophytes are locally common. Freshwater algae and fungi are known in the Rhynie Chert of Scotland. The first known forests are of late Middle Devonian age.

The Psylotophytopsida is the most primitive group of the pteridophytes (ferns and other seedless vascular plants). This group did not survive the Late Devonian. *Cooksonia*, *Rhynia*, and others possessing a naked stem with terminal sporangia (spore cases) belong here. In other members, sporangia were borne laterally but no true leaves were developed, and the branching was often of a primitive dichotomous type. Psylotophytopsids form a basic stock from which other groups apparently evolved. *Asteroxylon*, which occurs with *Rhynia*, and other Rhynie plants in the Lower Old Red Sandstone Rhynie Chert of Scotland form a link with the lycopsids by having lateral sporangia and a dense leafy stem. Psylotophytopsids soon gave rise to treelike forms and later to the important lepidodendrids of the Carboniferous flora. Another apparent derivative, the sphenopsids, which has jointed branches, is represented by *Hyenia* and *Pseudobornia*. Pteropsids also appeared in the Devonian. Primitive gymnosperms are known, and trunks of *Archaeopteris* up to 1.8 metres (6 feet) in diameter are present in Upper Devonian deposits of the eastern United States and the Donets Basin of Russia and Ukraine. These trunks apparently were carried by water to their current positions.

The rich record of land plants may be related to the fact that the Old Red Sandstone represents the first widespread record of continental conditions. However, the primitive nature of the stocks seen and the absence of a long earlier record, even of detrital fragments of vascular plants, suggest that the colonization and exploitation of land environments were real Devonian events. Fortuitous finds, such as the silicified flora of the Rhynie Chert and the pyritized tissue from the Upper Devonian of New

York, have enabled the intimate anatomy of many of these plants to be elucidated in detail equivalent to that of modern forms.

FAUNAL REALMS AND MIGRATIONS

There is a marked similarity in the fauna and flora of the Devonian continental facies the world over. Records from such deposits in China containing Early Devonian genera of the armoured fish *Cephalaspis* and *Pterichthys* or the widespread Australian records of *Bothriolepis*, a Late Devonian antiarch, correspond closely to those of the Old Red Sandstone in Europe. Yet, when studied in more detail, specific differences become apparent. It has been suggested that the Baltic fish succession is so rich that the area must have formed a migration centre. This may be so, but the wide distribution of supposed estuarine and fresh-water fishes raises many problems. Many of these can be resolved if the continents were closer together during the Devonian than at present.

The marine life of the Devonian gives little evidence of faunal provinces. It is true that in the Lower Devonian the brachiopod *Australocoelia* has been recognized only in the Antarctic, the Falkland Islands, South America, South Africa, and Tasmania and that *Australospirifer*, *Scaphiocoelia*, and *Pleurothyrella* share parts of this distribution. These genera are not known in the marine Lower Devonian of northern continents and seem to establish an "austral" fauna of limited circum-Antarctic distribution at this time (if the southern continents were then united as Gondwana). Elements of this fauna are often called "Malvinokaffric" after the Falkland (Malvinas) Islands and the South African Bokkeveld Beds. At other levels in the Devonian, however, provincial distinctions are not apparent, with the exception of local coral provinces that are distinguishable in areas of Asia.

DEVONIAN EXTINCTION EVENTS

Throughout the Devonian there were periods of widespread hypoxic or anoxic sedimentation (that is, sedimentary events indicated that little free oxygen or no oxygen at all was dissolved in Devonian seas). Some of these are known to be periods of significant extinction, and all are associated with some faunal anomaly in marine strata. These events are named according to the taxa involved. Some are associated with very wide distribution of certain taxa, such as the *Monograptus uniformis*, *Pinacites jugleri*, and *Platyclymenia annulata* events. The Lower Zlichov Event is associated with the extinction of the graptoloids and the appearance of the coiled cephalopod goniatites. Three events are very significant extinction episodes. The Taghanic Event, which formerly was used to draw the boundary between the Middle and Upper Devonian, was a marked period of extinction for goniatites, corals, and brachiopods. The Kellwasser Event saw the extinction of the beloceratid and manticoceratid goniatite groups, many conodont species, most colonial corals, several groups of trilobites, and the atrypid and pentamerid brachiopods at the Frasnian-Famennian boundary. And the Hangenberg Event saw the extinction of phacopid trilobites, several groups of goniatites, and the unusual late Devonian coiled cephalopods, the clymeniids, at the end of the Famennian Stage.

Earlier, certain writers sought to link these events with thin layers of iridium, characteristic of meteorite or bolide impacts. Evidence of a bolide impact, in the form of possible impact ejecta, has been reported in Middle Devonian deposits and is associated with a pulse of extinction. An impact crater about 65 kilometres (about 40 miles) in diameter, the Siljan structure in Sweden, has been dated to approximately 377 million years ago. This places the impact within the error range for the estimated boundary between the Frasnian-Famennian stages (about 374.5 million years ago) and also within the Kellwasser extinction. Nevertheless, the connection between this impact and the Kellwasser Event is still being debated.

A stronger environmental link to Devonian extinctions involves the layers of black shale characteristic of low oxygen conditions. Environmental stress is thought to take place when high global temperatures slow the mixing rate between the ocean's surface and deeper layers. Bottom waters experience a lowered re-oxygenation rate, which may result in the extinction of many marine species. It is still debated whether these events were caused by climatic extremes caused by an increase in the amount of solar energy from the Sun, an amplified greenhouse effect, or by processes wholly confined to the Earth. For example, greater production of organic matter, perhaps owing to an increased influx of nutrients related to the colonization of landmasses by rooted plants, may have made continental seas more susceptible to anoxia.

There is also evidence that extinctions may be associated with rapid global warming or cooling. Particularly in the Late Devonian, extinction events may relate to periods of abrupt cooling associated with the development of glaciers and the substantial lowering of sea level. It has been argued that patterns of faunal change at the Kellwasser Event are consistent with global cooling.

At present it is not possible to connect Devonian extinctions definitively with any single cause, and, indeed, it is probable that extinctions may record a combination of several stresses.

Significant Devonian Life-Forms

Extinctions aside, Devonian ecosystems contained an increasingly diverse assemblage of organisms. Devonian seas were habitats for different types of cephalopods and lamp shells, as well as a number of armoured fishes. Above sea level, terrestrial plants spread throughout the continents, and the first true tetrapods (four-legged land vertebrates) emerged.

Ammonoids

The ammonoids were a group of extinct cephalopods (of the phylum Mollusca), forms related to the modern pearly nautilus, that are frequently found as fossils in marine rocks from the Devonian Period (416 million to 359 million years ago) to the Cretaceous Period (145.5 million to 65.5 million years ago). The ammonoids were shelled forms, many predacious in habit. Ammonoid shells, which are either straight or coiled, served as protective and supportive structures as well as hydrostatic devices, enabling the animal to compensate for varying water depths. Ammonoids are characterized and distinguished from nautiloids by the highly crenulated and complex suture that occurs where internal partitioning walls come in contact with the outer shell wall. Ammonoids are important index fossils because of their wide geographic distribution in shallow marine waters, rapid evolution, and easily recognizable features. Three groups of ammonoids succeeded one another through time, each group having a more complex suture pattern. Ammonoids with a simple suture pattern, called goniatite, flourished during the Paleozoic Era (542 million to 251 million years ago). Ammonoids characterized by a more highly folded suture, called ceratite, replaced the goniatites and were most abundant in the Triassic Period (251 million to 200 million years ago). Most ammonoid genera became extinct at the end of that period, but a few survived and evolved into many diverse forms during the Cretaceous Period (146 million to 66 million years ago). These forms are characterized by an interwoven suture called the ammonite pattern.

ANTIARCHS

Antiarchs belonged to order Antiarchi, a group of extinct, mainly freshwater, jawed fishes in class Placodermi. They were abundant during Middle and Late Devonian times (387 to 359 million years ago). Members of such genera as *Bothriolepis* and *Pterichthys* were representative. Antiarchs were small and weak-jawed and had closely set eyes on top of the head. Armour shields covered the front part of the body as in the earliest known vertebrates, and armoured, jointed appendages extended from the shoulder regions. The hind part of the body was naked in *Bothriolepis* and covered with scales in *Pterichthys*.

Antiarchs may have been bottom dwellers that fed upon small animals and on plants and swam with the pectoral appendages. The presence of paired sacs suggests that lungs were evolved earlier than was once thought.

ARCHAEOPTERIS

This genus of plants was probably the first true tree to form forests during the Late Devonian Epoch (about 385 to 359 million years ago). Fossils of *Archaeopteris* confirm the presence of a woody trunk and branching patterns similar to those of modern conifers, but with fernlike foliage and reproduction based on spores. The largest fossil specimens possess trunk diameters of close to 40 centimetres (about 16 inches). *Archaeopteris* reproduced by two different-sized spores. The larger ones, the megaspores, produced egg cells, whereas the smaller ones, the microspores, produced sperm cells. This feature has led some authorities to believe that *Archaeopteris* was closely related to seed plants. This genus lived on the floodplains of rivers and in coastal lowlands until it became extinct at the end of the Devonian Period.

ARCTOLEPIS

An extinct genus of placoderms (fishlike animals) present during the early part of the Devonian Period, *Arctolepis* was a member of a group known as the arthrodires, or jointed-neck fishes. It had a bony head and trunk shield but was unarmoured behind the trunk region. The body tapered to a pointed tail, and a tail fin was developed only on the lower margin of the tail. *Arctolepis* was a small animal, less than 30 centimetres (12 inches) in length but with enormously developed pectoral spines that must have been some aid to swimming and possibly a deterrent to keep from being swallowed.

ARTHRODIRES

Arthrodires were extinct, armoured, jawed fishes (placoderms) found in Devonian freshwater and marine deposits that belonged to order Arthrodira. Early arthrodires, such as the genus *Arctolepis (see above),* were well-armoured fishes with flattened bodies. They had hollow, backward-curved shoulder spines and may have used the long spines to anchor themselves or to move about on the bottom.

Later arthrodires, such as the Middle Devonian genus *Coccosteus,* tended toward marine habitats. Coccosteans were less heavily armoured than *Arctolepis,* and the bony head and body shields were connected by a joint on each side allowing free head movement. They were predators and had bony jaws. Two toothplates were present on each side of an arthrodire's upper jaw, and one toothplate was present on each side of its lower jaw. The back of the body and the tail were apparently naked, and its headshield was reduced, which was possibly reflective of its predatory habits. The shoulder spine was shortened or, in some forms, absent.

Arthrodires became extinct during the Late Devonian. The genus *Dinichthys* (sometimes included with *Dunkleosteus*), representative of this period, was similar to coccosteans but grew much longer, about 9 metres (30 feet) against 0.6 metres (2 feet) for coccosteans.

There were many arthrodire offshoots during the Devonian. Members of the genus *Phyllolepis* lost most of their head armour. They were formerly considered ostracoderms. The ptyctodonts, relatives of the arthrodires, lived in the sea and possibly fed upon mollusks.

BACTRITES

Bactrites is a genus of extinct cephalopods (animals related to the modern pearly nautilus) found as fossils in marine rocks from the Devonian to the Permian periods (between 408 and 245 million years ago). Some authorities have identified specimens dating back to the Silurian Period (beginning 438 million years ago), but their classification is uncertain. The shell consists of a linear series of chambers, each successively occupied by the body of the animal. *Bactrites* fed on animals it caught in its tentacles. It is possible that *Bactrites* gave rise to more advanced cephalopods of later geologic periods, notably the ammonoids and the belemnoids.

BOTHRIOLEPIS

This genus of extinct fishes of the order Antiarcha, class Placodermi, is characteristic of the Middle and Late Devonian (from about 387 million to 360 million years ago). The front end of *Bothriolepis* (also spelled Bothryolepis) was very heavily encased in bony armour.

The eyes were located on top of the head shield and situated very close to the light-receptive pineal eye. The shield was separated into two parts: one for the head, the other for the thorax. The posterior portions of the body were naked, lacking even scales. Very strongly developed bony spines in the shoulder region appear to have had a serrated edge and were movable. *Bothriolepis* was a bottom-dweller inhabiting streams and lakes. With its small jaws and teeth, *Bothriolepis* was clearly not a pursuit predator but probably fed on bottom-dwelling invertebrates.

CEPHALASPIS

Another extinct genus of very primitive jawless, fishlike vertebrates found in Early Devonian rocks, *Cephalaspis* was found in Devonian rocks in Europe and North America. It is one of an early group of vertebrates called ostracoderms, possessed an external bony head shield, but probably its internal skeleton was not ossified to any great extent. Its eyes were situated on the dorsal side of the flat head. The ventral placement of its mouth indicates that *Cephalaspis* was a bottom-feeding animal. It is probable that *Cephalaspis* lived by straining organic matter from the bottom sediments of the freshwater streams it inhabited, a feeding method that persisted from its ancestors.

Cephalaspis differed from its predecessors in that the head shield was freed from the rest of the body, allowing for greater mobility, and it also possessed paired pectoral fins. Sensory structures, perhaps electric organs of a sort, were present along the margins of the head shield.

CHEIROLEPIS

Cheirolepis is an extinct genus of primitive fishes whose fossils are found in European and North American rocks of the Devonian period. The genus is representative of the paleoniscoids, a group of primitive ray-finned fishes, and may represent the common ancestor of more recent ray-finned fishes. *Cheirolepis* was slim and streamlined, with many teeth, indicating that it was an active predator. The tail was upturned, and the tail fin was supported beneath it. The dorsal fin was single, whereas the pectoral fins were broadly attached and had limited flexibility. The eyes were large and placed well forward in the skull.

CLADOSELACHE

A genus of extinct sharks, known from fossilized remains in Late Devonian rocks in North America and Europe, *Cladoselache* is a good representative of early sharks. Unlike larger forms, its mouth opened at the front of the skull, rather than beneath it, and both its pectoral and pelvic fins were broadly attached to its body. These features suggest that while this shark was less maneuverable than larger sharks, it was a high-speed predator. Two dorsal fins were present along the midline, and strong spines were developed behind the head and at the base of the pectoral fins.

CLIMATIUS

Climatius is a genus of extinct, primitive jawed vertebrates common as fossils in Devonian rocks in Europe and North America. *Climatius* is representative of the acanthodians, spiny fishlike vertebrates related to the true "bony" fishes and their relatives from class Osteichthyes. Acanthodians are characterized by diamond-shaped scales and fins that possessed a strong bony spine at their leading edges. *Climatius* had two dorsal fins and numerous paired ventral fins, each with a supporting spine.

DINICHTHYS

An extinct genus of arthrodires, *Dinichthys* lived during the Late Devonian Period. It is found fossilized in rocks of that age in Europe, northern Asia, and North America. *Dinichthys*, which is also called Dunkleosteus, grew to a length of about 9 metres (30 feet), more than 3 metres (9.8 feet) of which consisted of an armoured head shield that was hinged in the neck region, permitting the upper jaw to be raised in relation to the lower. *Dinichthys* was clearly the dominant marine predator of its time.

DIPTERUS

Dipterus is a genus of very primitive lungfish, among the earliest known, found as fossils in European and North American Devonian rocks. Lungfishes, along with coelacanths, tetrapods, and their relatives, are part of a unique lobe-finned group of jawed vertebrates. This group is distinct from ray-finned (or "true") fishes (Actinopterygii), sharks, placoderms, and acanthodians. *Dipterus* retained many archaic features, including two dorsal fins and a tail that resembled a lobe-finned tail. Functional lungs were probably present in *Dipterus,* and a freshwater habitat is indicated. The skull bones of *Dipterus,* though still primitive, consist of a mosaic of small bones. *Dipterus* had already initiated the unusual bone pattern seen in more advanced lungfish. Similarly, *Dipterus* evidences the beginnings of the lungfish trend toward extreme deossification of skeletal elements.

ENDOTHYRA

Endothyra is an extinct genus of Foraminifera, protozoans with a readily preservable shell, which is found as fossils in Devonian to Triassic marine rocks. *Endothyra* is characterized by a tightly coiled shell, and it is sometimes found in very large numbers. It is especially abundant in some rocks of the Mississippian Subperiod (359 million to 318 million years ago).

EUSTHENOPTERON

A genus of extinct lobe-finned fishes (crossopterygians) preserved as fossils in rocks of the late Devonian Period (about 370 million years ago), *Eusthenopteron* was near the main line of evolution leading to the first terrestrial vertebrates, the tetrapods. It was 1.5 to 1.8 metres (5 to 6 feet) long and was an active carnivore, with numerous small teeth in its broad skull.

The overall pattern of the skull bones is similar to that of early tetrapods, but the vertebral column was not very well developed in that the vertebral arches were not strongly fused to the vertebral spools, and the arches did not interlock between vertebrae, as they do in tetrapods. The shoulder girdle was still attached to the skull, but the hip girdle was only rudimentary and was not attached to the vertebral column. The fleshy fins had a series of stout bones supporting them, including elements that correspond to the limb bones of modern land vertebrates — the humerus, radius, ulna, femur, tibia, and fibula. However, the limbs ended in a series of bony rays much like those supporting the fins of ray-finned fishes (actinopterygians) today. *Eusthenopteron* was not built for land life. Rather, it seems to have lived in shallow fresh to brackish waterways, where it could have clambered among rocks and plants in search of food. It obtained oxygen in two ways — by breathing it from the air with its lungs and by absorbing it from the water through its gills.

GREENOPS

Greenops is a genus of trilobites found as fossils in Middle and Upper Devonian deposits. Easily recognized by its distinctive appearance, *Greenops* has a well-developed head and a small tail with a fringe of extended segmental rays. Long spinous processes are present at the terminal margins of the head shield and extend well back into the thoracic region.

Heliophyllum

A genus of extinct coral found as fossils in Devonian marine rocks, *Heliophyllum* was a solitary animal rather than a colonial form. The distinctive laminated form of its structure is clearly periodic, its growth being a function of time. This factor has been employed to calculate the length of the Devonian day and year. Several species of *Heliophyllum* are known.

Hyenia

Hyenia is a genus of herbaceous plants from the Middle Devonian Epoch (about 398 to 385 million years ago). It grew as a robust rhizome up to 5 centimetres (2 inches) in diameter and parallel to the soil surface. Upright branches up to 15 centimetres (about 6 inches) in height arose from the rhizome in a low spiral. Some branches divided several times to form flattened leaflike structures. Others bore additional smaller branches tipped with a pair of elongate sporangia that opened along a lateral slit to release spores. Little is known about its vascular system. However, its prostrate, creeping rhizome and leaflike appendages have led some authorities to suggest that *Hyenia* may be an early member of the fern lineage.

Ichthyostega

Ichthyostega is a genus of extinct animals, closely related to tetrapods (four-legged land vertebrates) and found as fossils in rocks in eastern Greenland from the late Devonian Period (about 370 million years ago). It was about one metre (three feet) long and had a small dorsal fin along the

Ichthyostega, model by J. S. Collard (H. R. Allen Studios). Courtesy of the Royal Scottish Museum, Edinburgh; phtograph, the Natural History Photographic Agency

margin of its tail. The tail itself possessed a series of bony supports, typical of the tail supports that are found in fishes. Other traits retained from earlier aquatic vertebrates include the relatively short snout region, the presence of a preopercular bone in the cheek region (which serves as part of the gill cover in fishes), and many small scales on the body. Advanced traits shared with tetrapods include a series of robust bones supporting the fleshy limbs, a lack of gills, and strong ribs. *Ichthyostega* and its relatives represent forms slightly more advanced than the aquatic *Eusthenopteron* and appear to be near the evolutionary line leading to the first tetrapods on land. It is possible that the ichthyostegids persisted into the following Carboniferous Period.

MONOPLACOPHORANS

Monoplacophorans belong to class Tryblidia and constitute a group of primitive marine mollusks characterized by a single, cap-shaped shell and bilateral symmetry. The term Tryblidia is preferred over Monoplacophoran and Galeroconcha, because both latter terms are taken to include several fossil groups of uncertain relationships.

In 1952 several live monoplacophorans were dredged from a depth of 3,570 m (about 11,700 feet) off the coast of Costa Rica. Until then it was thought that they had become extinct 400 million years ago. Existing monoplacophorans are represented by fewer than 10 species, including *Neopilina galatheae, N. ewingi,* and *N. valeronis.* They have been found to depths of about 5,800 metres (19,028 feet) off the coasts of Central and South America.

Monoplacophorans are unusual because of the combination of primitive characteristics that they possess. In addition to the single, cap-shaped shell, they have paired multiple organs, reflecting at least partial segmentation (metamerism). The gill structure and the type of metamerism suggest a much closer affinity of the mollusks with the annelid worms than was previously believed to exist. These features may also associate the mollusks more closely with the arthropods (e.g., insects, crustaceans).

MUCROSPIRIFER

A genus of extinct brachiopods found as fossils in Middle and Upper Devonian marine rocks, *Mucrospirifer* forms are characterized by an extended hinge line of the two valves, or shells, of the brachiopod and a prominent fold and sulcus—a bow-shaped ridge and depressed trough, respectively. The many species of *Mucrospirifer* are abundant Devonian fossils. Evolutionary trends within the genus and related forms are relatively well-known and studied.

OSTEOLEPIS

Osteolepis is an extinct genus of lobe-finned fishes from the Late Devonian. Osteolepiformes is a variation of this name that was given to a group of vertebrates that contained the closest relatives of the tetrapods. *Osteolepis* survived into later Devonian time. Its body was covered with large rhomboid scales. The upper lobe of the tail was more strongly developed than the lower lobe. The general bone pattern in the skull and jaws closely resembles that of the first tetrapods.

OSTRACODERMS

The word *ostracoderm* is an archaic and informal term for a member of the group of armoured, jawless, fishlike vertebrates that emerged during the early part of the Paleozoic Era . Ostracoderms include both extinct groups, such as the heterostracans and osteostracans, and living forms, such as hagfishes and lampreys.

PALAEOSPONDYLUS

A genus of enigmatic fossil vertebrates that were very fishlike in appearance but of uncertain relationships, *Palaeospondylus* lived during the Middle Devonian epoch (398 million to 385 million years ago). Specimens have been found in the Old Red Sandstone rocks in the region of Achannaras, Scot. Hundreds of specimens are known, yet the position of this genus in relation to other fishlike vertebrates is still poorly understood. *Palaeospondylus* was about 5 centimetres (about 2 inches) long. Unlike most of the contemporary forms of the Middle Devonian, the skeleton of *Palaeospondylus* was very well ossified, and no dermal armour was present, a feature prominent among the placoderms. A well-developed caudal, or tail, fin was present.

PLACODERMS

Placoderms (class Placodermi) are primitive jawed fishes known only from fossil remains. Placoderms existed throughout the Devonian period, but only two species persisted into the succeeding Carboniferous period.

During the Devonian they were a dominant group, occurring in all continents except South America in a variety of marine and freshwater sediments.

Most placoderms were small or moderate in size, but a few may have reached a length of 4 metres (13 feet). The name is derived from their characteristic armour of dermal, or skin, bones. This armour formed a head shield and a trunk shield, the two commonly connected by a paired joint in the neck region. The arrangement of bones is so different from that of modern fishes with bony skeletons that it is unlikely that the bones of the two groups are homologous (similar in origin).

The earliest placoderms were heavily armoured and were bottom-dwelling. Many later forms became highly specialized for this way of life. Others became adapted for fast swimming between the surface and the bottom. Bottom-dwelling placoderms, such as the antiarchs, had small, ventrally placed mouths and presumably fed on bottom detritus and small invertebrates. Fossil remains indicate that some species had heavy, blunt jaw plates adapted for crushing hard-shelled invertebrates, while others were able to open their jaws wide enough to swallow smaller fish. Some placoderms, such as members of the genus *Dunkleosteus*, reached sizes of 10 metres (30 feet) or more and were the dominant predators of the Devonian seas.

The origin of the placoderms is unknown, although it is possible that they may have shared a common ancestor with sharks, skates, and rays, as well as with true "bony" fishes.

POLYGNATHIFORMS

Polygnathiforms are conodonts (primitive chordates with tooth-shaped fossil remains) that resemble or may be derived from the genus *Polygnathus,* a genus found in rocks of Early Devonian to Early Carboniferous age (416 million to 318 million years ago). *Polygnathus* is clearly a key conodont genus. From this form a wide variety of distinct conodont genera evolved, including many forms that are important index, or guide, fossils.

PTERASPIS

Pteraspis is a genus of extinct jawless fishlike vertebrates found as fossils in Early Devonian rocks (those 416 million to 398 million years old) in North America and Europe. *Pteraspis* was approximately 16 centimetres (6.5 inches) in length and had a heavy, rounded, bony shield that covered the anterior parts of the body. The remainder of the body was encased in small scales. It is probable that *Pteraspis* was an active, though inefficient, swimmer.

RENSSELAERIA

A genus of extinct brachiopods found as fossils in Lower Devonian marine rocks, the shell of *Rensselaeria* is large and elongated. Its surface markings include fine costae (i.e., lines that radiate from the narrow apex of the shell to the distal, or terminal, margins) and arcuate (bowlike) growth lines. Because of its restricted time range, relative abundance, and ease of recognition, *Rensselaeria* serves as a reliable guide, or index, fossil for the Lower Devonian.

RHIPIDISTIA

An extinct group of lobe-finned bony fishes of the order Crossopterygii that included the ancestors of amphibians and the other terrestrial vertebrates, the Rhipidistia were common during the Devonian but became extinct during the Early Permian (the Permian Period began 299 million years ago). They were typical of early crossopterygians. Anatomical details, including skull-bone patterns, infolded (labyrinthodont) tooth enamel, and elements in the paired fins that correspond somewhat with tetrapod

Devonian rhipidistian
(*Eusthenopteron foordi*)

Encyclopædia Britannica, Inc.

limb bones, support the hypothesis that rhipidistians, such as *Osteolepis*, mentioned previously, were very closely related to the land-living vertebrates.

RHYNIE PLANTS

These rootless, leafless, spore-bearing plants are so named by virtue of their preservation in the Rhynie Chert, a mineral deposit that has been dated to the early part of the Devonian Period, near present-day Aberdeen, Scot. *Rhynia*, one of the most common forms, was about 18 centimetres (about 7 inches) tall and possessed water-conducting cells called tracheids in its stem, much like those of most living plants. Underground runners connected its aboveground stems. These stems were photosynthetic, branched evenly many times, and produced elliptical sporangia at the tip of every branch. Another genus, *Horneophyton*, resembled *Rhynia*, but its sporangia were cylindrical and formed in pairs at the branch tips. A third type, *Asteroxylon*, had kidney-bean-shaped sporangia located along the stem rather than at its tip. Small flaps of tissue along the stem may have increased its photosynthetic surface. The most unusual Rhynie plant is *Aglaophyton*, which resembled *Rhynia* in most respects. However, its tracheids were more like those of modern mosses.

Along with several genera of plants, the Rhynie Chert preserves other organisms from the same interval of geologic time. These include the fungus *Palaeomyces*, which may have been either a parasite or a decomposer of the Rhynie vegetation. The Rhynie Chert also preserves a variety of arthropods that may have fed on the spores and tissues of the Rhynie plants.

SCHIZODUS

Schizodus is an extinct genus of small mollusks found as fossils in rocks from the Devonian to the Permian Period (416 million to 251 million years ago). *Schizodus* is representative of a group of clams, the schizodonts, with a distinctive method of shell articulation. The shell of *Schizodus* is relatively smooth and unornamented except for fine growth lines.

SPHENOPHYLLUM

Sphenophyllum is a genus of extinct plants that lived from the end of the Devonian Period to the beginning of the Triassic Period (about 359 to 251 million years ago). It is most commonly reconstructed as a shrub or a creeping vine. *Sphenophyllum* had a strong node-internode architecture, which has led some authorities to ally it with modern horsetails. Branches and leaves were arranged in whorls at each node much like the later *Calamites*. However, the leaves of *Sphenophyllum* were triangular in shape. Spore-bearing cones were also similar to those of *Calamites* and modern horsetails. However, *Sphenophyllum* lacked the hollow central stem that characterizes horsetail relatives because its tracheids, or water-conducting cells, were arranged in a central triangle surrounded by wood. *Sphenophyllum* grew in floodplain swamps, away from the margins of rivers.

STRINGOCEPHALUS

An extinct genus of large brachiopods found as fossils in Devonian marine rocks, *Stringocephalus* is widely distributed and occurs in western North America, Asia, and northern Europe. Several forms are known. The shell is characterized by a well-developed, curved, beaklike structure.

STROPHEODONTA

Stropheodonta is a genus of small, extinct brachiopods (lamp shells) found as fossils in Devonian marine rocks. It has a distinctive internal structure and a shell form with fine linear and arcuate (bowlike) markings on its concavo-convex shell. *Stropheodonta* is characteristic of an important group of brachiopods, the strophomenids. It is a useful Devonian index fossil.

THEODOSSIA

Theodossia is a genus of extinct brachiopods (lamp shells) the fossils of which are restricted to Early Devonian marine rocks. The genus is characterized by a moderate-sized, rounded shell, the surface of which is covered with fine lines. Because of its temporal restriction, *Theodossia* is a good index fossil and aids in the correlation of sometimes widely separated rock units.

TIKTAALIK ROSEAE

A taxonomic name given to an aquatic, fishlike animal that lived about 380–385 million years ago (during the earliest late Devonian Period), *Tiktaalik roseae* was a very close relative of the direct ancestors of tetrapods (four-legged land vertebrates). The genus name, *Tiktaalik*, comes from the Inuktitut language of the Inuit people of eastern Canada and is a general term for a large freshwater fish that lives in the shallows. The species name, *roseae*, honours a benefactor of the research that led to the finding of the fossils in 2004 on southern Ellesmere Island, Nunavut, northern Canada. The fossil find consisted of a few nearly complete skeletons and several dozen partial specimens.

T. roseae is one of a series of fossil forms discovered since the 1960s that have greatly improved scientific knowledge of the transition between aquatic vertebrates and the first land vertebrates. The aquatic *Eusthenopteron* and the (at least partly) terrestrial *Ichthyostega*, both of late Devonian age, are now understood to be bridged by forms such as *Panderichthys*, *Elpistostege*, and *Acanthostega* as well as *Tiktaalik*. However, it is inaccurate to claim that *Tiktaalik* and the other forms represent some sort of "fish-amphibian transition" or are a "missing link" between fishes and amphibians. *Tiktaalik* and the other animals looked nothing like conventional ray-finned fishes such as trout and were not closely related to them. Likewise, the first tetrapods on land were nothing like familiar amphibians of today such as frogs and salamanders. *Tiktaalik* and the other forms were actually akin in many respects to the ancient lungfish and coelacanth species that survive to this day. For this reason, they are better described as representing the "emergence of vertebrates onto land."

T. roseae had nearly square, narrowly overlapping scales on its dorsal area, and it retained primitive features such as bony fin rays, which are lost in animals that mainly walk on land. In general form, it had a broad, flat skull with dorsally facing eye sockets, a long, crocodile-like body (some specimens reach almost 3 metres, or 10 feet, in length), and limbs that were intermediate in many respects between fins and legs. The forelimbs, for example, showed a common pattern of a central limb axis bifurcating at each new joint into two bones, the anterior one being smaller and generally unbranched and the posterior one being robust and branched. However, in *Tiktaalik* there was more branching on both axes, and it is tempting to see in this pattern the beginnings of bones that eventually would become some of the forearm and hand bones of tetrapods. The structure of the limb joints and the enlarged ribs of *Tiktaalik* show that the animal could flex enough to clamber about, at least in the shallows, and perhaps a bit on land, although its skeleton was not otherwise broadly adapted for that purpose. The fin rays covering the ends of its limbs and its flattened, streamlined body plan indicate that *Tiktaalik* retained the ability to swim. Its long snout and lack of gill covers suggest that it snapped up prey rather than inhaling it as fishes do.

TORNOCERAS

An extinct genus of cephalopods, forms related to the modern pearly nautilus, *Tornoceras* is a form that emerged during the Devonian Period. The shell is circular in outline and rather flat. The final whorl covers earlier whorls. The sutural pattern between successive chambers of the shell is gently rippled.

TREPOSPIRA

An extinct genus of gastropods (snails) found as fossils in rocks of Devonian to Late Carboniferous age (between 416 million and 299 million years old), its shell has a low spire, and the length of the coiling axis is short relative to the shell's width. The shell is smooth but is ornamented by nodules next to the sutures between the whorls.

TROPIDOLEPTUS

A genus of extinct brachiopods found as fossils only in marine rocks of the Devonian Period, *Tropidoleptus* serves as a useful guide, or index, fossil, allowing correlation of widely separated rocks. The shell is roughly elliptical and distinctively ornamented with many prominent costae, riblike thickenings of the shell arranged in a linear manner and radiating from the apex to the margins. Arcuate (bow-shaped) growth lines are also present.

WORTHENIA

Worthenia is a genus of extinct gastropods (snails) preserved as common fossils in rocks of Devonian to Triassic age (416 million to 200 million years old) but especially characteristic of Late Carboniferous deposits (318 million to 299 million years old) in the midcontinent region of North America. *Worthenia* is characterized by a turban-shaped shell in which a raised ridge follows the margin of the whorls. Small nodes occur along the ridge, and the opening of the shell is oval and large.

XENACANTHUS

A long-surviving but now extinct genus of freshwater sharks, *Xenacanthus* survived from the end of the Devonian Period, some 360 million years ago, to about the end of the Triassic Period, 208 million years ago. *Xenacanthus* had a slim, elongated body with a low dorsal fin that extended down most of it, almost merging with the triangular, pointed tail. From the back of the skull, a long, sharp, movable spine projected. This spine was made of bone. Though bone manufacture is not commonly associated with cartilaginous fishes, it is possible in certain tissues, such as the vertebrae, of certain shark species.

DEVONIAN GEOLOGY

What we know of Devonian life has, in large part, of course, come from the study and excavation of Devonian geology. Devonian rocks are relatively well studied in many regions of the world, and sedimentation and igneous activity characterize several continents of this period. The Caledonian orogeny, which left its mark across portions of three continents, occurred during the interval, and commercially valuable materials, such as copper, tin, petroleum, and natural gas, appear in rocks of Devonian age.

SIGNIFICANT GEOLOGIC EVENTS

As previously mentioned, the union of the paleocontinents of Laurentia and Baltica occurred near the beginning of the Devonian to form a single landmass that has been referred to both as Laurussia and as Euramerica.

Old Red Sandstone conglomerates, Devonian age, from the Ardennes, Belg Courtesy of Ernst ten Haaf

The northern portion of the combined landmass gave rise to widespread areas of continental desert, playa, and alluvial plain deposits that form one of the earliest documented large areas of nonmarine sedimentation. These terrestrial deposits, known as the Old Red Sandstone, covered much of the then-united areas of North America, Greenland, Scandinavia, and the northern British Isles. These deposits contain remarkable documentation of the colonization of land by vertebrates as well as that of freshwater rivers and lakes by plants and fish. The two latter groups existed prior to this time, but they had their earliest extensive evolutionary radiation during the Devonian.

The areas south of the Old Red Sandstone, including sectors of eastern and western North America, central and southern Europe, and parts of European Russia, were often covered by shallow continental shelf seas with local deeper marine troughs.

The continental collision that united these paleocontinents, which began during the Silurian Period, resulted from the closing of the Iapetus Ocean (which was the precursor of the Atlantic Ocean) and is known as the Iapetus suture. It was marked by a mountain-building event, the Caledonian orogeny, that established a mountain chain stretching from present-day eastern North America through Greenland, western Scandinavia, Scotland, Ireland, and northern England and south to the fringes of western North Africa. Considerable igneous activity was associated with the Caledonian orogenic belt, both intrusive (emplacement of magmatic bodies at depth) and extrusive (volcanic activity at the surface). Sediments derived from erosion of the mountain belt formed locally important strata such as the European deposits laid down during the Lower Devonian and the Catskill Delta in New York state begun in the Middle Devonian.

The present-day southern continents of South America, Africa, Australia, and Antarctica and the Indian subcontinent were joined together as the enormous continental mass called Gondwana during the Devonian. Large areas of Asia east of the Ural Mountains were divided into separate landmasses at this point in Earth history. Their distribution is poorly understood, but many of them may have been attached to the margins of Gondwana. Also during the Devonian Period, Gondwana began impinging upon Laurussia. There is evidence that these two land-masses completely fused together during the Late Carboniferous or Early Permian periods.

The sea level rose (transgressed) and fell (regressed) frequently during the Devonian. Some of these episodes were accompanied by a brief period of deposition of anoxic (oxygen-depleted) black shales or limestones. Many of these deposits are quite widespread. Some are associated with the extinction of important groups of fossil organisms.

THE ECONOMIC SIGNIFICANCE OF DEVONIAN DEPOSITS

In many countries Devonian rocks have provided building stone, refractory and building brick, glass sands, and abrasive materials. Marble of Devonian age has been quarried in France and Belgium. German medieval castles are mostly clad with Devonian slates. In areas of European Russia and in Saskatchewan, Can., evaporites, including anhydrite and halite, are commercially exploited. Lodes of tin, zinc, and copper occur in several areas where Devonian rocks have been subject to orogenic (mountain-building) processes, such as in Devon and Cornwall in England and in central Europe. Since the 19th century, oil and natural gas have been produced from Devonian rocks in New York and Pennsylvania. In the 1930s, oil was found in Devonian sandstones in the Ural-Volga region and later in the Pechora area of northern European Russia. In 1947 oil was discovered in an Upper Devonian reef at Leduc, Alta., Can.. This was followed by vigorous exploration, and oil production from the area remains significant today.

THE MAJOR SUBDIVISIONS OF THE DEVONIAN SYSTEM

The rocks formed during Devonian time are known as the Devonian System. These rocks occur on all continents both at the surface and as substrata. Extensive areas of North America, South America, Europe, and Asia are underlain by Devonian rocks. Subsequent folding has made such rocks common in many ancient fold belts.

The rocks of the Devonian System are divided into series. The first is the Lower Devonian Series (416–397.5 million years ago), which comprises the Lochkovian, Pragian, and Emsian stages. The Middle Devonian Series (397.5–385.3 million years ago) comprises the Eifelian and Givetian stages. And the Upper Devonian Series (385.3–359.2 million years ago) comprises the Frasnian and Famennian stages.

ESTABLISHING DEVONIAN BOUNDARIES

During the last half of the 20th century, the International Union of Geological Sciences (IUGS) defined the boundaries and subdivisions of the Devonian System using a series of Global Stratotype Sections and Points (GSSPs). The base of the Lochkovian Stage—that is, the Silurian-Devonian boundary—is in a section at Klonk, Czech Rep. A point at La Serre in southern France has been identified as the Devonian-Carboniferous boundary. All stages and series of the Devonian were ratified by the International Commission on Stratigraphy (ICS) using GSSPs during the period 1972 to 1995. The base of the Pragian Stage is defined at Velká Chuchle, near Prague. The base of the Emsian Stage is defined in the Zinzil'ban Gorge in Uzbekistan. The base of the Eifelian Stage is defined near

Wetteldorf in the Eifel Hills of Germany, while the base of the Givetian Stage is defined at Mech Irdane, near Erfoud in southern Morocco. And the bases of the Frasnian and Famennian stages are both defined near Cessenon in southern France.

Stratigraphic boundaries within the Devonian System are correlated using various fossil groups. In Devonian marine deposits, small toothlike conodonts and chambered cephalopod ammonites are especially important, but spores, brachiopods, and corals are also useful. In nonmarine deposits, freshwater fish and plant spores are employed for correlation. In the past, considerable difficulty was encountered in correlating the Silurian-Devonian boundary, and serious errors were made. This situation resulted because of the misconception that graptolites became extinct at the boundary. It is now known that these invertebrates range into the Emsian. In areas where graptolites range into the Early Devonian, especially in mainland Europe and Asia, much miscorrelation occurred. Today the base of the graptolite zone of *Monograptus uniformis* is regarded as marking the base of the Devonian.

THE OCCURRENCE AND DISTRIBUTION OF DEVONIAN DEPOSITS

Establishing the boundaries of any geologic era, series, or stage is done by examining the deposits from that time. Correlations can be made across continents based on the geology of rock deposits and the incidence of certain fossils in these deposits. Europe and North America were united approximately along their present continental slope margins during the Devonian Period. The collision of these two landmasses resulted in the Caledonian orogeny, , which was mentioned above. At the close of the Silurian and continuing in the Early Devonian, considerable igneous activity (both extrusive and intrusive) occurred in the Caledonian mountain belt, which stretched from New England, Nova Scotia, Newfoundland, Scotland, and Scandinavia to eastern Greenland. Radiometric dating of granitic intrusions associated with the Caledonian orogeny yields ages between about 430 million and 380 million years. The igneous activity that produced such intrusions constituted the final stages of subduction and obduction (that is, overthrusting of the edge of one lithospheric plate over another at a convergent boundary), leading to the union of the constituent parts of Laurussia.

The Caledonian mountains were undergoing active uplift during the Devonian. The Old Red Sandstone deposits appear to be the detritus produced by the erosion of these mountain areas. Clastic material from the belt dominated the European Lower Devonian but was local and limited after that point. In eastern North America similar activity near the Silurian-Devonian boundary was followed by renewed activity during the Middle Devonian that was associated with the Acadian orogeny and the commencement of the Catskill Delta. The easterly derived fan clastics of the latter are increasingly dominant eastward across New York state, and its mostly nonmarine alluvial rocks are best seen in the Catskill Mountains near Albany.

Marine Devonian rocks provide evidence that marine waters encircled Laurussia. These rocks are now located in western Canada and the Arctic islands of Canada, in a belt from Montana to New York in the United States, in Europe from Devon to the Holy Cross Mountains of Poland, and on the Russian Platform and Novaya Zemlya.

It is clear that there was probably easterly directed subduction in western North America during the Devonian. Relics of this process are incorporated into the Cordilleran mountain chain as discrete terranes that were accreted to the continent during or after the Devonian. The clearest evidence is from the mid-Famennian Antler orogeny, during which a tectonic event resulted in clastic material being shed eastward. This event is well documented, especially in Nevada.

In many areas Devonian rocks have been heavily deformed and folded by subsequent tectonic activity. These fold belts may be distinguished from cratonic areas where sediments remain much as they were when formed. The main fold belts in North America are the Cordillera (western mountain ranges, including the Rocky Mountains) and the Appalachian belts to the east. In contrast, the Devonian of the Midwestern United States and adjoining areas is flat-lying. In South America the main fold belt is the Andes and sub-Andes. East of this line, the Devonian rocks are little disturbed. In Australia the main fold belt is in the east from Queensland to Tasmania. In Europe the Armorican fold belt stretches eastward from Cornwall and Brittany. To the south of this line from the Pyrenees to Malaysia, Devonian rocks are caught up in the Alpine-Himalayan fold belt. Similarly, the Devonian of the Ural Mountains is disturbed, whereas to the west, on the Russian Platform, and to the east there is less deformation. In all these cases the folding occurred well after the Devonian, but there is evidence that Devonian sedimentation contributed to the oceanic belts that were sites of the mountain building that occurred later.

In the regions that have suffered severe deformation, the Devonian sediments are frequently metamorphosed into slates and schists and often lose all the characteristics by which they may be dated. In areas where little change has taken place, all rock lithologies occur, from those characteristic of continental and desert conditions to the varied lithologies associated with continental shelf and deep-sea accumulation. Contemporary igneous activity was widespread in the form of extrusive lavas, submarine pillow lavas, tuffs, agglomerates, and bentonites, as well as igneous intrusions. Extrusive activity is found in both continental and marine environments, whereas plutonic intrusions are usually linked with areas of uplift such as the Caledonian and Acadian belts of Europe and eastern North America.

SEDIMENT TYPES

A wide range of terrestrial and marine sediments of Devonian age are known internationally, and there is a corresponding variety of sedimentary rock types. Devonian igneous activity was considerable, albeit localized. Laurussia is thought to have been near-tropical and sometimes arid. Playa facies, eolian dunes, and fan breccias are known. Fluviatile sediments, deposited by water under flash-flood conditions, have been identified, and these are correlated to alluvial sediments of broad coastal flats. There are lacustrine deposits of freshwater or super-saline type. Similar facies are known in other continental areas of the Devonian. Similarly, nearshore clastic, pro-delta, and delta sandstones and offshore mud facies are comparable to those known in other periods.

Devonian sedimentary rocks include the spectacular carbonate reef deposits of Western Australia, Europe, and western Canada, where the reefs are largely formed of stromatoporoids. These marine invertebrates suddenly vanished almost entirely by the end of the Frasnian Age, after which reefs were formed locally of cyanobacterian stromatolites. Other areas have reefs formed by mud mounds, and there are spectacular examples in southern Morocco, southern Algeria, and Mauritania.

Also distinctively Devonian is the development of locally extensive black shale deposits. The Upper Devonian

Antrim, New Albany, and Chattanooga shales are of this variety, and in Europe the German Hunsrückschiefer and Wissenbacherschiefer are similar. The latter are frequently characterized by distinctive fossils, though rarely of the benthic variety, indicating that they were formed when seafloor oxygen levels were very low. Distinctive condensed pelagic limestones rich in fossil cephalopods occur locally in Europe and the Urals. These form the facies termed Cephalopodenkalk or Knollenkalk in Germany and griotte in France. In former times the latter was worked for marble. Evaporite deposits are widespread, but coals are rare. There is no firm evidence for glacial deposits except in the late Devonian of Brazil. Various types of volcanic rocks have been observed in the areas that were converging island-arc regimes. Some volcanic ash horizons, such as the Tioga Metabentonite of the eastern United States, represent short-term events that are useful for correlation.

EUROPE

A line passing from the Bristol Channel eastward to northern Belgium and Germany roughly demarcates the Devonian marine area from the Old Red Sandstone continental deposits to the south. The continental deposits, which characteristically are red-stained with iron oxide, extend also to Greenland, Spitsbergen, Bear Island, and Norway. The British geologist Robert Jameson coined the term Old Red Sandstone in 1808, mistakenly thinking it to be A.G. Werner's Aelter Rother Sandstein, now known to be of Permian age. The rocks of this wide area have a remarkable affinity in both fauna and rock type and are usually considered to have been united in Devonian times. The relationships with the underlying Silurian System are seen in the classic Welsh borderlands, where the Ludlow Bone Bed was taken as the boundary until international agreement placed it somewhat higher. In Wales, southern Ireland, and the Scottish Lowlands, thicknesses of detrital deposits, chiefly sandstones, accumulated to as much as 6,100 metres (20,000 feet) in places. These sediments are rich in fish and plants, as are the eastern Greenland and Norwegian deposits. Widespread volcanics occur in Scotland.

Devonian rocks in Devon and Cornwall are mostly marine, but there are intercalations of terrestrial deposits from the north. In northern Devon, at least 3,660 metres (12,000 feet) of shales, thin limestones, sandstones, and conglomerates occur. The latter two lithologies are typical of the Hangman Grits and Pickwell Down Sandstones, which are the main terrestrial intercalations. However, in southern Devon, reef limestones occur in Middle Devonian formations, and the Upper Devonian formation locally shows very thin sequences formed on submarine rises and contemporary pillow lavas in basinal areas. In northern Cornwall both the Middle and Upper Devonian formations primarily occur in slate facies. Fossils found in these rocks have permitted detailed correlations with the Belgian and German sequences.

Devonian rocks of mixed terrestrial and marine type are known from boreholes under London, and these form a link with the Pas de Calais outcrops and to the classic areas of the Ardennes. There, between the Dinant Basin and Namur Basin to the north, is evidence of a northward landmass, as in Devon. Both the Lower and Upper Devonian formations consist of nearshore and terrigenous sediments that reach thicknesses of 2,740 metres (9,000 feet) and 460 metres (1,500 feet), respectively. The Middle Devonian and lower Upper Devonian (that is, the Eifelian, Givetian, and Frasnian stages, whose former type sections are here) structures consist mainly of limestones and shales and reach at least 1,500 metres (4,900 feet) in the south. Reefs are especially well developed in the Frasnian and occur as isolated masses, usually less than about 800 metres (2,600 feet) in length, separated by shales. Equivalents to the north show red and green silts and shales of marginal continental marine sediments. Because the Belgian Devonian rocks are well exposed along a north-south line, their changes in thickness, lithology, and fauna have been well documented.

The Eifel forms a natural eastern extension of the Ardennes, and a somewhat similar succession occurs there. The Lower Devonian pattern is nonmarine, and the Middle Devonian and Frasnian formations have a poor reef development, but the calcareous shales and limestones carry a rich and famous fauna. The GSSP defining the Lower-Middle Devonian boundary and base of the Eifelian Stage is at Schöenecken-Wetteldorf in the Eifel. The uppermost Devonian structure is not preserved.

The Rhine Valley, along with the Middle Rhine Highlands to the east, has been the subject of extensive study by the numerous German universities that surround it since the early days of geology. Again, a northern sediment source is generally indicated, but a borehole well to the north near Münster has encountered Middle and lower Upper Devonian marine limestones. To the south, approaching the Hunsrück-Taunus mountains, there is also evidence of a landmass. Between these areas a rich Devonian sequence is exposed in folded terrain. The maximum thickness is 9,140 metres (30,000 feet). The Lower Devonian formation consists of slates and sandstones. The slate has been much worked to clad houses and castles. A ledge of Emsian sandstone in the Rhine gorge is the setting for the Lorelei legend According to this legend, the enchanting singing of a Rhine maiden drove sailors to drown in the river. Limestones are common in the Givetian and are termed Massenkalk. Middle and Upper Devonian areas of thin sedimentation, as in Devon, are interpreted as deposits on submarine ridges. These are commonly nodular limestones that are rich in cephalopods and that occur between thick shale sequences. Evidence of volcanic activity is common, and this has been invoked to explain the concentrations of sedimentary hematite iron ores in the Givetian and Frasnian. The Harz Mountains show a more calcareous Lower Devonian section. Here, copper, lead, and zinc have been exploited from lodes in the famous Wissenbach Slate.

A calcareous Lower Devonian succession, the Bohemian facies, occurs in the Prague Basin of eastern Europe. A continuous marine succession formed from the Silurian into the Devonian, and the boundary is drawn at the top of the Silurian Series with the crinoid genus *Scyphocrinites*. The overlying Lochkovian and Pragian formations include the Koneprusy Limestone, which contains substantial reef deposits. The GSSP defining the base of the Devonian System and the Lochkovian Stage is at Klonk, and that defining the base of the Pragian is at Velká Chuchle, near Prague. The Upper Devonian structure is not preserved. In Moravia, complete successions of calcareous and basinal volcanic sediments occur.

Devonian rocks of a type analogous to those of southern England and the Ardennes crop out in Brittany. Farther south, outcrops occur in France, Spain, and Portugal. The GSSPs defining the Middle-Upper Devonian boundary and base of the Frasnian Stage, the base of the Famennian Stage, and the Devonian-Carboniferous boundary are drawn near Cessenon in southern France. The successions of the Pyrenees, Noire Mountains, and Carnic Alps include deepwater limestones. Marine deposits occur in the Balkan Peninsula, including Macedonia as well as Romania. The southern Polish outcrops of the Holy Cross Mountains are especially famous. They include a lower marine and continental series with a calcareous Middle Devonian section and an Upper Devonian section of reefs and shales rich in ammonites and trilobites.

In Podolia along the Dniester (Dnestr) River are fine marine sections that go up well into the Lower Devonian and are overlain by the Dniester Series of the Old Red Sandstone type. During the entire Devonian, the Ural Mountains formed a depressional trough linked northward to Novaya Zemlya and southward to the Crimean-Caucasian geosyncline that, along with the southern European outcrops already mentioned, formed part of the original Tethyan sediments of the Alpine-Himalayan fold system of the present day. In European Russia, Old Red Sandstone deposits are widespread, but marine tongues stretched westward from the Urals to reach Moscow in the Middle Devonian and St. Petersburg in the lower Upper Devonian. A remarkable series of boreholes revealed these relationships in great detail, and there is widespread evidence for salt lakes. Apart from the St. Petersburg outcrop and those along the Don River south of Moscow, the salt lakes are known from subsurface data only. Of economic importance here are the Timan-Pechora oil and gas field and the oil and potash of the Pripet Marshes. The North African areas of Algeria and especially Morocco are noted for their wealth of Devonian fossils. The GSSP defining the base of the Givetian Stage is at Mech Irdane, near Erfoud in southern Morocco.

ASIA

Devonian rocks are widespread in Asia east of the Ural Mountains. However, in Devonian time Asia was composed of separated microcratons, or terranes, that appear to have been attached or adjacent to the northern margin of Gondwana. The coalescence into present-day Asia took place after the Devonian. Devonian rocks are well known to fringe the central Siberian craton (a Devonian microcontinent), particularly in some of the northern coastal islands, the Kolyma River basin, and even farther east in Siberia. A particularly good record has been found in Kazakhstan. Devonian rocks occur in the Caucasus and Tien Shan mountains along the southern border of Kyrgyzstan, and there is an excellent carbonate sequence in the Salair and a full marine sequence in the Altai. The Altai-Sayan area contains a wealth of Old Red Sandstone fishes and plants. The GSSP defining the base of the Emsian Stage is in the Zinzil'ban Gorge of Uzbekistan.

Scattered Devonian sequences occur in Turkey, Iran, and Afghanistan, but the Himalayan records need revision, as it has now been determined that reported significant fossils are spurious and come from quite different areas. Isolated Devonian rocks are known in Vietnam, Myanmar (Burma), and Malaysia.

The Greater Khingan Range has a good record of Middle and Upper Devonian marine deposits. China is especially noted for its Devonian rocks. Both marine and nonmarine facies occur. Reefs and carbonate deposits also are well developed, and the photographically spectacular sugar-loaf hills near Guilin are of Devonian age. Much research by Chinese geologists since the early 1980s has led to great advances in knowledge of the Devonian in the many outcrops in China. Devonian rocks in Japan contain the plant genus *Leptophloeum*, which is also widespread in China.

SOUTHERN HEMISPHERE

In New Zealand the Lower Devonian is known in the Reefton and Baton River areas. The brachiopods in the faunal assemblages include European elements and have few typical austral types.

Devonian rocks are known in eastern Australia in a belt from Queensland to Tasmania as part of the Tasman geosyncline. Fluviatile sediments are found to the west. Thicknesses of 6,100 metres (20,000 feet) are known. *Leptophloeum* is found in the Upper Devonian portion. Devonian rocks occur in central Australia in Lake Amadeus and along the western coast in the Carnarvon, Canning, and Bonaparte Gulf basins. Complex facies changes are known, and the Canning Basin reef complexes show every detail of forereef, reef, and backreef structures exposed by modern erosion.

In the Antarctic both marine and continental Devonian strata occur, the latter rich in fossil fishes of European genera. The marine Lower Devonian shows some affinity with the Bokkeveld in South Africa, which in turn has strong links with South America. No Devonian strata are known in Africa between the Bokkeveld and sections in Ghana and northwestern Africa.

Early Devonian marine rocks are well developed in South America, but the Late Devonian is poorly documented. In the western mountains of the Andes and sub-Andes, Devonian remnants are preserved from southern Chile north to Peru, Ecuador, Venezuela, and Colombia. The Devonian rocks of Uruguay, Argentina, and Brazil are thought to represent marine transgression from the west. Both continental and marine fossils have been documented. The fauna of the Falkland Islands as well as of the Paraná and Parnaíba basins include many genera of brachiopods and trilobites that are common within the circum-Antarctic region but unknown in the Northern Hemisphere. In Venezuela and Colombia, however, plant, animal, fungus, and microorganism fossils of Appalachian type dominate, although austral elements such as the brachiopod *Australospirifer* linger.

NORTH AMERICA

The Appalachian area of eastern North America shows spectacular and historically famous Devonian rocks that were first described by James Hall in New York state between 1836 and 1855. A source of sand and other clastics in the east provided a flood of sediment from an eastern land area, which formed the Devonian Catskill Delta that filled a broad sedimentary trough. In the area encompassing Ontario, Michigan, and Indiana, early thin calcareous sequences give way to deeper-water marine black shales, which were formed especially in the area of the Great Lakes and south beyond Indiana. The central area of the United States formed a mid-continental rise during the Devonian, and the Devonian rock record there is thin and incomplete. Devonian rocks are well developed in New Mexico, Utah, Nevada, and north to Montana, where evaporites in the subsurface are known to extend into Saskatchewan. In the mountainous area of the eastern United States, Devonian rocks are scattered and may have coalesced from separate microcratons or microplates over a long period of time. Very thick sequences of Devonian volcanics are known, for example, in the Sierra Nevada of California. In western Canada, flat-lying Devonian rocks are well known in the subsurface of Saskatchewan, and in Alberta they include oil-bearing Devonian reefs. Devonian reef complexes also occur along the Canadian Rocky Mountains. Involved in the thrusting of the Rockies, they can be seen in Alberta's Banff and Jasper national parks. In more-scattered outcrops to the east, it would appear that deeper-water facies are represented. Following the discovery of oil in a Devonian reef at Leduc, Alta., much detailed exploration was undertaken. Rocks of Devonian age are widespread from there northward to the Canadian Arctic islands and Alaska. Their faunal assemblages show many similarities with those of Europe.

THE CORRELATION OF DEVONIAN STRATA

Most groups of fossil forms contribute to the establishment of a faunal and floral chronology that enables Devonian rocks to be correlated. For the continental deposits, fish and plant spores are most important. The fishes give a very precise zonation in parts of the system. The Baltic Frasnian, for example, can be divided into at least five time zones using psammosteids (Agnatha), thus probably equaling the precision possible for the better-known marine Frasnian sequences. Many problems remain, however, in the correlation of the continental and the marine deposits.

The faunal succession in marine strata has been established for many groups, but only those of significance for international correlations are mentioned here. Traditionally, the goniatites and clymenids (ammonites) form the standard. The succession established first in Germany by the paleontologist Rudolf Wedekind in 1917 has been found to hold for all continents where representatives have been discovered.

Rivaling the ammonites in most parts of the Devonian and useful for defining the divisions of the system are the conodonts. The Late Devonian was characterized by a spectacular evolutionary radiation of *Palmatolepis* and its relatives.

The brachiopods, although more restricted, are also important. This is particularly true of the spiriferids of the Early Devonian and of the entry and evolution of the cyrtospiriferid types in the Late Devonian. The rhynchonellids also are of great value in the subdivision of the Late

Devonian. Some brachiopods, however, show diverse distribution patterns. *Stringocephalus*, a well-known Middle Devonian guide fossil in the western United States, Canada, Europe, and Asia, is entirely absent from the rich New York succession. Yet *Tropidoleptus*, elsewhere confined to the Lower and Middle Devonian, ranges high in the Devonian of New York. Corals also have been used for correlation, but further work suggests they were particularly sensitive to changing local environments and thus are poor time indicators.

STAGES OF THE DEVONIAN PERIOD

The Devonian Period is divided into seven individual stages that together span almost 56 million years of geologic time. Conodonts and graptolites are common guide fossils that separate Devonian strata.

LOCHKOVIAN STAGE

The lowermost of the three standard worldwide divisions of Early Devonian rocks and time, the Lochkovian Stage is the lowest division of the Devonian Period and the Lower Devonian Series. The Lochkovian Stage spans the interval between 416 million and 411.2 million years ago. The name is derived from Lochkov in the Czech Republic. As formally ratified in 1972 under the authority of the ICS, the Global Stratotype Section and Point (GSSP) defining the lower boundary of this stage is at Klonk near Suchomasty, 35 kilometres (22 miles) southwest of Prague. The Silurian-Devonian boundary had been subject to many different interpretations in various parts of the world. The GSSP for this boundary represented the first decision on a boundary stratotype under the ICS and played an important role in formalizing the ratification process.

The section itself contains many fossils within limestones made up of sediments deposited from the open ocean, the quiet water of mud flats, and the muddy water of riverine environments. The marker fossil is the graptolite *Monograptus uniformis uniformis*. Overlying this bed, the marker trilobite *Warburgella rugulosa rugosa* appears. A large crinoid, *Scyphocrinites*, occurs near the Silurian-Devonian boundary in many areas of the world and continues into the lowest 10 metres (33 feet) of the Lochkovian stratotype section. The top of the Lochkovian is drawn at the base of the overlying Pragian Stage. The base of the Lochkovian Stage is drawn to coincide with the boundary between the Devonian System above and the Pridoli Series of the Silurian System below.

PRAGIAN STAGE

The Pragian Stage is the second of the three standard worldwide divisions of Early Devonian rocks and time. Pragian time spans the interval between 411.2 million and 407 million years ago. The name is derived from Prague, the capital of the Czech Republic. The section is made up of fine-grained gray limestones containing biodetrital (decomposed organic material) and bituminous particles. The boundary is drawn at the appearance of the conodont *Eognathodus sulcatus*. This taxon is also identified in Germany, Austria, China, Australia, the United States (Nevada and Alaska), and Canada. Rocks of this age are known worldwide. As formally ratified in 1989 under the authority of the ICS, the Global Stratotype Section and Point (GSSP) defining the lower boundary of this stage is in the section of Veklá Chuchle in southwestern Prague. The Lochkovian Stage underlies the Pragian. The top of the Pragian Stage is defined by the base of the overlying division, the Emsian Stage.

EMSIAN STAGE

The uppermost of the three standard worldwide divisions of Early Devonian rocks and time, Emsian time spans the interval between 407 million and 397.5 million years ago. The Emsian Stage was named for exposures studied in the region of the Ems River in western Germany, where it consists of wackes (dirty sandstone) noted for their rich fossil faunas. Limestones dominate the Emsian in the Bohemian region of central Europe and in the foothills of the Altai Mountains of Russia, whereas limestones, cherts, and tuffs occur in the Emsian of Australia. The Emsian is well developed in the northeastern portions of the United States, where the Esopus Shale, Schoharie Grit, and Onondaga Limestones provide excellent exposures in New York state. As formally ratified in 1995 under the authority of the ICS, the Global Stratotype Section and Point (GSSP) defining the lower boundary of this stage is located in the Zinzil'ban Gorge, 170 km (105 miles) south-southeast of Samarkand, Uzbekistan. The Emsian Stage underlies the Eifelian Stage of the Middle Devonian Series and overlies the Pragian Stage of the Lower Devonian Series.

EIFELIAN STAGE

The Eifelian Stage is the lowermost of the two standard worldwide divisions of Middle Devonian rocks and time. Eifelian time spans the interval between 397.5 million and 391.8 million years ago. The name of the Eifelian Stage is derived from the Eifel Hills in western Germany, near Luxembourg and Belgium. As formally ratified in 1985 under the authority of the ICS, the Global Stratotype Section and Point (GSSP) defining the lower boundary of this stage is established in a trench section across pastureland near the town of Schönecken-Wetteldorf, Ger. The trench exposes siltstones and mudstones in the upper part of the Heisdorf Formation and alternating limestones and mudstones in overlying strata of the Lauch Formation. The boundary point is situated 1.9 metres (6.2 feet) below the base of the Lauch Formation, which is fixed by the first occurrence of the conodont *Polygnathus costatus partitus*, known worldwide from Eifelian strata in Morocco, Spain, Germany, Austria, the Czech Republic, Central Asia, China, Malaysia, Australia, the U.S. states of Nevada and Alaska, and the Canadian Arctic. The top of the Eifelian Stage is defined by the base of an overlying subdivision, the Givetian Stage of the Middle Devonian Series, while the bottom is underlain by the Emsian Stage of the Lower Devonian Series.

GIVETIAN STAGE

The uppermost of the two standard worldwide divisions of Middle Devonian rocks and time, Givetian time spans the interval between 391.8 million and 385.3 million years ago. It was named for exposures studied near Givet in the Ardennes region of northern France and is characterized by a zone (a smaller subdivision of geologic time) whose rocks include the ammonite genus *Maenioceras*.

In the Ardennes, limestones predominate and form escarpments about the town of Givet. Their rich fossil invertebrate fauna is characterized by the coral genus *Favosites* as well as gastropods and brachiopods (lamp shells). Important Givetian sections also occur in Great Britain, where limestones and gray, slaty goniatite-bearing rocks predominate; in Germany and Russia, where limestones and shales include fossils of the widely distributed brachiopod genus *Stringocephalus*; in northeastern North

America, where the richly fossiliferous limestones and shales include the upper formations of the Hamilton Group; and in Australia. As formally ratified in 1994 under the authority of the ICS, the Global Stratotype Section and Point (GSSP) identifying the lower boundary of this stage is located at Jebel Mech Irdane ridge, 12 kilometres (about 7 miles) southwest of Rissani, Morocco. The Givetian Stage is overlain by the Frasnian Stage of the Upper Devonian Series and underlain by the Eifelian Stage of the Middle Devonian Series.

FRASNIAN STAGE

The Frasnian Stage is the lowest of the two standard worldwide divisions of Late Devonian rocks and time. Frasnian time occurred between 385.3 million and 374.5 million years ago. The stage's name is derived from the town of Frasnes in the Ardennes region of southern Belgium. The lower boundary point of the Frasnian is defined on the basis of the first occurrence of the conodont *Ancyrodella rotundiloba*. Under the authority of the ICS, the Global Stratotype Section and Point (GSSP) defining the base of this unit was established in 1987 on a hillside exposure at Col du Puech de la Suque in the Noire Mountains region of southern France. The top of the Frasnian Stage records the Upper Kellwasser Event, a mass extinction of many marine invertebrates, especially among the colonial rugose corals; stromatoporoids (thought to be large fossilized sponges); orthid, pentamerid, and atrypid brachiopods (lamp shells); trilobites; and conodonts. This major extinction event defines the top of the Frasnian and thus the base of the overlying Famennian Stage. The Frasnian Stage is underlain by the Givetian Stage of the Middle Devonian Series.

FAMENNIAN STAGE

The uppermost of the two standard worldwide divisions of Late Devonian rocks and time, Famennian time spans the interval between 374.5 million and 359.2 million years ago. The name of the Famennian Stage is derived from the region of Famenne in southern Belgium, which has served historically as the type district.

Under the authority of the ICS, the Global Stratotype Section and Point (GSSP) defining the base of this unit was established at Coumiac, 1.5 kilometres (about 1 mile) west-southwest of the village of Cessenon in the Noire Mountains region of southern France. The boundary sequence is preserved in a quarry exhibiting lower Frasnian to upper Famennian pelagic limestones. The boundary point corresponds to the extinction of all conodont species belonging to the genera *Ancyrodella* and *Ozarkodina* and to all but a few species in the genera *Icriodus, Ancyrognathus, Palmatolepis,* and *Polygnathus* during the Upper Kellwasser Event. The boundary point between the underlying Frasnian Stage and the Famennian also corresponds to the first appearance of the conodont *Palmatolepis triangularis.* Three-quarters of all known upper Frasnian trilobite genera are represented at the GSSP, many of which subsequently became extinct.

The Upper Kellwasser extinction event separating the Frasnian and Famennian stages is widely associated with the deposition of black shales and limestones known as the Upper Kellwasser Kalk, thought to have been produced as the result of a dramatic decrease in dissolved oxygen levels within the oceans at the time. Upper Frasnian brachiopods and goniatites are also well represented at Coumiac, indicating that they survived the Upper Kellwasser Event. The top of the Famennian Stage is defined by the base of the overlying Tournaisian Stage of the Carboniferous System.

CHAPTER 6

THE CARBONIFEROUS PERIOD

The Carboniferous Period is the fifth interval of the Paleozoic Era. It succeeded the Devonian Period and preceded the Permian Period. In terms of absolute time, the Carboniferous Period began approximately 359.2 million years ago and ended 299 million years ago. Its duration of approximately 60 million years makes it the longest period of the Paleozoic Era and the second longest period of the Phanerozoic Eon. The rocks that were formed or deposited during the period constitute the Carboniferous System. The name *Carboniferous* refers to coal-bearing strata that characterize the upper portion of the series throughout the world.

The Carboniferous Period is formally divided into two major subdivisions—the Mississippian (359.2 to 318.1 million years ago) and the Pennsylvanian (318.1 to 299 million years ago) subperiods—their rocks recognized chrono-stratigraphically as subsystems by international agreement. In Europe, the Carboniferous Period is subdivided into the Dinantian and suceeding Silesian subsystems, but the boundary between those divisions is below the internationally accepted Mississippian-Pennsylvanian boundary.

THE CARBONIFEROUS ENVIRONMENT

During the Carboniferous Period, many continents moved northward. Connections arising between these continents and Gondwana occurring later in the period altered the movement of ocean currents. Colder conditions predominated on Gondwana that allowed the development of large continental glaciers. In contrast, glaciers and ice sheets did not emerge in northern latitudes because they remained largely devoid of land.

PALEOGEOGRAPHY

The Early Carboniferous (Mississippian) world is characterized by Laurussia, a series of small cratonic blocks that occupied the Northern Hemisphere, and Gondwana, an enormous landmass made up of present-day South America, Africa, Antarctica, Australia, and the Indian subcontinent in the Southern Hemisphere. Lithospheric plate movement brought the continents close together on one side of the globe. The orogenies (mountain-building events) taking place during the Devonian Period had formed the "Old Red Sandstone" continent (Laurussia). The principal landmass of Laurussia was made up of present-day North America, western Europe through the Urals, and Balto-Scandinavia. Much of Laurussia lay near the paleoequator, whereas the cratons of Siberia, Kazakhstania, and most of China existed as separate continents occupying positions at high latitudes. During this time, the Tethys Sea separated the southern margin of the Old Red Sandstone continent completely from Gondwana.

By Late Carboniferous (Pennsylvanian) times, plate movements had brought most of Laurussia into contact with Gondwana and closed the Tethys. Laurussia and Gondwana became fused by the Appalachian-Hercynian orogeny, which continued into the Permian Period. The position of the landmass that would become the eastern

United States and northern Europe remained equatorial, while the China and Siberia cratons continued to reside at high latitudes in the Northern Hemisphere.

The distribution of land and sea followed fairly predictable limits. The continental interiors were terrestrial, and no major marine embayments apparently existed. Upland areas of the continental interiors underwent substantial erosion during the Carboniferous. Shallow seas occupied the continental shelf margins surrounding the continents. Fringe areas of Carboniferous continents may very well have become the continental interiors of the present day. Deeper troughs (geosynclines) lay seaward of the continental masses, and their sedimentary record is now characterized by mountains.

PALEOCLIMATE

During the Carboniferous Period, the climate of various landmasses was controlled by their latitudinal position. Since prevailing wind patterns were similar to those on Earth today, tropical conditions characterized the equatorial regions. The midlatitudes were dry, and higher latitudes were both cooler and moist. Although both western Europe and Balto-Scandinavia resided in latitudes low enough to produce evaporite (minerals in sedimentary rock deposits of soluble salts resulting from the evaporation of water) deposits in shallow continental settings, only North America occupied an equatorial setting during the Mississippian. Wetter areas on other continental blocks in higher latitudes of the Northern Hemisphere began to form coal swamps during this time.

In contrast, the bulk of Gondwana was below 30° south latitude and experienced colder conditions that allowed the formation of continental glaciers. These glaciations were similar to those occurring in the Northern Hemisphere during the Pleistocene Epoch. Coeval (parallel) continental glaciations did not occur in the high latitudes of the Northern Hemisphere, probably because the landmasses were too small to sustain large ice fields.

Paleogeography continued to control climates into Pennsylvanian times. As sea-level cyclicity became more pronounced, the equatorial settings changed from carbonate shelves to coal basins. Continental glaciation expanded in Gondwana, allowing glaciers to extend into lower latitudes that otherwise might have formed coal swamps. As mountains developed toward the close of the Pennsylvanian, rain-shadow effects became more influential, inhibiting the process of coal deposition in the basins of western Europe. Flora of the Carboniferous followed the same climatic gradients as glacial deposits. Fossil plants found in areas located in high latitudes during the Carboniferous exhibit seasonal growth rings, while those of the presumed equatorial coal swamps lack such rings, as do modern tropical trees.

CARBONIFEROUS LIFE

Despite the minor setbacks occurring as a result of the Devonian extinctions, terrestrial and marine environments continued to diversify during the Carboniferous Period. The first examples of many groups that commonly occur today (such as winged insects and squid) emerged during this time, whereas other groups (such as the bony and cartilaginous fishes) colonized freshwater environments. Amphibians diversified. Terrestrial ferns and other plants that lived during this time would later serve as the foundation for many of the world's modern coal deposits.

INVERTEBRATES

The Carboniferous was a time of diverse marine invertebrates. The Late Devonian Period experienced major extinctions within some marine invertebrate groups, and Carboniferous faunas reflect a different composition from what had prevailed earlier in the Paleozoic Era.

Most notably, reef-forming organisms, such as tabulate corals and stromatoporoids (large colonial marine organisms similar to hydrozoans), were limited. Consequently, Carboniferous reefs were poorly developed because of this lack of framework builders. Benthic, or sea-bottom, marine communities were dominated by the crinoids, a group of stalked echinoderms (invertebrates characterized by a hard, spiny covering or skin) that still lives today. These animals were solitary suspension feeders that grew in such great profusion that they affected bottom currents and water circulation. The calcareous (containing calcium carbonate) remains of these organisms are significant rock-forming materials.

A related, but extinct, group of stalked echinoderms, the blastoids, also characterize Carboniferous deposits. Areas favourable for crinoids and blastoids were occupied by other filter-feeding organisms. Colonies of stenolaemate bryozoans (small colonial animals that produce a skeletal framework of calcium carbonate) and articulate brachiopods (lamp shells) are common associates of the crinoids. The bryozoans attached their undersurfaces to the seafloor and formed either fanlike, twiglike, or small knobby colonies of calcium carbonate in areas characterized by low rates of sedimentation. Articulate brachiopods formed a bivalved shell of calcium carbonate that either rested free on the seafloor or was attached by a fleshy stalk. The brachiopods and bryozoans both pumped the water column and removed food and oxygen by a tentacular lophophore (a horseshoe-shaped feeding organ). Brachiopods are particularly common, and all orders except the Pentamerida are found in Carboniferous rocks. Both calcareous and agglutinate foraminifers (pseudopod-using unicellular organisms protected by a test or shell) are represented in Carboniferous deposits, particularly limestones.

In the Pennsylvanian, an unusual group of these protozoans (single-celled eukaryotic organisms), the fusulinids (single-celled amoeba-like organisms with complex shells), appeared and dominated assemblages through the Permian Period, when they became extinct. The fusulinids secreted a tightly coiled calcareous test that was chambered, but they lived free on the seafloor.

Some benthic organisms that were common to early and middle Paleozoic times began to decline during the Carboniferous. These included the trilobites (which became extinct at the end of the Permian), rugose corals, and sponges. The pelagic, or water column, environment was inhabited by a profusion of cephalopods. These included both straight and coiled nautiloids (early relatives of the chambered *Nautilus*), the ammonoids (extinct members of the same class), and the first squids. Carboniferous cephalopods were either predators or scavengers, and they swam by jet propulsion. Some of the straight nautiloids grew exceedingly large (greater than 3 metres [10 feet]). The ammonoids exhibit rapid evolutionary development through the Carboniferous and, along with the calcareous foraminifers, provide the biostratigraphic data for age dating and correlating the boundaries and various subdivisions of the period. Graptolites (small, colonial, planktonic animals) extend into the Carboniferous, but they became extinct during the Mississippian.

Insects had occupied terrestrial environments since the Devonian, but they diversified during the Carboniferous Period. No winged insects are known from Devonian or Mississippian times, but wings probably evolved during the Mississippian. By the Pennsylvanian subperiod, dragonflies and mayflies were abundant and had reached large sizes. Fossils of more advanced insects capable of folding their wings, particularly cockroaches, are well represented in rocks of the Pennsylvanian subperiod. Other Pennsylvanian insects include the ancestral forms of grasshoppers and crickets and the first terrestrial scorpions.

PLANTS

Carboniferous terrestrial environments were dominated by vascular land plants ranging from small, shrubby growths to trees exceeding heights of 30 metres (100 feet). The most important groups were the lycopods, sphenopsids, cordaites, seed ferns, and true ferns. Lycopods are represented in the modern world only by club mosses, but in the Carboniferous Period they included tall trees with dense, spirally arranged leaves. Reproduction involved either cones or spore-bearing organs on the leaves. *Lepidodendron*, with diamond-shaped leaf bases, and *Sigillaria*, with ribs and round leaf bases, were the dominant lycopod genera. They have produced fossil logs that exceed 1 metre (3.3 feet) at their bases. Sphenopsids are trees and shrubs with a distinctly jointed stem and leaves arranged in spirals from those joints. The horsetail rush (*Equisetum*) is the only living representative, but Carboniferous floras contained several members of the group. *Calamitesis* was the most common Carboniferous genus. Although small in comparison with lycopods,

Calamitesis grew in profusion in drier, more upland environments.

Cordaites are extinct members of the gymnosperms (nonflowering vascular plants), and they were the precursors to the conifers. They also favoured upland environments, where they grew tall and possessed tiny scalelike leaves and cones similar to modern conifers. *Walchia* is a typical genus that probably grew in forested areas in stands similar to where modern pines would grow.

Seed ferns, or pteridosperms, are gymnosperms with fernlike foliage, but they reproduce by using seeds rather than spores. They have no living representatives. This group includes trees, such as the Permian genus *Glossopteris*, but they are represented in Carboniferous floras by taxa such as *Neuropteris* and *Pecopteris*, both of which were low scrubs. Both seed ferns and true ferns formed the underfoliage associated with most Carboniferous coal swamps.

FISHES

The diversity of fish from the Devonian continued into the Carboniferous in both marine and freshwater environments. The arthrodires (armoured, jawed fish) became extinct almost immediately in the Mississippian, while both the chondrichthians (cartilage skeleton) and osteichthians (bony skeleton) are represented throughout the Carboniferous. The common Carboniferous shark, *Cladoselache*, dominated marine settings, which also included the bradyodonts (a group of shell-crushing, pavement-toothed cartilaginous fish). A freshwater shark, *Orthacanthus*, is also known from Pennsylvanian freshwater deposits in both Europe and North America. Osteichthians also occupied freshwater environments. These included the crossopterygians (lobe-finned fishes), dipnoi (lungfishes), and palaeoniscoids (small ray-finned fishes). In the Devonian, the crossopterygians and dipnoi were the dominant forms, but the palaeoniscoids dominated the Carboniferous assemblages. All these groups have living relatives.

AMPHIBIANS AND EARLY REPTILES

The Carboniferous Period was the time of peak amphibian development and the emergence of the reptiles. Among the amphibians, the labyrinthodonts are represented by members of order Embolomeri, such as *Calligenethlon*, *Carbonerpeton*, and *Diplovertebron*, and members of family Eryopoidae, such as *Eryops*, *Arkserpeton*, and *Amphibamus*. These forms had large skulls, small trunks, and stocky limbs. They were derived from the crossopterygians that emerged in the Devonian from freshwater settings. Embolomerians and Eryopodaens probably remained close to water, favouring the abundant coal swamps of the time. None of these forms have living representatives.

Another group of unusual forms, the lepospondylians, resembled amphibians but are not included within the class in most recent classifications. This group contained a great variety of semiaquatic forms such as the snakelike *Ophiderpeton*, the "horned" *Keraterpeton*, and the microsaurs, such as *Asaphestera*. The lepospondylians became extinct during the Pennsylvanian subperiod.

The development of the reptiles was characterized by the improvement of terrestrial reproductive systems during the Carboniferous, a feature not preservable in the record as such. The fossil record of early reptiles is poor, particularly in comparison with that of Permian and Mesozoic times. The earliest reptiles, the captorhinid

Hylonomus, were recovered from Lower Pennsylvanian lycopod tree stumps in Nova Scotia. These small animals, which measure less than 0.3 metre (1 foot), were preserved after becoming entrapped in the cavities left by rotting trees.

SIGNIFICANT CARBONIFEROUS LIFE-FORMS

Notable forms of this period include the vascular plants, such as the Cordaitales, the cone-bearing *Lebachia*, and others that dominate terrestrial environments. The Carboniferous is also known as the time in which the mammal-relatives, such as *Edaphosaurus*, appear.

CALAMITES

A genus of tree-sized, spore-bearing plants that lived during the Carboniferous and Permian periods (about 360 to 250 million years ago), *Calamites* had a well-defined node-internode architecture similar to modern horsetails, and its branches and leaves emerged in whorls from these nodes. Its upright stems were woody and connected by an underground runner. However, the central part of the stem was hollow, and fossils of *Calamites* are commonly preserved as casts of this hollow central portion. *Calamites* grew to 20 metres (about 66 feet) tall, standing mostly along the sandy banks of rivers, and had the ability to sprout vigorously from underground rhizomes when the upper portions of the plant were damaged. The remains of *Calamites* and other treelike plants from the Carboniferous Period were transformed into the coal used as a source of energy today. A virtually identical plant from the Triassic Period (about 250 to 200 million years ago) is called *Neocalamites*.

COMPOSITA

This genus of extinct brachiopods, or lamp shells, appears as fossils in marine rocks of the Carboniferous to Permian periods (from 359 million to 251 million years ago). *Composita* is abundant and widespread as a fossil, especially in Permian deposits. The shell is smooth, small, and distinctive in form. A fold and sulcus (groove) are present in the valves, and the pedicle opening (for the anchoring foot) is round.

CORDAITALES

Cordaitales is an order of coniferophytes (phylum, sometimes division, Coniferophyta), fossil plants dominant during the Carboniferous Period (359 million to 299 million years ago) directly related to the conifers (order Coniferales). Many were trees up to 30 metres (100 feet) tall, branched, and crowned with large, leathery, strap-shaped leaves. Three families are included— Pityaceae, Poroxylaceae, and Cordaitaceae—of which the Cordaitaceae is the best known. Its genera *Cordaites* and *Cordaianthus* are represented by fossil leaves, branches, and loosely formed cones, investigations of which have led to the formulation of the cordaite-conifer evolutionary sequence through the primitive conifer family Lebachiaceae (*see* Lebachia). The Pityaceae, from the Early Carboniferous, and the Poroxylaceae, geologically later but more primitive in wood structure, are closer in many respects to the seed ferns (pteridosperms). They are provisionally grouped with the Cordaitales until evidence displaces them.

CRYPTOBLASTUS

Cryptoblastus is an extinct genus of blastoids, a primitive group of echinoderms related to the modern sea lilies, found as fossils in Early Carboniferous marine rocks (the Early Carboniferous Period occurred from 360 to 320 million years ago).

DICTYOCLOSTUS

A genus of extinct brachiopods that were common invertebrate forms in the shallow seas of North America from the Carboniferous to the Permian periods (between 359 million and 251 million years ago), *Dictyoclostus* often grew to large size. Its distinctive shell is concavo-convex and is frequently highly ornamented with lines, grooves, and finely developed spines.

DIELASMA

Dielasma is a genus of extinct brachiopods that occur as fossils in rocks deposited in marine environments of Carboniferous to Permian age. The two small, rather smooth valves of the shell of *Dielasma* are slightly convex in profile, but the pedicle, or foot, valve is much larger than the brachial, or upper, valve. Growth lines are generally apparent. In some respects *Dielasma* is similar to *Composita,* a brachiopod with similar time range and habitat.

DIPLOVERTEBRON

Diplovertebron is a genus of extinct amphibians of North America and Europe known from fossils in Late Carboniferous rocks (from 318 million to 299 million years ago). *Diplovertebron* represents an early representative of the anthracosaurs, a group of tetropods with some reptile traits. Since they could not produce an amniotic egg, which is a defining characteristic of true reptiles, anthracosaurs are classified as reptilelike amphibians. *Diplovertebron* and other primitive anthracosaurs are characterized by a distinctively constructed vertebral column and skull pattern and five-toed feet.

EDAPHOSAURUS

Edaphosaurus is a primitive herbivorous relative of mammals that is found in fossil deposits dating from Late Carboniferous to the Early Permian periods (318 million to 271 million years ago).

Edaphosaurus was more than 3.5 metres (11.5 feet) long, with a short, low skull and blunt conical teeth. The head was very small in comparison with the massive barrel-like body. More distinctive, however, was the large "sail" on its back formed by elongated vertebral arches. The arches were probably connected by a membrane that had bony knobs or crossbars along its length. The sail may have functioned in thermoregulation and also may have served as a storehouse for phosphates, which could be easily mobilized from the bony projections supporting the sail. The sail also may have had a defensive function, giving the animal a much larger and more imposing appearance to predators.

A similar sail evolved independently in *Dimetrodon*. Although *Dimetrodon* was a voracious predator distantly related to *Edaphosaurus*, both creatures were pelycosaurs. Members of Pelycosauria were neither dinosaurs nor reptiles, but some may have given rise to the therapsids, a group that includes the class Mammalia.

EUPHEMITES

An extinct genus of gastropods (snails) abundant during the Late Carboniferous Period (between 320 and 286 million years ago) in the shallow seas that covered the midcontinental region of North America, *Euphemites* was a small, globular snail with a broad and arcuate (bow-shaped) aperture. Ornamentation consists of parallel ridges separated by troughs following the plane of coiling.

Particularly characteristic of the Early Carboniferous Period, Fenestella *was a small colonial animal that displayed a branching network of structures with relatively large elliptical and smaller spherical openings.* Colin Keates/ Dorling Kindersley/Getty Images

FENESTELLA

Fenestella, a genus of extinct bryozoans (small colonial animals that produce a skeletal framework of calcium carbonate), was especially characteristic of the Early Carboniferous Period. Close study of *Fenestella* reveals a branching network of structures with relatively large elliptical openings and smaller spherical openings that housed individual members of the colony. *Fenestella* was a marine form.

FUSULINA

Fusulina is a genus of extinct fusulinid foraminiferans (protozoans with a shell) found as fossils in marine rocks of Late Carboniferous age (318 million to 299 million years old). *Fusulina,* an excellent index fossil for Late Carboniferous rocks, enables widely separated rocks to be correlated.

FUSULINELLA

Fusulinella is a genus of extinct fusulinid foraminiferans found as fossils in Late Carboniferous marine rocks (those formed between 320 and 286 million years ago). Because of its narrow time range and wide geographic distribution, *Fusulinella* is an excellent guide fossil for Late Carboniferous rocks and time.

FUSULINIDS

Fusulinids make up a large group of extinct foraminiferans. The fusulinids first appeared late in the Early Carboniferous Epoch, which ended 318 million years ago, and persisted until the end of the Permian Period, 251 million years ago. Where they occur, the fusulinids have proven to be extremely useful for correlating different rock units in widely separated regions and for dividing geologic time into smaller units. Petroleum geologists also use them as keys to the locations of economically important deposits of oil and natural gas. Many forms of fusulinids are known, from barely visible species to forms that are easily seen with the naked eye and may be as much as 5 centimetres (2 inches) long. Many fusulinids resemble grains of wheat. The internal structure, however, is very complex and distinctive. The shell consists of a series of chambers formed about a central longitudinal axis. Complex patterns in the number and arrangement of internal walls and deposits are present and aid in classification and the working out of evolutionary relationships. Most fusulinids lived in clear marine water far from the shore.

GASTRIOCERAS

This genus of extinct cephalopods (animals related to the modern pearly nautilus) is found in Pennsylvanian marine rocks over a wide area, including North America and Great Britain (the Pennsylvanian Subperiod began 318 million years ago and lasted about 19 million years). The shell of *Gastrioceras* is round and coiled and consists of a series of chambers. The sutures between successive chambers are represented by a sinuous line of arches and troughs in a simple pattern known as a goniatite suture pattern.

LABYRINTHODONTS

A labyrinthodont is a type of tooth made up of infolded enamel that provides a grooved and strongly reinforced structure. This tooth type was common in the true amphibians of the Paleozoic Era, some lobe-finned fishes closely related to tetrapods, and in the early anthracosaurs— which were tetrapods closely related to the amniotes.

Labyrinthodont is also an archaic name for any member of the subclass Labyrinthodontia, an extinct group that served as a precursor to the amphibians. Labyrinthodonts lived during Carboniferous and Permian times (about

Eryops

top view

Encyclopædia Britannica, Inc.

359–251 million years ago) and may well have included the ancestors of all terrestrial vertebrates.

LEBACHIA

Lebachia is a genus of extinct cone-bearing plants known from fossils of the Late Carboniferous and Early Permian epochs (from about 320 to 258 million years ago). *Lebachia* and related genera in the family Lebachiaceae, order Coniferales (sometimes family Voltziaceae, order Voltziales), appear to be among the immediate ancestors of all extant conifers except the yews. A tree of uncertain size with pinnately arranged side branches (like the barbs of a feather), *Lebachia* apparently had a growth habit similar to that of the present-day Norfolk Island pine. It bore both pollen-bearing and seed-bearing cones (the latter, as detached fossils, are called *Gomphostrobus*) at the ends of the side branches.

LEPIDODENDRON

An extinct genus of tree-sized lycopsid plants that lived during the Carboniferous Period, *Lepidodendron* and its relatives—*Lepidophloios, Bothrodendron,* and *Paralycopodites*—were related to modern club mosses. They grew up to 40 metres (130 feet) in height and 2 metres (about 7 feet) in diameter. During their juvenile stages, these plants grew as unbranched trunks with a shock of long, thin leaves that sprouted near the growing tip. They branched at later stages, either in even dichotomies at the growing tip or in lateral branches that were later shed. After branching, the leaves became shorter and awl-shaped. As the plant grew, it shed leaves from older parts of the stem that left diamond-shaped leaf bases. Stems were characterized by a slender central strand of wood and a thick bark. Since *Stigmaria*—the underground parts of the

Fossil fragment of Lepidodendron.
Louise K. Broman/Root Resources

plant—resembled stems, they are not considered true roots. The shape of leaf bases and the arrangement of their vascular strands distinguish the different genera within the group of arborescent lycopsids.

Lepidodendron and its relatives reproduced by spores, with megaspores giving rise to the female (egg-producing)gametophyte and micro-spores giving rise to the male (sperm-producing) gametophyte. *Lepidophloios* wrapped its megasporangium in a layer of tissue much like that of the seed plants. This feature, however, was independently derived in the lycopsid lineage. In some genera, spore-bearing cones were produced at the tips of branches, suggesting that the plants could reproduce only once in their lifetime. *Lepidodendron* and its relatives lived in the extensive peat-forming swamps of the Early and Middle Pennsylvanian epochs (318 to 306 million years ago) and became extinct when these swamps disappeared.

LINOPRODUCTUS

Linoproductus is a genus of extinct articulate brachiopods found throughout the midcontinent region of North America as fossils in Early Carboniferous to Late Permian rocks (from about 359 million to about 251 million years ago). The genus *Linoproductus* is a distinctive invertebrate form distinguished by its strongly convex pedicle valve and its slightly concave brachial valve. Fine ribbing is present on the convex shell.

LOPHOPHYLLUM

An extinct genus of solitary marine corals found as fossils especially characteristic of the Late Carboniferous epoch (between 318 million and 299 million years ago) in North America, *Lophophyllum* is included in the horn corals (so named because of the hornlike form of the individual) and probably preferred warm, clear, shallow marine waters.

MYALINA

An extinct genus of clams found in rocks of Early Carboniferous to Late Permian age (dating from about 359 million to 251 million years ago), *Myalina* belongs to an ancient group of clams, the Mytilacea, that first appeared in the earlier Ordovician Period (beginning 505 million years ago). *Myalina* had a thicker shell than other mytilacids. *Myalina,* abundant in many rock formations, is important for stratigraphic correlations.

NEOSPIRIFER

Neospirifer, a genus of extinct brachiopods, is found as fossils in Late Carboniferous to Permian marine rocks (the period of time from the Late Carboniferous to the end of the Permian was about 251 million to 318 million years ago). Many species are known. The shell or valves of *Neospirifer* are robustly developed and frequently well preserved as fossils. A prominent furrow, or sulcus, and a distinctive ridge, or fold, are generally developed in the shell, aiding rapid identification. *Neospirifer* is a useful index fossil for stratigraphic correlations.

NUCULOPSIS

An extinct genus of clams found as fossils in rocks of the Pennsylvanian Subperiod (318 million to 299 million years ago), *Nuculopsis* was small, almost spherical, and ornamented with fine growth lines. Because *Nuculopsis* is similar to the longer lived and commoner genus *Nuculana,* it has been considered a subgenus of *Nuculana. Nuculopsis* inhabited the broad, shallow Pennsylvanian seas that covered much of midcontinental North America.

PENTREMITES

Pentremites was an extinct genus of stemmed, immobile echinoderms (forms related to the starfish) abundant as marine fossils in rocks of the Carboniferous Period, especially those in the midcontinent region of North America. The genus is mainly restricted to the Early Carboniferous Period (359 million to 318 million years ago). More than 80 species are known. Specimens are frequently well preserved, allowing detailed anatomical and evolutionary studies.

PHILLIPSIA

Phillipsia is a genus of trilobites uncommonly found as fossils in Carboniferous and Permian rocks (359 million to 251 million years old) in Europe, North America, and the Far East. One of the last known trilobite genera, *Phillipsia* is characterized by a relatively large head region and a large posterior region. Some forms are characterized by an unusual development of small surface nodes.

PLATYCRINITES

Platycrinites, a genus of extinct crinoids, or sea lilies, is especially characteristic as fossils of Early Carboniferous marine deposits (359 million to 318 million years ago). *Platycrinites,* of moderate size, had a columnar stem with a twisted pattern, an unusual feature.

SEED FERNS

Seed ferns are loose confederations of seed plants from the Carboniferous and Permian periods (about 359 million to 251 million years ago). Some, such as *Medullosa*, grew as upright, unbranched woody trunks topped with a crown of large fernlike fronds. Others, such as *Callistophyton*, were woody vines. All had fernlike foliage. However, they reproduced by seeds, with ovules and pollen organs attached to the fronds. Gamete-producing structures in the seeds were surrounded by a hard inner integument and a fleshy outer layer. These features have led some authorities to speculate that these seeds may have been dispersed by animals. Some seeds were large. (*Pachytesta gigantea*, a

Loose amalgamations of seed plants with fernlike foliage from the Carboniferous and Permian periods, seed ferns reproduced by seeds and their structure suggests to some experts that the seeds may have been scattered by animals. Ken Lucas/Visuals Unlimited/Getty Images

seed of *Medullosa*, grew up to 7 centimetres [2.7 inches] long.) Pollen organs of seed ferns were also large and complex and were commonly made up of many pollen sacs fused into a large structure. Some authorities suggest that these large structures and the large pollen grains they contained were evidence of pollination by animals.

SIGILLARIA

An extinct genus of tree-sized lycopsids from the Carboniferous Period, *Sigillaria* is related to modern club mosses. It had a single or sparsely branched trunk characterized by a slender strand of wood and thick bark. Long, thin leaves grew in a spiral along the trunk but persisted only near its growing tip. On lower portions of the plant where the leaves had fallen off, characteristic polygonal leaf scars remained. *Sigillaria* reproduced by spores of two distinct sizes. The larger megaspores produced egg cells, whereas the smaller microspores produced sperm cells. *Sigillaria* appears to have preferred mineral soils of river floodplains, in contrast to its relative, *Lepidodendron*, which grew in peat-forming swamps. This preference for better-drained soils may have allowed *Sigillaria* to survive the drying of the great coal swamps that led to the extinction of many tree-sized lycopsids during the middle of the Pennsylvanian Subperiod (318 to 299 million years ago).

WEDEKINDELLINA

Wedekindellina is a genus of fusulinid foraminiferans, an extinct group of protozoans that possessed a hard shell of relatively large size. They are especially characteristic as fossils in deposits from the Pennsylvanian Subperiod (318 million to 299 million years ago) of midcontinental

North America. The several species that are known serve as excellent guide, or index, fossils and enable Late Carboniferous time and rocks to be divided into smaller units.

CARBONIFEROUS GEOLOGY

The Carboniferous Period was a time of highly variable depositional settings. The many and varied types of life forms that existed during the Carboniferous Period were characterized by both shallow marine and continental environments. In the Northern Hemisphere, the Lower Carboniferous (Mississippian time) is typified by shallow-water limestones, while the Upper Carboniferous (Pennsylvanian time) possesses cyclical sedimentary deposits that reflect an alternation of marine and nonmarine conditions and a frequent occurrence of coal swamps. In contrast, the Southern Hemisphere experienced widespread continental glaciations during much of these same intervals.

Plants and animals were diverse during the Carboniferous and had a decisive effect on the accumulation of sedimentary materials. Most Mississippian limestones are composed of the disarticulated remains of stalked echinoderms known as crinoids. Bryozoans (small colonial animals that produce a skeletal framework of calcium carbonate) and brachiopods were also both common and diverse during this time. Coals and the associated rock strata of the Pennsylvanian subperiod contain abundant remains of unusual vascular plants, such as the sphenopsids, lycopods (or lycopsids), and seed ferns. More coal was formed during Pennsylvanian times than at any other time in the entire geologic record. In the Southern Hemisphere a cold-climate flora, typified by seed ferns, dominated upland environments and became a source of coal deposits as well. Amphibians, which appeared in the Devonian Period, were joined on land by a great variety of insects. In addition, the first reptiles appeared in the late portion of the Pennsylvanian.

Pulses of orogenic activity occurred in the Cordilleran (Rocky Mountain) region of North America, in the Hercynides and Ural Mountains of Europe, and in Asia and Africa. The preservation of these physical and biological events is one of the most extensive in the entire Phanerozoic record, and Carboniferous strata are well exposed on all continents.

SIGNIFICANT GEOLOGIC EVENTS

The Carboniferous was a time of relative continental stability. Continental margins, and some continental interiors, such as that of North America, were covered by shallow, epicontinental seas that resulted in the development of the most extensive carbonates since those occurring in the lower latitudes of the Ordovician Period. No mountain building is associated with the Mississippian, but the isostasy following the orogenies that closed the Devonian Period certainly affected the continental blocks of Laurussia and Gondwana.

Widespread continental ice sheets had developed in Gondwana to the point that their expansion and contraction began to drive the rise and fall of sea level, producing cyclic depositions that characterize the later part of the Carboniferous. A major drop in sea level produced the unconformity (an interruption in the deposition of sedimentary rock) at the Mississippian-Pennsylvanian boundary and an associated global extinction event, particularly among the crinoids and ammonoid cephalopods. The Pennsylvanian record reflects the continued

Gondwanan glaciations, which produced the extensive coal cyclothems (repeated sequences of distinctive sedimentary rock layers) throughout the Northern Hemisphere. These cyclothems produced the most extensive coal deposits in the entire geologic record. The Pennsylvanian concludes with the Ouachita-Alleghenian-Herycnian orogeny, which developed mountains through the collision of the major landmasses of Laurussia and Gondwana.

The movement of Gondwana toward the paleoequator closed the remaining salient of the Tethys Sea and formed the Ouachita Mountains (Arkansas, Oklahoma, Texas), southern Appalachians (southeastern United States), Hercynide Mountains (southern Europe), and Mauritanide Mountains (northern Africa). These events continued the creation of a supercontinent, Pangea, that would finally end in the Permian Period.

Less-significant orogenic events occurred in the Cordilleran region of present-day North and South America with a pulse of the Antler orogeny that elevated the ancestral Rocky Mountains, precordilleran movements in western South America, and similar tectonism in northern Asia (as in the Tien Shan and Kunlun ranges), Australia, and New Zealand. The ancestral Ural Mountains also date from this time.

THE MAJOR SUBDIVISIONS OF THE CARBONIFEROUS SYSTEM

The Carboniferous System is divided into two subsystems—the Mississippian and Pennsylvanian—and seven depositional stages that also correspond to time units (ages) of the same name. The Mississippian subsystem is made up of the Tournasian (359.2 to 345.3 million years ago), Viséan (345.3 to 328.3 million years ago), and

Serpukhovian (32 8.3 to 318.1 million years ago) stages. The Bashkirian (318.1 to 311.7 million years ago), Moscovian (311.7 to 307.2 million years ago), Kasimovian (307.2 to 303.4 million years ago), and Gzhelian (303.4 to 299 million years ago) stages make up the Pennsylvanian subsystem.

THE ECONOMIC SIGNIFICANCE OF CARBONIFEROUS DEPOSITS

Most of the great coal basins of the world are of Carboniferous age. These include the famous coal basins of central and eastern North America, England, western and eastern Europe, Russia, Ukraine, China, and Australia. Coal powered the Industrial Revolution, and mining has exploited coal in most of these regions for more than 200 years. In addition, major accumulations of natural gas and liquid petroleum are associated with the strata of the Carboniferous Period throughout the Northern Hemisphere. Furthermore, where Carboniferous strata (both limestones and sandstones) occur near the surface, they are utilized for high-quality building stone and aggregate for the manufacture of concrete and asphalt. Other commercially valuable materials derived from Carboniferous rocks include fertilizer and refractory clays and gypsum.

THE OCCURRENCE AND DISTRIBUTION OF CARBONIFEROUS DEPOSITS

The Mississippian is characterized by shallow-water limestones deposited on broad shelves occupying most continental interiors, particularly in the Northern Hemisphere. Turbidite facies, deep-water sandstones, and shales deposited as submarine fans by ocean floor currents formed in deeper troughs (geosynclines) along continental margins. Terrigenous clastic facies (sedimentary rock exposures composed of fragments of older rocks), such as sandstone and shale, are more poorly developed during this time, and coals are rare. The Southern Hemisphere preserved a similar record of carbonates until, during the later portion of the Mississippian, cold-water conditions prevailed and terrigenous clastics predominated.

The Pennsylvanian strata of the Northern Hemisphere are characterized by cyclothemic deposits reflecting the alternating advance and retreat of shallow seas into continental interiors. These widespread deposits included both terrigenous clastics and limestones. Nonmarine strata typically became coal beds, and Pennsylvanian cyclothems contain the major portion of world coal reserves. Oceanic troughs continued to receive clastic facies, particularly turbidites (sedimentary rock formed by a turbidity current), and pulses of mountain-building began to markedly affect the depositional sequences and their thicknesses. In the Southern Hemisphere, glacial deposits reflecting the Gondwanan continental glaciation were common, although shelf deposits of terrigenous clastics and even limestones were present in some areas. All Gondwanan strata reflect cold-water conditions. The sections below will go into greater detail on the makeup of Mississippian and Pennsylvanian deposits.

MISSISSIPPIAN LIMESTONES

Mississippian limestones are composed of the disarticulated remains of crinoids. Upon their death, the plates of individual crinoids accumulated as sand-sized sediment on the seafloor to be cemented later by calcium carbonate. Crinoid fragments were frequently reworked by currents, and their associated deposits exhibit both crossbedding and ripple marks. Deposits of crinoidal limestone approaching 150 metres (500 feet) are not uncommon in intervals of Mississippian age, particularly in North America, and they are exploited as quarry stone. In addition to the crinoidal limestones, oolitic limestones and lime mudstones also formed in shallow-water marine environments of the Mississippian. Ooliths are concentric spheres of calcium carbonate inorganically precipitated around a nucleus. They were deposited on warm marine shelf margins receiving high wave energy similar to the present-day Bahama Shelf and northern Red Sea. These deposits also exhibit cross-bedding and ripple marks reflective of high-energy conditions. Mixtures of ooliths and abraded fossil fragments, particularly foraminifers (pseudopod-using unicellular organisms protected by a test or shell), are common in the Mississippian strata.

Lime mudstones reflect quiet shallow-water environments, such as are found in Florida Bay and on the west side of Andros Island, Bahamas, that may have been exposed by tidal change. The carbonate mud was produced through the life cycle of green algae, but fossils are not particularly common in these lithologies. Deposits of these Mississippian limestones are frequently used as quarry stones as well. In the upper portion of the Mississippian, marine cycles are developed, probably reflecting the beginning of mountain building in the Appalachian region of eastern North America. Quartz sandstones typically began each of these cycles as the seas transgressed across the continental interiors. Shales may have succeeded the sandstones and were followed by limestone development reflecting the clearance of the water and the establishment of carbonate production by animals and plants.

Limestones of Mississippian age are typically associated with lenses and beds of chert (silicon dioxide). The origin of this chert is somewhat uncertain, but it appears to reflect either primary or secondary origin. Chert of both origins may occur within a single limestone unit but reflect different times of silicification. Primary cherts formed penecontemporaneously (with small folds and faults) with deposition of the limestones in slightly deeper water settings. Secondary chert formed as a later replacement by groundwater usually involving shallower water deposits. Penecontemporaneous cherts are frequently dark coloured (flint) and disrupt the bedding rather than follow it. They usually lack fossils. Later chert is light coloured, follows the bedding, and is usually fossiliferous.

Deeper, intracontinental basins and deep ocean troughs (geosynclines) are characterized by Mississippian terrigenous clastics deposited as turbidites.

PENNSYLVANIAN CYCLOTHEMS, TILLITES, AND TURBIDITES

Cyclothems occur on a worldwide basis throughout Pennsylvanian strata. However, they have been most widely studied in North America. The cyclothems display one of two types of development. In the eastern interior of North America, where they were first studied, one cyclothem may consist of as many as 10 separate beds reflecting a single advance and retreat by shallow seas. The lower portion of the cyclothem is predominantly nonmarine and consists of (in ascending order) a sandstone, shale, "freshwater" limestone, underclay (buried soil), and a coal bed. The upper portion of the cyclothem reflects marine conditions and exhibits alternating shale and limestone beds, both of which usually contain fossils. The nonmarine sequence probably represents deltaic conditions associated with the regression that allowed swamp conditions to develop on a delta plain. Marine transgression began with the shale beds overlying the coal. Rapid retreat ends each cycle, which is capped by an unconformity. Most cyclothems are incomplete. They do not exhibit the full sequence of beds.

Cyclothems of the Appalachian Basin coal fields in Ohio, Pennsylvania, and West Virginia typically have good representation of the nonmarine portion of the sequence with thick coals. These coals formed from the carbonization of plant debris, and it is generally held that 1 metre (3.3 feet) of coal equals the compaction of approximately five times as much plant material. Some coals exhibit remarkable thicknesses. The Mammoth coal bed of the Anthracite Belt in eastern Pennsylvanian has an average thickness of 10–12 metres (35–40 feet) throughout its extent. The Pittsburgh seam in western Pennsylvania averages 4 metres (13 feet) thick and is reported workable over 15,540 square kilometres (6,000 square miles). More than 60 coal seams have been identified in Pennsylvania, although only about 10 have ever been exploited. Coeval cyclothems in the western midcontinent have better development of the marine portion of the sequence with fewer and thinner coals.

In contrast to the coal cyclothems, predominantly marine intervals of Pennsylvanian age in the western midcontinent (Kansas, Iowa, and Missouri) exhibit cyclothems involving alternations of limestone and shale. These cyclothems also reflect transgression and regression by shallow seas, but the lower portion of the cycle is the transgressive event, followed by regression in the upper part. The cyclothem begins with a sandy shale containing marine fossils. It is succeeded by dark, carbonate mudstones that are, in turn, overlain by black shale. The black shale marks the maximum marine transgression. Above the black shale, marine carbonate mudstones and grainstones occur, followed by a return to sandy shale. One striking feature of both coal and marine cyclothems is the tremendous lateral persistency of beds within the sequence. Tracing of a single bed from outcrop to outcrop over a distance of hundreds of kilometres is not uncommon in the midcontinent.

Depositional cycles similar to those of eastern North America can be recognized in Europe, but distribution of those sediments is confined to small isolated basins instead of a broad cratonic shelf. Nonmarine sequences predominate, and indeed some sequences exhibit no marine influence at all. Positioning of the basins is the result of folding and faulting reflective of the mountain-building of the Hercynian orogenic belt. The Middle and Upper Carboniferous record of western Russia and Ukraine is similar to that of North America.

In the Southern Hemisphere, there is a marked cooling event beginning near the boundary separating the Mississippian and Pennsylvanian subperiods. Faunas and floras after that time are highly provincial, impoverished, and adapted to the cold climates that persisted into the Permian Period. Pennsylvanian glacial deposits of the Gondwana Realm are characterized by tillites resting on polished and striated bedrock surfaces. Striated cobbles, glacio-fluvial deposits, and varved (deposited in still water) lacustrine (lake) sediments occur over large areas of present-day South America, Africa, India, Australia, and Antarctica. The extensive development of these unusual deposits has been used to support the theory of continental drift. The timing of these glacial episodes is still uncertain, and they may have actually begun during Mississippian times. Furthermore, many glacial advances and retreats occurred that were not necessarily simultaneous over the whole of Gondwana.

Areas marginal to continental masses continued to receive turbidites, particularly in the Ouachita-Marathon region of Arkansas, Oklahoma, and Texas and the Cordilleran geosyncline in the western United States. Evaporites formed in restricted basins, such as those in Montana-North Dakota (Williston) and the Four Corners area in Utah-Colorado (Paradox Basin), that lay near the Pennsylvanian paleoequator. Igneous and metamorphic rocks of Pennsylvanian age reflect the Hercynian orogeny and its equivalents in North America, Europe, and North Africa.

THE CORRELATION OF CARBONIFEROUS STRATA

The type of regions characterizing the subperiods of the Carboniferous Period lie within the eastern United States. Mississippian rocks generally occur in formations throughout the valley of the Mississippi River and its tributaries, whereas Pennsylvanian rocks generally occur in Pennsylvania and its adjacent states. In the western United States, rocks of both subperiods appear in the Grand Canyon and Rocky Mountain regions. Examples of Mississippian and Pennsylvanian rocks also occur in several locations in Europe.

MISSISSIPPIAN SUBSYSTEM

The type region for the Mississippian Subsystem lies in the central Mississippi Valley of the United States. Most of the formations representing the type sequence are found in Missouri, Iowa, and Illinois. The Kinderhookian Series includes the Hannibal Formation and the Chouteau Group. It is succeeded by the Osagean Series, which includes the Burlington Limestone and overlying Keokuk Limestone. The Meramecan and Chesterian series overlie previous layers. Other well-known Mississippian units in North America include: the Pocono Group and Mauch Chunk Shale of the Appalachian region; Fort Payne Chert of

Tennessee and Alabama; the Caney and Goddard shales of the Arbuckle region, Oklahoma; the Stanley Shale of the Ouachita Mountains of Arkansas and Oklahoma; the Madison Group and Big Snowy Groups of the northern Rocky Mountains; Redwall Limestone of the Grand Canyon region; and the Lisburne Group of the Brooks Range of northern Alaska.

Mississippian units exposed at the famous Avon Gorge section at Bristol, Eng., include (in ascending order): Shirehampton beds, Lower Limestone Shale, Black Rock Limestone, Gully Oolite, Clifton Down Mudstone, Goblin Combe Oolite, Clifton Down Limestone, Hotwells Limestone, and the Upper Cromhall Sandstone. Other well-known Mississippian formations outside North America include: limestones at Waulsort and the Black Marble of Dinant, Belg.; Montagne-Noire of the French Massif; and limestones in Spain, the Ural Mountains, the Moscow Basin in Russia, and the Donets Basin of Ukraine.

PENNSYLVANIAN SUBSYSTEM

The type region for the Pennsylvanian Subsystem is located in central West Virginia. There the interval is represented by the following groups or formations (ascending order): Pocahontas, New River, Kanawha, Charleston Sandstone, Conemaugh, Monongahela, and basal Dunkard. Other well-known Pennsylvanian units in North America include: the Jackfork and Johns Valley shales of Oklahoma and Arkansas; the Atoka Formation of Arkansas and Oklahoma; the Supai Group of the Grand Canyon region; the Amsden and Tensleep formations of the northern Rocky Mountains; Fountain Arkose of the central Rocky Mountains; and the Haymond and Gaptank formations of the Marathon region, west Texas. Major coal fields in the United States include the Appalachian region (Pennsylvania, West Virginia, and Ohio), Illinois Basin, midcontinent region

(Iowa, Missouri, and Kansas), Arkoma Basin (Arkansas and Oklahoma), and north-central Texas.

The Pennsylvanian part of the type Carboniferous in Great Britain includes the Millstone Grit and the Coal Measures—names in use since the naming of the system. Local names are applied to specific intervals, and marine horizons, called bands, are named either for their characteristic fossil occurrence (i.e., Listeri Marine Band) or for a geographic locality (i.e., Sutton Marine Band). This process is followed in most areas outside North America. Major Pennsylvanian coal fields occur throughout Europe, especially in the central Pennines (Lancashire coal basin), Scottish border, southern Wales, Great Britain; Franco-Belgian Basin, northern France; Saar-Lorraine Basin, border of France and Germany; central French Massif (St. Etienne and Gard coal basins); Ruhr and Westphalian basins, Germany; Silesian Basin, Poland; Moscow Basin, Russia; and Donets Basin in Ukraine.

STAGES OF THE CARBONIFEROUS PERIOD

The Carboniferous is divided into seven rock stages. The first three stages make up the Mississippian Subperiod, and the final four stages make up the Pennsylvanian Subperiod. Below, information pertaining to each rock stage follows a brief description of the subperiod containing it.

MISSISSIPPIAN SUBPERIOD

The Mississippian is the first major subdivision of the Carboniferous Period, lasting from 359.2 to 318.1 million years ago. As previously mentioned, it is characterized by shallow-water limestone deposits occupying the interiors of continents, especially in the Northern Hemisphere. These limestones exhibit a change from calcite-dominated grains and cements to aragonite-dominated ones. This change is reflective of an increase in the ratio of magnesium to calcium in seawater due to decreased rates of seafloor spreading. During this time, sea level began a cyclic retreat from the continental interiors that would end in a worldwide lowstand at the Mississippian–Pennsylvanian boundary. The Mississippian Subperiod is also recognized as the interval in which armoured fishes, plentiful during the Devonian Period (416 to 359.2 million years ago), went largely extinct.

TOURNAISIAN STAGE

The lowest and first of three intercontinental stages of the Mississippian Subsystem, Carboniferous System, the Tournaisian Stage encompasses all rocks deposited during the Tournaisian Age (359.2 to 345.3 million years ago). The name is derived from exposures of fine-grained limestone with shaly intervals surrounding the town of Tournai in southwestern Belgium, near the French border.

By international agreement, the coterminous bases of the Carboniferous, the Mississippian, and the Tournaisian stages are drawn at the first appearance of the conodont (primitive chordate with tooth-shaped fossil remains) *Siphonodella sulcata* in sequence with its evolutionary precursor *S. praesulcata*. This horizon is also about the level of the appearance of the ammonoid *Gattendorfia*. Ratified by the International Commission on Stratigraphy (ICS) in 1990, the Global Stratotype Section and Point for that horizon has been selected at the base of bed 89 in the La Serre section, Montagne Noire, of southern France. This horizon can also be recognized by appearances of ammonoids, smaller calcareous foraminifers (pseudopod-using unicellular organisms protected by a test or shell), and palynomorphs (microfossils composed of microscopic remains of plant and animal structures).

The top of the Tournaisian is characterized by the base of the Viséan Stage, currently indicated by the first appearance of the foraminifer *Eoparastaffella simplex*, which occurs very close to the first appearance of the conodont *Gnathodus homopunctatus* in the fossil record. The Tournaisian overlays the Famennian Stage of the Devonian Period.

VISÉAN STAGE

The Viséan Stage is the second of three internationally defined stages of the Mississippian Subsystem, Carboniferous System. It contains all rocks deposited during the Viséan Age (345.3 to 328.3 million years ago). The name is derived from the town of Visé in eastern Belgium on its border with The Netherlands, although most of the understanding of the stage comes from exposures surrounding the town of Dinant, Belg. There the base of the Viséan is placed at the lowest marbre noir, a black limestone facies with few macrofossils. The base of the Viséan has been historically characterized by the first appearance of the conodont *Gnathodus homopunctatus* in the fossil record. However, the primary tool used to identify the boundary between the Viséan and the Tournaisian stages is the first appearance of the foraminifer (a pseudopod-using unicellular organism protected by a test or shell) *Eoparastaffella simplex*. The ICS has proposed that the Global Standard Section and Point (GSSP) for the base of this stage be located in the Penchong section of Guangxi province in southern China.

The Viséan Stage overlies the Tournaisian Stage of the Mississippian Subsystem. The top of the Viséan and the bottom of the overlying Serpukhovian Stage are currently undefined but are roughly approximated near the first appearance of the conodont *Lochriea ziegleri*. There is increasing evidence that the boundary between the Viséan and Serpukhovian Stages corresponds to a major episode of glaciation in the ancient supercontinent of Gondwana. Recognition of the Viséan Stage by other fossil groups is somewhat problematic, and there is no international agreement on the biostratigraphic horizons defining its boundaries.

SERPUKHOVIAN STAGE

The Serpukhovian Stage is the third of three internationally defined stages of the Mississippian Subsystem, Carboniferous System, accounting for all rocks deposited during the Serpukhovian Age (328.3 to 318.1 million years ago). The Serpukhovian is the shortest of the Carboniferous stages. The name is derived from the Russian city of Serpukhov, near Moscow in the Moscow Basin—although the type section is not complete there, and the principal reference exposures are in the Russian Ural Mountains. Serpukhovian strata yield abundant and varied fossil assemblages that have been studied extensively in Russia.

Currently the base of the Serpukhovian is roughly approximated near the first appearance of the conodont *Lochriea ziegleri*. This falls at a horizon that matches the base of the Namurian Series of rocks in western Europe and is above the base of the Chesterian Series in North America. The base of the stage in the Moscow Basin relates to the appearance of the foraminiferans *Pseudoendothyra globosa* and *Neoarchaediscus parvus*. The top of the Serpukhovian is overlain by the Bashkirian Stage of the Pennsylvanian Subsystem and corresponds to the internationally accepted boundary drawn at the appearance of the conodont *Declinognathodus noduliferus*. The boundary also reflects a significant drop in global sea level, which was produced by extensive glaciation on the ancient supercontinent of Gondwana.

Pennsylvanian Subperiod

The Pennsylvanian Subperiod is the second major interval of the Carboniferous Period, lasting from 318.1 to 299 million years ago. The Pennsylvanian is recognized as a time of significant advance and retreat by shallow seas. Many nonmarine areas near the Equator became coal swamps during the Pennsylvanian. These areas are mined for coal today.

Bashkirian Stage

The first of four internationally defined stages of the Pennsylvanian Subsystem, Carboniferous System, the Bashkirian Stage contains all rocks deposited during the Bashkirian Age (318.1 to 311.7 million years ago). The name is derived from Gornaya Bashkiriya in the southern Ural Mountains of Russia.

The base of the Bashkirian Stage is defined to correspond to the internationally accepted Mississippian-Pennsylvanian boundary, drawn at the appearance of the conodont *Declinognathodus noduliferus*. The ICS has located the GSSP for the base of Bashkirian Stage, and thus the Pennsylvanian Subsystem, at Arrow Canyon near Las Vegas in the southwestern United States. The stage can be recognized and subdivided readily by calcareous foraminiferans, ammonoid cephalopods, conodonts, and palynomorphs (microfossils composed of tiny remnants of plant and animal structures) on a worldwide basis.

A definition for the top of the Bashkirian Stage is currently being evaluated. It appears to be coincident with the appearance of the conodonts *Idiognathoides postsulcatus* and *Declinognathus donetzianus* and advanced forms of *Neognathodus nataliae*. The Bashkirian Stage overlies the Serpukhovian Stage of the Mississippian Subsystem and is itself overlain by the Moscovian Stage of the Pennsylvanian Subsystem.

MOSCOVIAN STAGE

This stage is the second of four internationally defined stages of the Pennsylvanian Subsystem, Carboniferous System. It encompasses all rocks deposited during the Moscovian Age (311.7 to 307.2 million years ago). The name is taken from exposures in the Moscow Basin, Russia. There the section is dominated by fossiliferous limestones and dolomites, although thin intercalated shales and sandstones also occur.

In the Moscow Basin, the base of the Moscovian Stage is indicated by the appearance of the calcareous fusulinid foraminiferan *Aljutovella aljutovica* and the conodont *Declinognathus donetzianus*. On the Russian Platform and in the Ural Mountains, however, the ammonoid *Winslowoceras* is used to define the stage. The Moscovian Stage overlies the Bashkirian Stage and underlies the Kasimovian Stage of the Pennsylvanian Subsystem.

KASIMOVIAN STAGE

The third of four internationally defined stages of the Pennsylvanian Subsystem, Carboniferous System, the Kasimovian Stage is made up of all rocks deposited during the Kasimovian Age (307.2 to 303.4 million years ago). The name is taken from the Russian city of Kasimov, which lies east of Moscow in the Moscow Basin. The section is cyclic but consists mainly of limestones and dolomitic mudstones with intercalated siltstones.

The base of the stage is historically defined by the appearance of the advanced fusulinids *Protriticites pseudomontiparus* and *Obsoletes obsoletus*, with the ammonoid zone defined by the genus *Parashumardites*. This layer appears to correspond to the Westphalian-Stephanian Series boundary of western Europe and the Desmoinesian-Missourian boundary in the midcontinent of North

America. The ICS has not yet established a GSSP for correlation at the base of this stage. The Kasimovian Stage is underlain by the Moscovian Stage and overlain by the Gzhelian Stage of the Pennsylvanian Subsystem.

GZHELIAN STAGE

The Gzhelian Stage, also spelled Gzelian, is the last of four internationally defined stages of the Pennsylvanian Subsystem, Carboniferous System. It contains all rocks deposited during the Gzhelian Age (303.4 to 299 million years ago). The name is taken from the Russian city of Gzhel, which lies just southeast of Moscow in the Moscow Basin. Gzhelian strata are cyclic but consist mainly of dolomite, dolomitic marls, and intercalated siltstones.

The base of the stage has been historically drawn at the appearance of the advanced fusulinid (single-celled amoeba-like organisms with complex shells) species *Rauserites rossicus, R. stuckenbergi, Jigulites jigulensis*, and *Daixina sokensis*. However, working groups of the ICS now believe that using the first appearances of the conodont *Idiognathodus simulator* is more useful for the global correlation of basal Gzhelian strata. To date, no Global Stratotype Section and Point (GSSP) section for the base of this stage has been submitted to the ICS.

In contrast, the top of the Gzhelian, and thus the Carboniferous-Permian boundary, has been demarcated by a GSSP at the Aidaralash Creek section in northern Kazakhstan. This section was ratified by the ICS in 1996. The Gzhelian Stage lies above the Kasimovian Stage of the Pennsylvanian Subsystem, Carboniferous System, and is overlain by the Asselian Stage of the Permian System.

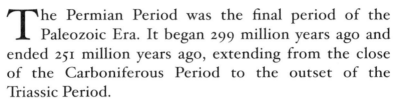

CHAPTER 7

THE PERMIAN PERIOD

The Permian Period was the final period of the Paleozoic Era. It began 299 million years ago and ended 251 million years ago, extending from the close of the Carboniferous Period to the outset of the Triassic Period.

At the beginning of the period, glaciation was widespread, and latitudinal climatic belts were strongly developed. Climate warmed throughout the Permian times, and, by the end of the period, hot and dry conditions were so extensive that they caused a crisis in Permian marine and terrestrial life. This dramatic climatic shift may have been partially triggered by the assembly of smaller continents into the supercontinent of Pangea, into which most of Earth's land area was consolidated.

Terrestrial plants broadly diversified during the Permian Period, and insects evolved rapidly as they followed the plants into new habitats. In addition, several important reptile lineages first appeared during this period, including those that eventually gave rise to mammals in the Mesozoic Era. The largest mass extinction in the Earth's history occurred during the latter part of the Permian Period. This mass extinction was so severe that only 10 percent or fewer of the species present during the time of maximum biodiversity in the Permian survived to the end of the period.

Permian rocks are found on all present-day continents. However, some have been displaced considerable distances from their original latitudes of deposition by tectonic transport occurring during the Mesozoic and Cenozoic eras. Some beds dated from the latest Permian ages are renowned for their fossils. Strata (rock layers) in the Russian Platform contain a remarkable vertebrate faunal assemblage as well as fossil insects and plants.

The Permian Period derives its name from the Russian region of Perm, where rocks deposited during this time are particularly well developed.

THE PERMIAN ENVIRONMENT

The Permian Period constitutes an important crossroads both in the history of the Earth's continents and in the evolution of life. The principal geographic features of the Permian world were a supercontinent, Pangea, and a huge ocean basin, Panthalassa, with its branch, the Tethys Sea (a large indentation in the tropical eastern side of Pangea).

PALEOGEOGRAPHY

During the Early Permian (Cisuralian) Epoch, northwestern Gondwana collided with and joined southern Laurussia (a craton also known as Euramerica). This resulted in the Alleghenian orogeny, occurring in the region that would become North America, and the continuance of the Hercynian orogeny, its northwestern European counterpart. The assembly of Pangea was complete by the middle of the Early Permian Epoch following its fusion to Angara (part of the Siberian craton) during the Uralian orogeny.

On the periphery of Pangea was Cathaysia, a region extending beyond the eastern edge of Angara and comprising the landmasses of both North and South China. Cathaysia lay within the western Panthalassic Ocean and at

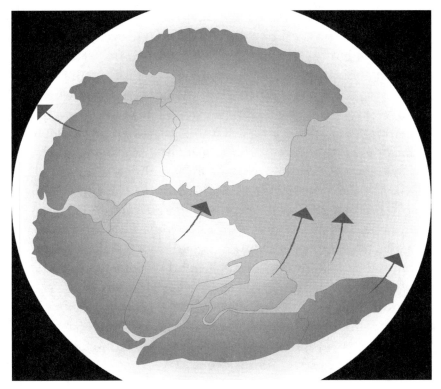

Earth's continental drift is substantiated by distribution of glacial deposits, plants, and mesosaurs. De Agostini/Getty Images

the eastern end of Tethys (sometimes called Paleotethys) Sea. The Panthalassa and Tethys also contained scattered fragments of continental crust (microcontinents), basaltic volcanic island arcs, oceanic plateaus, and trenches. The island arcs featured extensive fringing limestone reefs and platforms that were subsequently displaced by seafloor spreading. These isolated landmasses were later welded onto the margins of Pangea, forming accreted terranes.

Evidence of sea-level rise and fall is well displayed in Permian strata. Fluctuations in sea level are often associated with changes in climate. Some fluctuations with large magnitudes and short durations, such as near the base of the Permian Period, are likely the result of glaciation. For others, the possibility that Milankovitch cycles (adjustments in Earth's axis and the long-term orbital patterns of Earth about the Sun) directly affect sea level is still being investigated, though their periodic occurrence has been linked to episodes of glaciation. Global sea-level events are marked by four long lowstands (times when sea level falls below the level of the continental shelf) within the Early Permian Epoch, a major lowstand near the base of the Middle Permian (Guadalupian) Epoch, and four long lowstands within and at the top of the Middle Permian Epoch. Lowstands are also recorded at various times within the Late Permian (Lopingian) Epoch and at the terminus of the Permian Period. Extended global withdrawal of seas from continental shelves and platforms led to significant unconformities (gaps in the geologic record) and to extensive evolutionary turnovers (events of species diversification and extinction) in shallow marine faunas at the family and superfamily levels.

PALEOCLIMATE

The assembly of the various large landmasses into the supercontinent of Pangea led to global warming and the development of dry to arid climates during Permian times. As low-latitude seaways closed, warm surface ocean currents were deflected into much higher latitudes (areas closer to the poles), and cool-water upwelling developed along the west coast of Pangea. Extensive mountain-building events occurred where landmasses collided, and the newly created high mountain ranges strongly influenced local and regional terrestrial climates.

Extensive glaciation persisted from the Carboniferous Period into the initial stage of the Early Permian Epoch over vast areas of present-day southern India, Australia, Antarctica, and northeastern Siberia. Middle Permian climates generally were warmer and moist. Climates of the Late Permian (Lopingian) Epoch were typically hot and locally very dry. Deserts became widespread in various tropical and subtropical areas during this time.

The orogenies that marked the assembly of Pangea strongly influenced both climate and life. East-west atmospheric flow in the temperate and higher latitudes was disrupted by two high mountain chains—one in the tropics oriented east-west and one running north-south—that diverted warm marine air into higher latitudes. The continental collisions also closed various earlier marine seaways and isolated parts of the tropical shallow-water realms that were home to marine invertebrates. These realms eventually became endemic (regionally restricted) biological provinces.

Volcanism may have strongly influenced climate at the end of the Permian Period. Extensive Siberian flood basalts (the Siberian traps) in northeastern Siberia and adjacent western China erupted about 250 million years ago and for about 600,000 years extruded 2,000,000 to 3,000,000 cubic kilometres (480,000 to 720,000 cubic miles) of basalt. These eruptions contributed great amounts of volcanic ash to the atmosphere, probably darkening the skies and lowering the efficiency of plants in taking up carbon dioxide from the atmosphere during photosynthesis.

PERMIAN LIFE

Life during the Permian Period was very diverse—the marine life of the period was perhaps more diverse than that of modern times. The gradual climatic warming that took place during the Early Permian (Cisuralian) Epoch encouraged great evolutionary expansion (diversification) among both marine and terrestrial faunas that had survived the relatively cold conditions of the Carboniferous Period. Many lineages entering Early Permian times with only a few species and genera progressively diversified into new families and superfamilies as the climate warmed. Communities became increasingly complex, and generic diversity (diversity of organisms at genus level) increased through the midpoint of the Middle Permian (Guadalupian) Epoch. Within the tropical shallow-water marine communities, significant environmental changes occurring at the end of the Middle Permian Epoch were so abrupt that many groups became extinct, and only a few of the remaining groups survived into the Late Permian (Lopingian) Epoch.

Terrestrial life in Permian times was closely keyed to the evolution of terrestrial plants, which were the primary food source for land animals. The fossil plant record for the Early Permian Epoch consists predominantly of ferns, seed ferns, and lycophytes (a group of vascular plants containing club mosses and scale trees), which were adapted to marshes and swampy environments. A less abundant Middle and Late Permian fossil record of early coniferophytes (a group of vascular plants containing cycads, ginkoes, and gnetophytes) and protoangiosperms (precursors to flowering plants) suggests a broad adaptation of these plant groups to progressively drier areas.

Evidence of broad plant diversification also is found in the rapid evolution of insects, which quickly followed plants into new habitats. As these insects adapted to their new surroundings and formed very specialized associations with plants, many new species emerged. Permian insects included at least 23 orders, 11 of which are now extinct.

THE EMERGENCE OF IMPORTANT REPTILES

Several important reptile lineages, which descended from several orders of relatively large amphibians, first appeared during the Permian Period. Although a few primitive and generalized reptile fossils are found in Carboniferous deposits, Permian reptile fossils are common in certain locations. They include the protorosaurs, aquatic reptiles ancestral to archosaurs (dinosaurs, crocodiles, and birds) and the captorhinomorphs, "stem reptiles" from which most other reptiles are thought to have evolved. They also include eosuchians, early ancestors of the snakes and lizards; and early anapsids, ancestors of turtles. Early archosaurs, ancestors of the large ruling reptiles of the Mesozoic, and synapsids, a common and varied group of mammal-like reptiles that eventually gave rise to mammals in the Mesozoic are also common finds in rocks laid down during this period.

Captorhinomorphs are common in Lower Permian beds of North America and Europe. Massively built and large for their day, they reached lengths of 2 to 3 metres (about 7 to 10 feet). Captorhinomorphs are less common in Upper Permian beds, and only one small group survived into the Triassic Period.

Synapsids (mammal-like reptiles) are divided into two orders: pelycosaurs and therapsids. They show a remarkably complete transition in skeletal features from typical early reptiles (Early Permian Epoch) into true mammals (in the Middle and Late Triassic epochs) through a fossil record lasting about 80 million years. The Early Permian pelycosaurs included carnivores and herbivores that developed long spines on their vertebrae that supported a membrane, or "sail." Pelycosaurs reached 3.5 metres (about 11.5 feet) in length and had large, differentiated teeth. Their remains are common in the Lower Permian red beds of central Texas in North America but are rare in Europe.

Therapsids were advanced synapsids known from the Middle and Upper Permian and Triassic Karoo beds of South Africa and equivalent beds in South America, India, Scotland, and Russia. Therapsids were highly diversified and had remarkably mammal-like dentition and bone structure. Their skeletal structures merge with early mammals with no apparent morphological breaks. The point at which mammal-like reptiles pass into mammals is generally placed at forms with cheek teeth having only two roots instead of three. The success of therapsids in the relatively high paleolatitudes of Gondwana has strengthened the view that they were able to maintain an elevated body temperature.

Reconstructed skeleton of Dimetrodon, a primitive mammal-like reptile of the Permian Period. Courtesy of the American Museum of Natural History, New York

PERMIAN MASS EXTINCTION

The greatest mass extinction episodes in Earth's history occurred in the latter part of the Permian Period. Shallow warm-water marine invertebrates show the most protracted and greatest extinctions during this time. Starting from the maximum number of different genera in the middle part of the Middle Permian Epoch, extinction within these invertebrate faunas significantly reduced the number of different genera by 12 to 70 percent by the beginning of the Capitanian Age (the latest age of the Middle Permian Epoch). The diversity levels of many of these faunas plummeted to levels lower than at any prior time in the Permian Period. Extinctions at the Middle Permian–Late Permian boundary were even more severe—bordering on catastrophic—with a reduction of 70 percent to 80 percent from the Middle Permian generic maxima. A great many invertebrate families, which were highly successful prior to these extinctions, were affected. By the early part of the Late Permian Epoch (specifically the Wuchiapingian Age), the now substantially reduced invertebrate fauna attempted to diversify again, but with limited success. Many were highly specialized groups, and more than half of these became extinct before the beginning of the Changhsingian Age (the final subdivision of the Late Permian Epoch). Late Permian faunas accounted for only about 10 percent or less of the Middle Permian faunal maxima—that is, about 90 percent of the Permian extinctions were accomplished before the start of the last age of the period (the Changhsingian Age).

The extinction events taking place during both the last stage of the Middle Permian Epoch and throughout the Late Permian Epoch, each apparently more severe than the previous one, extended over about 15 million years. Disruptive ecological changes eventually reduced marine invertebrates to crisis levels (about 5 percent of their Middle Permian maxima)—their lowest diversity since the end of the Ordovician Period. The final Permian extinction event, sometimes referred to as the terminal Permian crisis, while very real, took 15 million years to materialize and likely eliminated many ecologically struggling faunas that were already greatly reduced by previous extinctions.

TEMPERATURE CRISES AND THE PERMIAN EXTINCTION

Although other single event causes have been suggested, current explanations of Permian extinction events have focused on how biological and physical causes disrupted nutrient cycles. Hypotheses of temperature crises, especially of those occurring in shallow marine (surface) waters, are based in part on studies of oxygen isotopes and the ratios of calcium to magnesium in Permian fossil shell materials. The highest estimated temperatures of ocean surface waters (estimated to be 25–28°C [about 77–82°F]) until that time occurred during the end of the Middle Permian and the beginning of the Late Permian Epoch. Subsequently, by the end of the Late Permian Epoch, calcium-to-magnesium ratios suggest that water temperatures may have dropped to about 22–24°C (about 72–75°F), decreasing further during the very beginning of the Triassic Period. One hypothesis proposes that water temperatures greater than 24–28°C (about 75–82°F) may have been too warm for many invertebrates. Only those specialized for high temperatures, such as those living in shallow lagoons, survived.

Another temperature-related hypothesis posits that photosynthetic symbionts, which may have lived within the tissues of some marine invertebrates, were unable to survive the higher ocean temperatures and abandoned their hosts. Some of the data have been interpreted to show that an increase in seawater temperature of about 6°C (10.8°F) occurred—perhaps increasing the overall temperature of seawater to about 30–32°C (about 86–90°F)—near the Permian-Triassic boundary.

THE ALTERATION OF THE CARBON CYCLE

Temperature crises account for some of the possible causes of the Permian extinctions. The ratio between the stable isotopes of carbon ($^{12}C/^{13}C$) seems to indicate that significant changes in the carbon cycle took place starting about 500,000 to 1,000,000 years before the end of the Permian Period and crossing the boundary into the Induan Age (the first age of the Triassic Period). These changes appear to coincide closely with two Permian extinction events, suggesting some cause-and-effect relationship with changes in the carbon cycle.

Several studies have suggested that changes in the carbon isotope record may indicate a disrupted biological cycle. Some scientists consider the unusually high amounts of ^{12}C trapped in Permian sediments to be a result of widespread oceanic anoxia (very low levels of dissolved oxygen). They associate this anoxia with the prolonged eruption of the Siberian flood basalts, which probably led to higher levels of carbon dioxide in the atmosphere. Clouds of volcanic ash may have worsened the situation by restricting the amount of sunlight available for photosynthesis, thereby inhibiting the process of carbon fixation by plants and lowering the extraction rate of carbon dioxide from the atmosphere. In addition, high amounts of carbon dioxide may have been injected into the atmosphere directly by the venting of volcanic gases from the eruption of flood basalts or indirectly by the ignition of forests by hot lava. Other hypotheses suggest that the warming and drying of the terrestrial environments during the Permian Period reduced the amount of organic matter buried in sediments as coal or petroleum, shifting the amount of organically fixed carbon dioxide that was recycled through the atmosphere.

OTHER POTENTIAL CAUSES OF THE PERMIAN EXTINCTION

A few scientists have suggested that a large icy meteoritic impact caused a sudden cooling of the Earth, but such an impact lacks supporting evidence. A glacial episode at the end of the Permian has been suggested because of the general lowering of the sea level during the Late Permian Epoch. However, that theory remains unproved—no Late Permian glacial deposits have been identified, despite extensive searching.

SIGNIFICANT PERMIAN LIFE-FORMS

Before the onset of the mass extinction events detailed above, marine environments diversified throughout the Permian Period. Meanwhile, Permian terrestrial faunas included several important amphibians, reptiles, and mammal-like reptiles. Increasingly, these groups had members that grew to relatively large sizes. For example, *Eryops*, probably the best known amphibian of Permian times, was roughly two metres (six feet) long, whereas the pareiasaurs had the distinction of being the world's largest vertebrates of the time. In addition, some Permian vertebrates (such as *Dimetrodon*, *Moschops*, and the cynodonts) displayed mammal-like characteristics.

BRADYSAURUS

Bradysaurus is a genus of extinct early reptiles found in South Africa as fossils in deposits from the Permian Period. *Bradysaurus* belonged to a larger group of reptiles called pareiasaurs, which were characterized by massive bodies, strong limbs and limb supports, and grotesque skulls with many bony protuberances. Pareiasaurs were not dinosaurs, but they were the first very large land vertebrates and were unusual for their time in that they were herbivorous. *Bradysaurus*, like the other pareiasaurs, had leaf-shaped crenulated teeth along the jaw margins, palatal teeth, and a thick skull that was about 0.5 metre (about 1.6 feet) long.

CACOPS

Members of the extinct amphibian genus, *Cacops,* are found as fossils in Early Permian, or Cisuralian, rocks in North America (the Early Permian Period, or Cisuralian Epoch, lasted from 299 million to 271 million years ago). *Cacops* reached a length of about 40 centimetres (16 inches). The skull was heavily constructed, and the otic notch, the region in the hind part of the skull that housed the hearing mechanism, was extremely large and closed behind by a bony bar. With its strongly developed legs and limb girdles, the animal was well equipped to move about on land. The tail was relatively small, and the thick plating of bony armour on the back was probably an adaptation against attack.

CAPTORHINUS

A genus of extinct reptiles found as fossils in Permian rocks of North America, *Captorhinus* was small with slender limbs. Its full length was about 30 centimetres (12 inches), and its skull was only about 7 centimetres (2.75 inches) long. It bore some resemblance to a modern lizard. *Captorhinus* was one of the earliest and most primitive reptiles. In form it was representative of the captorhinomorphs, a group of early reptiles with nearly solid skulls that had no openings for the attachment of jaw muscles.

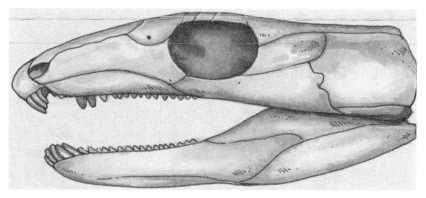

Small and lean-limbed Captorhinus *was one of the earliest and most primitive reptiles and appears strikingly like the modern lizard.* Peter Bull/ Getty Images

The captorhinomorphs were eventually succeeded by reptiles with more advanced skulls and stronger jaws for biting and chewing food. Only one small group of captorhinomorphs persisted into the Triassic Period (251 million to 200 million years ago) before becoming extinct.

CYNODONTS

Cynodonts are members of the suborder or infraorder Cynodontia. They are mammal-like reptiles of the order Therapsida that existed from the Late Permian to the Early Jurassic Epoch (258 to 187 million years ago). Cynodont fossils have been found in China, South Africa, South America, and North America. (Examples in North America were not reported until 1989, from sites in Virginia, U.S.)

The cynodont skull has many features anticipating that of a mammal. Notably, it has a secondary palate, as in a mammal, allowing it to simultaneously chew food and breathe, making for quicker digestion. (Most reptiles do not chew food but swallow it in large pieces, digesting slowly.) Thus cynodonts probably had a metabolic rate and large food requirement similar to mammals. They also had differentiated teeth, jaw bones, and jaw muscles suitable for chewing. Though the brain remained small, the braincase had an almost mammalian appearance, presaging the enlargement of the brain in mammalian descendants. Otherwise, the skeleton remained largely reptilian (the front and back limbs were appended on the sides, not underneath the body), signifying a sprawling posture and gait.

The suborder Cynodontia contains, according to some classifications, five families — Procynosuchidae, Galesauridae, Tritylodontidae, Chiniquodontidae, and Trithelodontidae. The first mammals probably derived from small carnivorous chiniquodontids or trithelodonts sometime in the Middle Triassic Epoch (240 to 230 million years ago).

DIADECTES

Diadectes is an extinct genus of tetrapods closely related to the first amniotes (mammals, birds, reptiles, and their relatives). Members of this genus have been found as fossils in Carboniferous and Lower Permian rocks in North America (360 million to 270 million years ago). *Diadectes* shares a mixture of features from both amniotes and primitive tetrapods, but it did not possess an amnion, which is a protective membrane surrounding the developing embryo and a defining characteristic of reptiles. Its classification — along with that of other related forms such as *Seymouria* — has been long controversial. *Diadectes* grew to be about 2 metres (6 feet) long. The skeleton was heavily constructed, with massive limbs, limb girdles, backbone, and ribs. The skull was relatively high and short. It was broad in the back and featured a constricted snout. The teeth were blunt and peglike. *Diadectes* was probably one of the earliest terrestrial herbivores. The front teeth were longer than the cheek teeth and probably served to nip off plant material. The cheek teeth probably served to grind the plant material.

DIMETRODON

Dimetrodon is an extinct relative of primitive mammals that lived from about 286 million to 270 million years ago during the Early Permian Period, fossils of which are found in North America.

Dimetrodon was a carnivore that grew to a length of more than 3.5 metres (11.5 feet) and had a large "sail" on its back that may have functioned in temperature regulation. The sail was presumably formed by elongated vertebral spines connected by a membrane containing many blood vessels. The skull of *Dimetrodon* was high and narrow, and the region in front of the eyes was long. Its many teeth were differentiated into several sizes.

A similar sail is found on the related but herbivorous *Edaphosaurus*, a herbivore with a smaller head and more modest teeth. Given the physiological importance of thermoregulation, there arises the question of why all the various members of *Dimetrodon* and *Edaphosaurus*'s taxonomic group, Pelycosauria, did not have sails. Pelycosaurs were not dinosaurs and in fact were not even reptiles. Although pelycosaurs became extinct by the end of the Permian, it is probable that therapsids, a group that would eventually include the mammals, were descended from pelycosaurs similar to *Dimetrodon*.

ERYOPS

A genus of extinct primitive amphibians found as fossils in Permian rocks in North America, *Eryops* was a massive animal more than 2 metres (6 feet) long. Its large skull had thick and uneven bones, with wrinkles. The eye sockets were large and directed upward. Large and pointed teeth grew along the margins of the jaws and on the palate. The strength and size of the vertebral column and the skeletal limb elements indicate that *Eryops* was well suited to moving about on land. Although short, the limbs were very broad, and the shoulder and hip girdles were massive. The skin bore bony nodules that probably provided a sort of protective armour against predators. *Eryops* was a predator that subsisted to a large extent upon fish, although it probably preyed upon land vertebrates as well. The structure of its limb girdle and ribs suggests that it was among the most successful of early amphibians in traversing terrestrial environments.

GLOSSOPTERIS

Glossopteris is a genus of fossilized woody plants known from rocks that have been dated to the Permian and Triassic periods (roughly 300 to 200 million years ago),

The multi-continental distribution of the seed-bearing Glossopteris *(seed fern), with its tongue-shaped leaf, prominent midrib, and reticulate venation, is among the first of several arguments for continental drift.* Ken Lucas/ Visuals Unlimited/Getty Images

deposited on the southern supercontinent of Gondwana. *Glossopteris* occurred in a variety of growth forms. Its most common fossil is that of a tongue-shaped leaf with prominent midrib and reticulate venation. *Glossopteris* leaves are commonly found in thick mats, and thus some authorities speculate that the plants were deciduous. It reproduced by seeds, and a tremendous variety of both ovule-bearing and pollen-bearing reproductive structures are borne on characteristic *Glossopteris* leaves. Before the last of this group finally succumbed to extinction at the end of the Triassic Period, *Glossopteris* became one of the major features of the flora of Gondwana. The distribution of this plant was among the first evidence for continental drift.

LEPTODUS

Leptodus, an extinct genus of articulate brachiopods, also lived during the Permian period. *Leptodus* was a very specialized form characterized by an aberrant morphology. It had an oysterlike pedicle valve, which anchored the shell to the substrate and was probably attached to other shells by cementation. The brachial (upper) valve was flat and very thin. It is likely that *Leptodus* inhabited the flanks of reefs developed in shallow Permian seas of North America.

LIMNOSCELIS

An extinct genus of tetrapod that appeared very close to the origin of amniotes (mammals, birds, or reptiles), *Limnoscelis* may have been a stem form from which more advanced reptiles may have descended. It occurs as fossils in Permian rocks (those 251 million to 299 million years old) of North America. *Limnoscelis* was about 1.5 metres (5 feet) long, with a robust skeleton and a rather long and solid skull. An opening for the pineal organ, which was in effect a third eye, was present between the parietal bones of the skull roof. The nostrils were placed well forward, and the margins of the jaws contained numerous sharp teeth. The anteriormost teeth were larger than the others and labyrinthine in internal structure. Teeth also were present on the bones of the palate. The body and tail were long, and the limb girdles were massive. In life, the limbs were splayed outward from the body in a sprawling pose, a relatively primitive reptilian condition.

MESOSAURUS

Mesosaurus was an early aquatic relative of reptiles, found as fossils from the Early Permian Period (299 million to 271 million years ago) in South Africa and South America.

Mesosaurus lived in freshwater lakes and ponds. Elongated and slim, it measured about 1 metre (3.3 feet) long. The skull and tail were both long and narrow, and the animal probably undulated through the water as it fed on small crustaceans and other prey with its jaws, which were full of long, thin, pointed teeth. The ribs were large and banana-shaped, possibly reinforcing the ribcage for diving. Mesosaurs may have seldom, if ever, ventured onto land. Because it is unlikely that the mesosaurs could have traversed broad stretches of saline open ocean, their geographic distribution provided paleontological evidence corroborating the hypothesis that the continents of the Southern Hemisphere were once joined. The distribution of mesosaurs was thus some of the earliest proof of continental drift.

MOSCHOPS

Moschops, an extinct genus of mammal-like reptiles (Therapsida), is found as fossils in rocks of Permian age in southern Africa. *Moschops* is representative of a group that became adapted to a diet of plant food; it was about 2.6 metres (8 feet) long. The body was massive. The skull was high and shortened front to back. Numerous chisel-edged teeth suitable for cropping vegetation were present in the jaws. The animal's back characteristically sloped downward from the front to the back in giraffelike fashion. The limb girdles or supports were massive, especially in the shoulder region, and the bone on the top of the skull was greatly thickened.

PARAFUSULINA

Parafusulina is a genus of extinct fusulinid foraminiferans (single-celled animals with a hard, complexly constructed shell) found as fossils in Permian marine rocks (the Permian Period began 286 million years ago and ended 245 million years ago). *Parafusulina* is more specifically restricted to the Leonardian and Guadalupian stages, smaller divisions of Permian rocks and time, and is thus an excellent index, or guide, fossil. The shell is characterized by distinct flutings, and the details of internal structure are best studied in thin sections.

PARASCHWAGERINA

Paraschwagerina, a genus of extinct fusulinid foraminiferans, appears as fossils restricted to marine rocks. The animal probably lived in clear water, far from the shoreline. The various species are excellent index, or guide, fossils for the Early Permian and allow the correlation of sometimes widely separated rock units.

PSEUDOSCHWAGERINA

Pseudoschwagerina is an extinct genus of fusulinid foraminiferans found as fossils in Early Permian marine rocks.

The shell is spherical with localized thickening as a sort of lip. In thin section, the shell structure consists of widely spaced inner walls and distinctive wall deposits. *Pseudoschwagerina* is a guide, or index, fossil for the Wolfcampian Stage, a division of Permian rocks.

SCHWAGERINA

Schwagerina is an extinct genus of fusulinid foraminiferans that serves as a useful guide, or index, fossil for Early Permian rocks and time. Various forms or species of *Schwagerina* are recognized on the basis of distinctive shell form and internal structure. Many extensive petroleum deposits are associated with *Schwagerina.*

SEYMOURIA

An extinct genus of terrestrial tetrapod found as fossils in Permian rocks in North America and named for fossil deposits near Seymour, Texas, *Seymouria* had many skeletal characteristics in common with amniotes (reptiles, mammals, and certain sets of their more primitive relatives), but it is not included in this group.

Some seymouriamorphs pursued an almost exclusively aquatic life, whereas others, such as the genus *Diadectes,* became early terrestrial plant-eating animals. In *Seymouria,* the skull was deep and much like that of early amniotes and amphibians. An opening was present in the roof of the skull for the pineal eye, a light-receptive organ found in many primitive vertebrates. Numerous teeth grew around the margins of the jaws and several in the palate. The teeth had a complexly folded internal structure, or labyrinthodont configuration, of the sort present in early tetrapods and their relatives. *Seymouria* was about 60 centimetres (24 inches) long, and the body was capable of being raised well off the ground in a stance more reptilian than amphibian. The structure of the vertebrae and limb girdles suggests a strong adaptation to terrestrial life.

TAPINOCEPHALUS

Tapinocephalus, an extinct genus of therapsids, relatives of mammals, is found as fossils in Permian rocks of South Africa. The genus *Tapinocephalus* is representative of the Tapinocephaloidea, characterized by many herbivorous specializations. A large and bulky animal, *Tapinocephalus* also is characteristic of a distinctive assemblage of lowland animals that are useful as a horizon marker for a part of the middle Permian in South Africa known as the *Tapinocephalus* zone.

VENYUKOVIA

Venyukovia is a genus of extinct mammal-like reptiles (therapsids) that are found as fossils in Permian deposits in eastern Europe. It was herbivorous, with primitive teeth. It is thought that *Venyukovia* (also spelled Venjukovia) may well have been the ancestor of an important group of plant-eating therapsids, the Dicynodontia. *Venyukovia* and the dicynodonts did not give rise to more advanced forms, however.

PERMIAN GEOLOGY

The study of Permian life-forms only gives us one part of the geologic picture. Scientists also must examine the rock deposits from this time to uncover the major and minor geologic events that shaped Earth and, thereby, the organisms living during this period. Although volcanism was relatively limited during most of the Permian, sedimentary rock laid down throughout the interval occurs worldwide. Phosphorites, petroleum, salts, and coal are characteristic of Permian formations along with reef limestones and tillites. Petroleum-rich Permian deposits occur in the United States and Russia, whereas coal-rich deposits occur in Asia, Africa, and Australia.

THE MAJOR SUBDIVISIONS OF THE PERMIAN SYSTEM

The Permian Period is subdivided into Early (Cisuralian), Middle (Guadalupian), and Late (Lopingian) epochs corresponding to the Cisuralian, Guadalupian, and Lopingian rock series. Rocks laid down during these epochs and ages have been assigned to corresponding depositional series and stages, respectively. The Cisuralian Epoch takes its name from its type region on the western slopes of the Ural Mountains in Russia and Kazakhstan and is subdivided into four internationally recognized ages: the Asselian (299 million to 294.6 million years ago), Sakmarian (294.6 million to 284.4 million years ago), Artinskian (284.4 million to 275.6 million years ago), and Kungurian (275.6 million to 270.6 million years ago). The Guadalupian Epoch takes its name from its type area in the Guadalupe Mountains of the West Texas region in the United States and contains three internationally recognized ages: the Roadian (270.6 million to 268 million years ago), Wordian (268 million to 265.8 million years ago), and Capitanian (265.8 million to 260.4 million years ago). The Lopingian Epoch takes its name from its type area in China and contains two internationally recognized ages: the Wuchiapingian (260.4 million to 253.8 million years ago) and Changhsingian (253.8 million to 251 million years ago). Lower Triassic beds overlie the Lopingian Series.

The establishment of time equivalence of Permian strata between different areas has been a serious problem since the mid-19th century. Most Permian invertebrate faunas from marine environments are strongly endemic (localized in one or a few nearby areas) and thus difficult to correlate between different paleobiotic provinces. However, in the type regions of each of these series, all located within the paleoequatorial warm-water conodont (a primitive chordate with tooth-shaped fossil remains) province, a succession of these pelagic faunas continues to undergo description. While this will not lead to the global correlation of certain fossils, it is useful enough to define some regional patterns and assist in the general correlation of each particular rock series.

Subdivisions within the Permian Period are classified by the emergence of several species of conodonts. In the Cisuralian Series the first appearance of *Streptognathodus isolatus* marks the base of the Asselian Stage, the first appearance of *Sweetognathus merrilli* marks the base of the Sakmarian, *Sweetognathus whitei* and *Mesogondolella bisselli* mark the base of the Artinskian, and *Neostreptognathodus pnevi* and *N. exculptus* mark the base of the Kungurian. The first appearance of *Jinogondolella nankingensis* specifies the base of the Roadian Stage in the Guadalupian Series, the first appearance of *Jinogondolella aserrata* indicates the base of the Wordian, and the first appearance of *Jinogondolella postserrata* marks the base of the Capitanian. The emergence of *Clarkina postbitteri* marks the base of the Wuchiapingian Stage in the Lopingian Series; and the first appearance of *Clarkina wangi* characterizes the base of the Changhsingian. The base of the Triassic Period is indicated by the first appearance of *Hindeodus parvus*.

Different conodont zonations must be used for the colder waters surrounding Gondwana. These zones, which are in the process of being described and established, are based on different conodont species, and even different genera, from those found in the Northern Hemisphere. Even in the paleoequatorial belt, some of the conodont guide species do not appear in all areas, and certain successions of conodonts are rare (as in the sediments of the Tethys Sea) or do not appear at all. For these successions, local series and stage names remain useful, particularly in identifying different nonmarine successions.

THE ECONOMIC SIGNIFICANCE OF PERMIAN DEPOSITS

Permian rocks have long been economically important sources of evaporite minerals, such as halite (rock salt),

Plenty of Permian marine basins produce petroleum, which is an important economic source. The most famous are based in the United States and Russia. Joe Raedle/Getty Images

sylvite (potash salts), gypsum and anhydrite (calcium sulfate salts), petroleum, and coal. The distribution of these resources, in part, is related to the latitudes where they were deposited. Evaporites were particularly common in subtropical and tropical Permian paleolatitudes in what is now West Texas, New Mexico, and Kansas in North America and in northwestern Europe and the European part of Russia. Thick coals formed in cool temperate paleolatitudes, such as central and northern Siberia, Manchuria, Korea, peninsular India, eastern Australia, South Africa, Zimbabwe, and the Congo. These locations lay in higher latitudes during the Permian Period.

Many Permian marine basins produce petroleum. The most famous oil fields are in the United States—in Oklahoma and the Permian Basin of West Texas and New Mexico—and along the Ural orogenic belt in Russia.

Phosphorites (sedimentary rocks with economic amounts of various phosphate-bearing minerals) are common in Montana, Idaho, Wyoming, Utah, and Nevada. They were deposited in deepwater sedimentary wedges next to the Permian continental shelf margin at the western edge of the North American craton. In Europe, phosphorites occur along a deepwater trough marking the eastern edge of the Russian Platform.

Of significance to European civilizations is the Permian Kupferschiefer, a copper-bearing shale that has been mined for hundreds, perhaps even thousands, of years. In addition, pinnacle reefs composed of limestones from the Cisuralian Series occur along the southeastern margins of the Russian Platform. The Ishimbay oil fields of this region were a critical source of petroleum for the former Soviet Union during World War II after their fields to the west fell under German control.

THE OCCURRENCE AND DISTRIBUTION OF PERMIAN DEPOSITS

Permian rocks are common to all present-day continents. However, some have been moved—sometimes thousands of kilometres—from their original site of deposition by tectonic transport during the Mesozoic and Cenozoic eras. For example, Permian glacial terrestrial and marine deposits typical of the cold high latitudes of the Southern Hemisphere are now found in Antarctica, southern Africa, India, Thailand, and Tibet, and glacial deposits of the Northern Hemisphere laid down at that time are found in northeastern Siberia. By contrast, some Permian tropical and subtropical carbonate deposits, typical of deposition in low latitudes, were relocated to high latitudes. The present location of certain fossilized animals, endemic to the tropics during Permian time, suggests that other deposits were also moved great distances longitudinally (on a north-south axis). These deposits formed accreted terranes (smaller landmasses subsequently added onto continents) that became attached to the margins of some continents during Mesozoic and Cenozoic times. The present-day locations of Permian deposits are explained by the theory of plate tectonics. When the Permian globe is reconstructed, these apparent conflicts in rock deposition disappear, and a plausible arrangement of deposition, which is consistent with Permian climate patterns, emerges.

CARBONATE PROVINCES

Two tropical to subtropical carbonate provinces are recognized centred near the paleoequator but on opposite sides of Pangaea. One includes the southwestern United States and northwestern South America. The other, which is much larger and has a more diverse fauna, includes the

Tethys belt of rocks from Tunisia and the Carnic Alps of present-day Italy and Austria on the west through Turkey, Iran, southern China, Southeast Asia, and Japan to central British Columbia, Washington, Oregon, and California. The Tethys carbonate province was thoroughly disrupted by orogenic deformation (as the result of seafloor spreading and plate tectonics) after the Permian Period ended. Thus, the remains now reside in almost entirely dislocated fragments.

Sediments in Tectonically Active Regions

In terms of geologic setting, Permian sediments deposited as thick sedimentary wedges along the tectonically active

Exposed stratified rock of the Beacon Group in the Pensacola Mountains near the South Pole. Flat-lying Permian siltstone and coal measures are capped by Jurassic diabase sill. Courtesy of the U.S. Geological Survey

margins of the major cratons are least understood. Most of these Permian sediments have been thrust and involved in major geologic deformation. Much of the fossil evidence is from clastic material derived from shallow shelf environments or eroded from older rocks and deposited as deepwater debris fans. Thick deposits—perhaps originally 1 to 3 kilometres (0.6 to 1.9 miles) thick—are known in central Nevada, Idaho, and northward into Canada. Similar deposits occur in the Middle East, China, Japan, and eastern Siberia.

Interleaved with these thick clastic wedges are other thrust slices of ocean-floor deposits. These are thinner, about 0.5 kilometres (0.3 miles) thick or less, and are characterized by radiolarian-rich cherts, basaltic volcanic dikes, sills, and submarine lava flows, as well as silts and clays of the distal ends of turbidity flows. All Permian (and older) ocean-floor deposits and thick sedimentary wedges have been caught up in Mesozoic and Cenozoic subduction zones along plate boundaries and either form accretionary wedges or were lost to the Earth's mantle.

LIMESTONE

Associated with some oceanic basalts are thick accumulations of tropical and subtropical reef limestone that formed on seamounts and volcanic island arcs. Because limestone is comparatively less dense than adjacent oceanic rocks, such as basalt or chert, many of the Permian reef limestones were not as readily subducted. They are present in many accretionary wedges, such as those found in Tunisia, the Balkan Peninsula, Turkey, the Crimea (in Ukraine), the Middle East, northern India, Pakistan, Southeast Asia, New Zealand, China, Japan, eastern Siberia, Alaska, the western Cordillera of Canada and the United States, and a small part of northwestern Mexico.

Other limestones were deposited as reefs along the outer margins of sedimentary basins. Striking examples of these reefs form the Guadalupe Mountains of western Texas and New Mexico. Such reefs also occur in the subsurface along the Central Basin Platform in western Texas, where they are a source of petroleum. Similar reefs are found in northern England, Germany, and the subsurface of the North Sea. Lower Permian limestone reefs are found in the western and southern Urals of eastern Europe.

BASIN SEDIMENTATION

Cratonic shelf sedimentation in low paleolatitudes during Permian time was characterized by the gradual withdrawal of shorelines and the progressive increase in eolian (wind-transported) sands, red beds, and evaporites. Many intracratonic basins—such as the Anadarko, Delaware, and Midland basins in the western United States; the Zechstein Basin of northwestern Europe; and the Kazan Basin of eastern Europe—show similar general changes. In most basins the inner parts became sites of red bed deposition during the Early Permian, followed by periods of extensive evaporite production. Sand sources along the ancestral Rocky Mountains supplied eolian sand and silt in great quantities.

The outer portions of the intracratonic basin systems, as in the Delaware and Zechstein basins, were involved in some transform faulting (process where two tectonic plates slide past one another) and extensional tectonics (the stretching and rifting of a continental plate), which produced landforms of considerable relief in some areas. Although some of this relief was from rotated fault blocks, most of it resulted from the very rapid growth of limestone reefs on upthrown blocks (that is, the sides of faults that appear to have moved upward) and the slower accumulation of clastic sediments on downthrown blocks.

At higher paleolatitudes, limestone is rare, and clastic rocks dominate the succession (the progressive sequence of rocks). Australia, Namibia, South Africa, peninsular India, southern Tibet, and southern Thailand all report Permo-Carboniferous tillite. These areas, as the paleogeographic reconstruction indicates, would have been in relatively high Gondwanan latitudes (closer to the South Pole) during the Permian Period, and thus their geology was affected by the expansion and contraction of glaciers. Tillites are also known from the northern high paleolatitudes in northeastern Siberia.

Some areas of Gondwana were tectonically active during Permian time, as evidenced by extensive basaltic, andesitic, and other volcanic rocks in eastern Australia. In addition, intracratonic sedimentary marine basins, such as the Carnarvon Basin in Western Australia, where nearly 5 kilometres (3 miles) of Permian sediments accumulated, were formed.

Continental rocks were widespread on all cratons during the Permian Period. The Dunkard Group is a limnic (deposited in fresh water), coal-bearing succession that was deposited from the latest of Carboniferous times into Early Permian time along the western side of the then newly formed Appalachian Mountains. Coal-bearing Lower and Upper Permian beds—up to 3 kilometres (1.9 miles) thick—are widely distributed in Australia, peninsular India (the lower part of the Gondwana System), southern Africa (the lower part of the Karoo System), the Kuznetsk Basin of western Siberia, the Paraná Basin of southern Brazil, and the Precordillera Basin of western Argentina. Red beds were common in the continental beds of tropical and subtropical paleolatitudes.

THE CORRELATION OF PERMIAN STRATA

Major subdivisions of the Permian Period are identified by extended periods of lowered sea level and by major faunal change. To overcome problems of shallow-water marine provincialism, biostratigraphers have increasingly turned to more open-ocean fossils, including cephalopods (which also are surprisingly provincial) and conodonts (which appear to be less provincial but whose biological affinities are poorly known).

DELINEATING THE MAJOR BOUNDARIES AND SUBDIVISIONS OF THE PERMIAN SYSTEM

The history of the identification and acceptance of the Permian Period by geologists is in many ways the account of good deductive reasoning, a determined scientist, and an opportunity that was exploited to its fullest. Scottish geologist Roderick I. Murchison had been aware that the Coal Measures (unit of stratigraphy equal to the Pennsylvanian Series or Upper Carboniferous System) in northern England and Germany were overlain by red beds and poorly fossilized dolomitic limestones that had major unconformities at their base and top. Murchison reasoned that somewhere, perhaps outside northwestern Europe, a more complete stratigraphic succession would fill in these sedimentary gaps and would provide a more complete, better-preserved fossil assemblage.

In 1840 and 1841 Murchison found the missing stratigraphic succession in European Russia along the western flanks of the Ural Mountains, where he recognized a well-developed succession of rocks that both included rocks equivalent in age to the problematic red beds and dolomitic limestones of northwestern Europe and also filled the missing gaps below and above those sediments. He named these rocks the Permian System after the region of Perm, where they are particularly well developed.

Murchison included the red beds and evaporite beds now referred to as the Kungurian Stage in the lower part of his Permian System, while incorporating the nonmarine beds of the Tatarian Stage (a regional stage roughly equivalent to the Capitanian Stage plus a portion of the Wordian Stage) in its upper part. The upper portion of these nonmarine beds was subsequently shown to be Early Triassic in origin. The Ufimian-Kazanian Stage (a regional stage overlapping the current Roadian Stage and the remainder of the Wordian Stage) in between Murchison's upper and lower parts of the Permian System was considered to be a close lithologic and age equivalent of the Zechstein of northwestern Europe.

LATER WORK

A symposium organized by the American Association of Petroleum Geologists in 1939 established North American standard reference sections for the Permian consisting of four series—namely, the Wolfcampian, Leonardian, Guadalupian, and Ochoan—on the basis of the succession in West Texas and New Mexico.

Attempts in the 1950s and 1960s to unify the nomenclature within the Permian System into two (upper and lower) series based primarily on the Russian Platform and Ural successions proved unsuccessful. Currently the Permian System is subdivided into three series with global reference sections based on the Russian Cisuralian succession for the Lower Series, the West Texas Guadalupian for the Middle Series, and the Chinese Lopingian for the Upper Series.

Regional stages were considered necessary and important because they were based on strongly provincial faunal zonations that differ markedly from one region to the next. Within a single region or faunal province, the similarity of the succession of fossils and patterns of rock deposition permits ready age correlations. However, age correlations from one region to the next are more difficult and open to more questions. This differentiation of provincial faunas and their isolation from one another increase noticeably in the middle and later parts of the Permian Period.

THE PERMIAN-TRIASSIC BOUNDARY

Except for the central and eastern parts of the Tethys region, where local deposition was apparently continuous, the boundary between the Permian System and the overlying Triassic System is a hiatus of one to several million years. Outside of the Tethys region, the boundary between these two important systems — indeed, the boundary between the Paleozoic and Mesozoic eras — has not been readily defined. The latest Permian faunas were reduced to only a few remnant genera that were sensitive to stressful new environments. Typical Triassic lineages were mostly relicts from the latest Permian.

STAGES OF THE PERMIAN PERIOD

The Permian Period is made up of nine stages distributed among three epochs. The reference locations for the stages contained within the Cisuralian Epoch occur within Russia, whereas the reference locations for stages encompassed by the Guadalupian and Lopingian Epochs occur in the southern United States and southern China, respectively. At the boundaries of each stage, conodonts serve as the primary biological markers separating one stage from another.

ASSELIAN STAGE

The Asselian Stage is the first of the four stages of the Lower Permian (Cisuralian) Series. It encompasses all rocks deposited during the Asselian Age (299 million to 294.6 million years ago) of the Permian Period. The Asselian Stage is especially well-developed in the Perm region of Russia. Asselian deposits are shales and limestones interbedded with thin layers of sandstones and conglomerates. They were deposited on the eastern edge of the Russian Platform and the upper slope of the Uralian geosyncline in shallow marine environments. Asselian strata are characterized by the first appearance of the conodont (a primitive chordate with tooth-shaped fossil remains) *Streptognathodus isolatus*. Important fossil zones for the Asselian Stage, as well as the succeeding Sakmarian Stage, are those containing fusulinids (single-celled organisms with complex shells) of the genera *Sphaeroschwagerina* and *Pseudoschwagerina* and ammonites of the genus *Properrinites*. These fossil zones are extensive enough to permit worldwide correlation of Lower Permian strata. The Asselian Stage overlies the Gzhelian Stage of the Carboniferous Period and is overlain by the Sakmarian Stage.

SAKMARIAN STAGE

The second of the four stages of the Early Permian (Cisuralian) Epoch, the Sakmarian Stage contains all rocks deposited during the Sakmarian Age (294.6 million to 284.4 million years ago) of the Permian Period. Rocks deposited during the Sakmarian were marine sandstones, siltstones, shales, and limestones, interbedded with minor, thin conglomerates. Most were deposited as lateral sedimentary facies to one another. Conglomerates and sandstones belonging to this stage occur on the western flanks of the Ural Mountains in central Russia and may reach a thickness of more than 1,000 metres (3,300 feet). The base of the Sakmarian is marked by the first appearance of the conodont (primitive chordate with tooth-shaped fossil remains) *Sweetognathus merrilli*. The Sakmarian Stage overlies the Asselian Stage and is in turn overlain by the Artinskian Stage.

ARTINSKIAN STAGE

The third of the four stages of the Lower Permian (Cisuralian) Series, the Artinskian Stage represents those rocks deposited during Artinskian time (284.4 million to 275.6 million years ago) in the Permian Period. Rocks of Artinskian time were deposited in marine environments. In its type area in the Ural region of Russia, these strata were mainly sandstones, siltstones, shales, and conglomerates deposited on a steep inclined ramp near the edge of the Russian Platform. During the Artinskian, this ramp became a marine tectonic foredeep (a narrow trough filled with sediment) in the western part of the Ural geosyncline as the Uralian orogenic belt moved progressively westward. The base of the Artinskian is marked by the first appearance of the conodonts *Sweetognathus whitei* and *Mesogondolella bisselli*. The stage is also characterized by biostratigraphic zones containing fusulinids (single-celled organisms with complex shells) that are primitive members of the genus *Parafusulina* and ammonites of the genera *Metaperrinites* and *Perrinites*. The Artinskian Stage overlies the Sakmarian Stage and is overlain by the Kungurian Stage.

Kungurian Stage

The Kungurian Stage is the last of the four stages of the Lower Permian (Cisuralian) Series, encompassing all rocks deposited during the Kungurian Age (275.6 million to 270.6 million years ago) of the Permian Period. Rock exposures from this stage are well developed in the Ural region in both Kazakhstan and Russia.

In the Mughalzhar Hills (Kazakhstan) and southern Ural mountain regions (Russia), Kungurian deposits are primarily terrigenous (formed by erosion), consisting of red beds and lagoonal sediment types. Many different kinds of shallow marginal marine, evaporitic, and nonmarine strata were deposited here as lateral sedimentary facies to one another. Elsewhere, conglomerates, sandstones, and other red beds occur. To the east, thick evaporite sequences of gypsum, halite, and potash form the salt basin of the upper Kama River in Russia. Marine limestones occur in the Russian province of Perm, and reef carbonates occur in the western portions of the Mughalzhar Hills.

The Kungurian Stage represents the final phase of the Uralian geosyncline as the Uralian orogenic belt continued to move west, closed, and overrode part of the Uralian marine seaway. Evaporites became predominant after this time. In order to establish a consistent Cisuralian conodont-based zonal scheme that would include a definition of the Kungurian, the base of the stage was lowered from its traditional (nonfossiliferous) horizon to contain the first appearance of *Neostreptognathodus pnevi* and *N. exculptus*.

The Kungurian Stage overlies the Artinskian Stage and is, in turn, overlain by the Roadian Stage of the Middle Permian (Guadalupian) Series.

ROADIAN STAGE

The first of three stages of the Middle Permian (Guadalupian) Series, the Roadian Stage is made up of all rocks deposited during the Roadian Age (270.6 million to 265.8 million years ago) of the Permian Period.

In 2001 the International Commission on Stratigraphy (ICS) established the Global Stratotype Section and Point (GSSP) defining the base of this interval within the limestone portion of the Cutoff Formation located in the Guadalupe Mountains of Texas, U.S. The GSSP coincides with the appearance of the conodont *Jinogondolella nankingensis* in the fossil record. Other important fossil organisms characteristic of the stage include ammonoids of the genera *Demarezites* and *Waagenoceras*. Rocks of the Roadian Stage overlay those of the Kungurian Stage and sit below those of the Wordian Stage.

WORDIAN STAGE

The second of three stages of the Middle Permian (Guadalupian) Series, the Wordian Stage is made up of all rocks deposited during the Wordian Age (268 million to 265.8 million years ago) of the Permian Period. The name of this interval is derived from the Wordian Formation located in the Glass Mountains of western Texas in North America.

In 2001 the ICS established the Global Stratotype Section and Point (GSSP) defining the base of this interval in the Cherry Canyon Formation of the Guadalupe Mountains in Texas, U.S. The GSSP is located in a deposit of carbonate mudstone and coincides with the appearance of the conodont *Jinogondolella aserrata* in the fossil record. Other important fossil organisms characteristic of the stage include ammonoids of the genera *Timorites* and *Waagenoceras*. Rocks of the Wordian Stage rest above those of the Roadian Stage and sit beneath those of the Capitanian Stage.

CAPITANIAN STAGE

The Capitanian Stage is the last of three stages of the Middle Permian (Guadalupian) Series. It represents all rocks deposited during the Capitanian Age (265.8 million to 260.4 million years ago) of the Permian Period. This interval of geologic time is named for the Capitan Formation, which is located on Capitan Peak in New Mexico, U.S.

In 2001 the ICS established the Global Stratotype Section and Point (GSSP) defining the base of this interval in the Bell Canyon Formation of the Guadalupe Mountains in Texas, U.S. The GSSP is located in a limestone deposit just below the top of Nipple Hill. It marks the first appearance of the conodont *Jinogondolella postserrata* in the fossil record. The stage is also characterized by the presence of fusulinids of the genera *Yabeina* and *Polydiexodina* and ammonoids of the genera *Timorites* and *Strigogoniatites*. The Capitanian Stage resides above the Wordian Stage and is overlain by the Wuchiapingian Stage.

WUCHIAPINGIAN STAGE

The first of two stages of the Upper Permian (Lopingian) Series, the Wuchiapingian makes up all rocks deposited during the Wuchiapingian Age (260.4 million to 253.8 million years ago) of the Permian Period.

In 2004 the ICS established the Global Stratotype Section and Point (GSSP) defining the base of this unit along the southern bank of the Hongshui River southeast of Labin, China. The GSSP is located at the lowest reach of Bed 6k in the Labin Limestone and marks the first appearance of the conodont *Clarkina postbitteri post-bitteri* in the fossil record. Important fossil zones for the Wuchiapingian stage include those containing the fusuli-nid genera *Codonofusiella* and *Nanlingella* and the ammonoid genera *Roadoceras* and *Doulingoceras*. The Wuchiapingian Stage overlies the Capitanian Stage and is overlain by the Changhsingian Stage.

CHANGHSINGIAN STAGE

The Changhsingian Stage is the last of two internationally defined stages of the Upper Permian (Lopingian) Series. It contains all rocks deposited during the Changhsingian Age (253.8 million to 251 million years ago) of the Permian Period. The name of the interval is derived from the Chinese county of Changxing.

In 2005 the ICS established the Global Stratotype Section and Point (GSSP) defining the base of this unit in Bed 4 of the Changxing Limestone of Meishan, Changhxing county, Zhejiang province, China. It marks the first appearance of the conodont *Clarkina wangi* in the fossil record. Other important fossils characteristic of this interval include the fusulinids *Paleofusulina sinensis* and *P. minima*. The top of the Changhsingian, and thus the boundary between the Permian and Triassic periods, has been demarcated by a GSSP in Bed 27c at the same location. This GSSP was ratified by the ICS in 2001. The Changhsingian Stage lies above the Wuchiapingian Stage of the Permian System, and it is overlain by the Induan Stage of the Triassic System.

CONCLUSION

The Paleozoic was a time of great upheaval on Earth. Geographically, several continents moved northward and joined together with great force to form Pangea. The continents, once devoid of life, became overrun with plants and animals by the end of the era driven in part by the endless diversification taking place in the seas. More advanced forms of life, such as the fishes and tetrapods, emerged, and the descendants of the early tetrapods would become the first amphibians, reptiles, and the precursors to the mammals. The great extinction occurring at the close of the era took a terrible toll on marine as well as terrestrial ecosystems. However, it set the stage for the Mesozoic Era, the next chapter of life on Earth.

GLOSSARY

bathymetric Related to the the measurement of depths of water in oceans, seas, and lakes.

bioherms Moundlike bodies of rock consisting of skeletal grains of corals, algae, sponges, and other marine organisms.

biomineralization The process by which living organisms produce minerals that often harden or stiffen existing tissues.

biostromes Bedded masses of rocks composed entirely of skeletal remains.

bituminous A type of coal material containing any of various mixtures of hydrocarbons (as tar) often together with their nonmetallic derivatives.

calcareous Made up of calcium carbonate.

coelomic Related to the fluid-filled cavity between the body wall and the digestive tract of metazoans more advanced than the lower worms.

craton A stable region of Earth's crust forming the nucleus of a continent.

cryptospores Fossilised porelike structures dating to the Ordovician Period that are thought to be the direct ancestors of land plants.

dolomite A mineral $CaMg(CO_3)$ consisting of a calcium magnesium carbonate found in crystals and in extensive beds as a compact limestone.

endemism An organism that is restricted to a certain locality or region.

facies A part of a rock or group of rocks that differs from the whole formation (as in composition, age, or fossil content).

geosyncline A great downward flexure of Earth's crust.

intercalations Matter inserted between existing elements or layers.

isostasy General equilibrium of Earth's crust maintained by a yielding flow of rock material beneath the surface under gravitational stress.

isotopic Related to two or more species of atoms of a chemical element with the same atomic number and position on the periodic table but with differing atomic mass or mass number and different physical properties.

karst Landscape characterized by irregular irregular limestone with sinks, underground streams, and caverns.

lithified Cemented unconsolidated sediments into solid rock.

mafic intrusions Molten, dark-colored minerals rich in magnesium and iron that are forcibly inserted into or between other rock formations.

meiosis A process in which the number of chromosomes inside a cell is halved, forming a sex cell called a gamete.

morphological Related to the external structure of rocks in relation to the development of erosional forms or topographic features.

paleoclimactic To do with the climate of past ages.

paleomagnetic Related to the intensity and direction of residual magnetization in ancient rocks.

palynologists Scientists who study pollen and spores.

phylum One of the primary taxonomic divisions of the animal kingdom; it ranks below a kingdom and above a class.

pineal To do with the small, usually conical appendage of the brain of all craniate vertebrates that in a few reptiles has the essential structure of an eye, that functions in some birds as a time-measuring system, and that is postulated as a vestigial third eye or and endocrine organ.

rhizomes Somewhat elongate and usually horizontal subterranean plants that are often thickened by deposits of reserve food material, produce shoots above and roots below, and are distinguished from a true root in having buds, nodes, and usually scale-like leaves.

spicules Minute, slender, and pointed calcareous or siliceous bodies that support the tissue of various invertebrates.

stratigraphy Branch of geology that deals with layered rock, or the arrangement of layered rock.

taxa Groups of organisms that have been classified together based on their presumed natural relationships.

tillites Sedimentary rock made up of various material deposited by glaciers and other consolidated masses of unweathered rock.

trilete spores Spores with three-pronged scars thought to be the direct ancestors of land plants.

tuffs Rocks composed of the finer volcanic detritus and usually fused together by heat.

wackes Varieties of sandstone characterized by their hardness, dark color, and poorly sorted, angular grains of quartz, feldspar, and small rock fragments.

FOR FURTHER READING

Arnold Davis, Richard, and David L. Meyer. *A Sea without Fish: Life in the Ordovician Sea of the Cincinatti Region*. Bloomington, Indiana: Indiana Universtity Press, 2009.

Bartels, Christoph, Derek E.G. Briggs, and Ginter Brassel. *The Fossils of the Hunsrück Slate: Marine Life in the Devonian*. Cambridge: Cambridge University Press, 2009.

Carroll, Robert. *The Rise of Amphibbians: 365 Million Years of Evolution*. Baltimore: Johns Hopkins University Press, 2009.

Cerling, T.E., and Maria-Denise Dearing. *A History of Atmospheric CO2 and Its Effects on Plants, Animals, and Ecosystems*. Springer, 2005.

Clack, J.A. *Gaining Ground: the Origin and Evolution of Tetrapods*. Bloomington, Indiana: Indiana University Press, 2002.

Erwin, Douglas H. *The Great Paleozoic Crisis: Life and Death in the Permian*. New York: Columbia University Press. 1993.

Fedonkin, Michael A., James G. Gehling, Kathleen Grey, Guy M. Narbonne, and Patricia Vickers-Rich. *The Rise of Animals: Evolution and Diversification of the Kingdom Animalia*. Baltimore: Johns Hopkins University Press, 2008.

Gensel, Patricia G., and Dianne Edwards (eds.). *Plants Invade the Land*. New York: Columbia University Press. 2001.

Gradstein, Felix M., J.G. Ogg, and A.G. Smith. *A Geologic Time Scale 2004.* Cambridge: Cambridge University Press, 2004.

Haines, Tim, and Paul Chambers. *The Complete Guide to Prehistoric Life.* Ontario: Firefly Books, 2006.

Hou, Xian-guang, Richard Aldridge, Jan Bergstrom, David Siveter, Derek Siveter, and Xiang-Hong Feng. *The Cambrian Fossils of Chengjiang, China: The Flowering of Early Animal Life.* New York: Wiley-Blackwell, 2007.

McMenamin, Mark, A.S., and Dianna L. McMenamin. *The Emergence of Animals.* New York: Columbia University Press. 1990

Miall, Andrew D. (ed). *Sedimentary Basins of the United States and Canada.* Oxford: Elsevier B.V., 2008.

Ponder, Winston, and David R. Lindberg. *Phylogeny and Evolution of the Mollusca.* University of California Press, 2008.

Sengor, A.M. Celal, and Saniye Atayman. *The Permian Extinction and the Tethys: An Exercise in Global Geology.* Boulder, CO: Geological Society of America, 2009.

Stanley, S.M. *Earth System History.* New York: WH Freeman & Co., 1998.

Whitely, Thomas E., Gerald J. Kloc, Carlton E. Brett, and Rolf Ludvigsen. *Trilobites of New York.* New York: Cornell University Press, 2002.

Zhuralev, Andrey, and Robert Riding (eds). *The Ecology of the Cambrian Radiation.* New York: Columbia University Press, 2000.

INDEX